DYMOND GUIDE

THE LAKE DISTRICT

Cumbria

FOOD & DRINK

For Birthe, Jack and John Paul

DYMOND GUIDE

THE LAKE DISTRICT

Cumbria

FOOD & DRINK

CHRISTIAN DYMOND

Dymond Guide The Lake District Cumbria
Food and Drink
Copyright © Dymond Guides/Christian Dymond 2009

Editor: Chris Bagshaw, Little Spider Publishing, Kirkoswald, Cumbria
Design: Gary Burge at Walker Ellis Associates Ltd, Threlkeld, Cumbria
Main photographer: Helen Whitaker

Published by Dymond Guides, Cumbria
www.dymondguides.com

A CIP catalogue record for this book is available from the British Library

ISBN 978-0-9554726-1-9

Printed in England by The Amadeus Press, Cleckheaton, West Yorkshire

Christian Dymond has been a journalist for 30 years. After three years at the Press Association in London, he spent ten years at Border Television in Carlisle where he presented two series of *Hindsight* for ITV. As a freelance since 1992, he has written for *The Times*, *Sunday Times*, *Financial Times*, *Daily Telegraph* and other publications. For a number of years he wrote extensively on food and drink for *Cumbria Life* magazine.

He was the overall winner of the Cumberland News Countryside Awards 2004 for his proposal that led to the very first Cumbria and Lake District Food and Drink Festival in that year. He is on the committee of the Cumbria convivium of Slow Food. He also runs an independent production company, Dymond Productions, with his wife, Charlotte (*www.dymondproductions.co.uk*).

Contents

Preface 7

Restaurants 9
There's also information on food festivals

Pubs, Inns and Bars 43
You'll also find information on the Carlisle and District State
Management Scheme, the Campaign for Real Ale, Pub
is the Hub, beer festivals and the Cask Marque Trust

Food and Drink Producers 77
There's also information on Herdwick sheep, the Cumberland
sausage, Cumbria Organics, Saltmarsh lamb, Mutton
Renaissance, the Great Taste Awards, damsons in the Lyth
and Winster valleys and Slow Food

Food and Drink
Shops/Farm Shops 111
This chapter includes information on farmers' markets,
Borough Market in London and butchers in Cumbria as well

Cookery and Baking Courses 149

Cafés, Tea Rooms
and Café/Restaurants 159

Map 187

Index 188

Acknowledgements 191

Above: countryside near Glenridding, Ullswater

Page 8
Above left: table setting at Linthwaite House Hotel,
Bowness-on-Windermere (see p16)
Above right: dish at Rothay Manor (see p12)
Below left: dish at Storrs Hall (see p36)
Below right: restaurant at Holbeck Ghyll, Windermere (see p32)

Preface

Not long after I moved to Cumbria in 1982 I had dinner in a small restaurant in a village near Carlisle. The food was good and the service impeccable but it was the manifest enjoyment with which the host watched over his diners, imbuing the restaurant with a wonderful sense of well being, that remains in the memory after all these years.

Save for some fine and notable exceptions, Cumbria in the early 1980s was not generally known for its food and drink. But it certainly is now. Top restaurants (three of them Michelin-starred), great pubs in equally wonderful locations, nationally award-winning producers, about 25 small breweries, inviting tea rooms and cafés, an abundance of specialist food and farm shops and a distinctive variety of cookery and baking courses – collectively they give this area a well deserved national reputation for food and drink.

This book is a guide, a pointer, to about 300 different places. I could have included more but I wanted to visit as many of those listed as possible and in the end there was no flexibility left in the deadline. But if you've got suggestions for other places, or comments about the ones included, please let me know. The email address is at the back of the book.

Needless to say, travelling around Cumbria, writing a food and drink guide, has not been the most arduous of tasks. The landscape itself is pretty special, the major draw for visitors for a century and a half. That's why designer Gary Burge has thoughtfully included a few images of the countryside, just in case you need reminding of its beauty.

As for the memories from my months of research, there are many to savour: the restaurants and pubs where the chefs allow their top notch ingredients to sparkle on the plate; the startling range of producers, many of whom have set up their businesses since the dreaded foot and mouth epidemic of 2001; the places where you can feel the direction and presence of the owner or manager, even if they're not always present.

I've warmed to publicans who light their fires on chilly days and serve local ales at the bar; I love those food and farm shops where the shelves are full of artisan produce, and the owners can tell you all about it; I like it that when proprietors use Cumbrian food and drink, they'll give you its provenance; I like well trained, enthusiastic, knowledgeable and friendly staff; I admire the commitment to quality and service that's evident in so many places; and above all I love that pride and joy – despite the incredible hard work – that so many proprietors take in their work. Much like the man who ran that first restaurant I ever went to in Cumbria all those years ago.

Enjoy your visit here and savour as much as you can.

Christian Dymond

Restaurants

Alston

Lovelady Shield

Nenthead Road, near Alston CA9 3LF
Tel: 01434 381203
Website: www.lovelady.co.uk

This is almost splendid isolation because when you drop down the lane, cross the small bridge over the River Nent and pull up outside this Georgian property, you'll feel the rest of the world is a long way off. The 12-bedroom hotel is in the North Pennines Area of Outstanding Natural Beauty, and a short hop from Alston, a town so historic that it barely needed a facelift for the filming of ITV's *Oliver Twist* in 2002.

Peter and Marie Haynes have run Lovelady Shield since 1997 – they thought it was the stuff of dreams when they first saw the property – but head chef Barrie Garton has been here considerably longer, having previously worked at renowned Michael's Nook, near Grasmere (closed some years ago).

The peach and cream coloured restaurant has two AA Rosettes and is towards the back of the hotel, past a library with log fire on the left, past a lounge on the right and then a bar. The lounge has a log fire too. Dinner is a four-course affair, with a daily changing, seasonal menu (£42.50). For starters expect dishes like mousses of white and brown crabmeat, pickled cucumber and toasted sweet chilli bread; or steamed king scallops with lemon thyme, warm fragrant three rice salad, sweet pepper, spring onion and oriental dressing.

A sorbet or soup follows and then main courses could offer breast of guinea fowl, celeriac and chorizo mash, sweetcorn and leek and guinea fowl jus; whole grilled lemon sole, goat's cheese and spinach, and tomato dressed new potato; or hand-raised pie of Lune Valley mutton and kidney, rosemary jus, pease pudding and runner beans.

Guests have the option of cheese or dessert and if both are taken it's £5 extra. Desserts might be warm carrot cake, clotted cream and kumquat compote; dark chocolate and Grasmere gingerbread tart and lychee ice cream; or hot baked fig sponge pudding, butterscotch sauce and Greek yoghurt ice cream.

The informative wine list, grouped around grape varieties, runs to about 130 bins, with prices £15–£80. One of the biggest compliments guests have paid Peter is to ask to take it to bed to read. In 2001 and 2003 Lovelady Shield won Les Routiers *Wine List of the Year* for the north west of England.

Dinner: *19–20.30. Sunday lunch (£21 including coffee) is by appointment. There are 12 bedrooms and three self-catering cottages behind the hotel.*

Ambleside

The Bay Restaurant

The Waterhead Hotel, Ambleside LA22 0ER
Tel: 015394 30708
Website: www.elh.co.uk/restaurants/waterhead

John Lennon and Yoko Ono pitched up here in 1969 and ate Dover sole, but the restaurant of today is very different from 40 years ago. A £3.2 million redevelopment in 2004 turned an unremarkable 28-bedroom affair into a four star, 41-room town house hotel. The old cocktail bar has been transformed into the L-shaped, 80-seat Bay Restaurant.

You can see the shores of Windermere through the window (and the kitchen through another), there's art work on the walls, a polished slate floor, leather chairs and some rather attractive lighting. Next door is the Bay Bar, with its large glass frontage. A 2.5-ton piece of Elterwater slate makes for a striking water feature just by the bar entrance. Soup and sandwiches are served in here 12–18.00.

In 2007 the hotel's owners, English Lakes Hotels, asked Steven Doherty, former head chef of Le Gavroche in London, and Lee Jeynes, captain of the Welsh National Culinary Team, to look at the menus in both bar and restaurant, so expect some pretty good food, with increased use of locally sourced produce. Amongst the starters in the restaurant there might be Cartmel Valley smoked salmon (£6.95), Thornby Moor goats' cheese, walnut crust and compote of beetroot and apple (£6.25) and Cumbrian air dried ham, pickled fig and cantaloupe melon.

Main courses offer the likes of Holker venison (£19.95), Eden Valley chicken (£15.50), rack of fellbred lamb (£16.75), fillet of sea bass, and Cumbrian stumpy goats' cheese gnocchi. Desserts could include brown bread ice cream and fresh raspberries or iced passion fruit and marshmallow parfait. The 25 white wines go from £12.50 to £33.50, 24 red wines (including Mexican) £13.50–£33.95.

Lunch: *12.30–14.30. Dinner: 19–21.30. 41 bedrooms.*
Directions: *the Waterhead Hotel is on the right-hand side as you leave Ambleside heading south on the A591.*

Lucy's on a Plate

Church Street, Ambleside LA22 0BU
Tel: 015394 31191
Website: www.lucysofambleside.co.uk

It's over 30 years since Lucy Nicholson first visited the Lake District and 20 years since she opened her specialist grocers on Church Street. Lucy's on a Plate came in 1996, a café by day (with 'cakes to keep Cumbria curvy') and a restaurant by night. It's a well known and lively eatery with stripped pine floors, a fire in the main room, chapel chairs, pine tables, a conservatory at the back and a bar just inside the entrance. This is the area where the grocer's used to be before it moved to Compston Road (see p113).

Lucy's enthusiasm and personality are writ large in the restaurant and on the menu. Whether you're here for a 'Marvellous Monday Night', a 'Wonderful Wednesday' or a 'Thrilling Thursday', you'll quickly find out about your fellow diners from Lucy's notes at the top of the menu: such and such celebrating their 18th birthday, ruby wedding anniversary, a family relishing the last night of their holidays, someone else enjoying the Lake District in its autumnal splendour.

The 12–15 starters (£3.25–£7.50) might include pan-fried scallops; sardines stuffed with coriander and lemon; pan-fried prawns with sweet chilli sauce; Tuscan lamb balls; chicken goujons; and pan-fried pigeon. The 10–15 main courses go from £10.50 to £25 and offer such dishes as Tunisian tagine (with Lakeland lamb); Bluebird beef (braised beef in Coniston Bluebird Bitter); saffron seabass; racked and ready Lakeland lamb cutlets with a herb crust; pork fillet stuffed with Cumberland sausage and wrapped in air dried ham; and guinea fowl with a juniper berry jus.

The range of desserts (£3.95–£4.95) is impressive – over 30 in all, taking in the likes of raspberry pavlova, blackberry crumble cake, Mrs Bramley's apple pie, Bakewell tart, Lancashire lemon tart, sticky toffee pudding and chocolate and prune torte. Those with gluten and wheat intolerance are well catered for. Wines go from £11.50.

Open: *daily 10–21. Dinner: from 18 (last orders 21.00).*

Although the examples from menus - and the prices - were correct at the time of going to print, please be aware that they can change over the months.

Ambleside
Rothay Manor Hotel

Rothay Bridge, Ambleside LA22 0EH
Tel: 015394 33605
Website: www.rothaymanor.co.uk

One brother has a degree in physics, the other a degree in chemistry. They're not the most obvious qualifications for the hotel industry but, in the case of Nigel and Stephen Nixon, and for over 30 years, the alchemy most certainly worked. Stephen retired in 2008 so Nigel is now running the hotel, which is as relaxed and family friendly as it's always been.

Nothing changes in its reputation for food either. It's had 40 continuous years in the *Good Food Guide* – the sixth longest serving restaurant in the guide – and the head chef Jane Binns has been in charge of the kitchen for 25 of those years. Rothay Manor was also the Cumbria Tourist Board's *Small Hotel of the Year* in 2006 and in the top three for Cumbria Tourism's *Taste of Cumbria Awards* 2008.

Once the home of a Liverpool merchant, the hotel is a fine looking Regency building, with a listed frontage overlooking a large garden. Inside there are two lounges and a 34-seat main dining room, and in any of them you can take lunch. Lunch itself offers plenty of options – soup, sandwiches (most at £5) and light dishes (£7.50), like the smoked salmon, salmon and hake terrine with herb mayonnaise or ploughman's with assorted cheeses, most of them Cumbrian. For those who've worked up a bigger appetite there are more substantial dishes (£11), such as Holker Hall wild mallard, fillet of salmon or kidneys Madeira. A three-course Sunday lunch is £21.50.

At dinner, Rothay Manor gives you a choice of two–five courses (£34–£46). Starters might be an assiette of smoked fish, game terrine or fillet of red mullet. Mains could include escalopes of prime beef fillet, grilled fillet of lemon sole or roasted loin of fell-bred lamb. Lemon posset and chocolate tart are two possibilities for dessert.

Jane Binns being a big supporter of local produce, expect plenty of Cumbrian names on the menu, as with the cheeses: Kendal Creamy, Smoked Cumberland and so on. The 161 wines go from £16 to £154. Three bottled Cumbrian beers are available which is good to see. Don't forget you can come here for breakfast, morning coffee and the award winning afternoon tea as well. And the parking is free.

Lunch: 12.30–13.45. Dinner: 19.15–21. Afternoon tea: 15.30–17. Rothay Manor has 16 bedrooms and three suites. Good wheelchair accessibility. The hotel runs a number of special interest holidays – walking, gardening, antiques, chess, painting, Scrabble, bridge, music, interior design (new for 2010) and the like – between October and May every year.

Below: Rothay Manor Hotel. Pictures opposite, clockwise from top left: Zeffirellis, the Bay Restaurant at the Waterhead Hotel (see p11), a view of Windermere and Lucy's on a Plate (see p11)

Zeffirellis

Compston Road, Ambleside LA22 9AD
Tel: 015394 33845
Website: www.zeffirellis.com

Zeffirellis is named after the great Italian film director Franco Zeffirelli and has been a landmark in Ambleside for over 25 years, attracting a regular and devoted clientele. Owned by brothers Derek and Raymond Hook and their sister Dorothy Smith, the complex houses two cinema screens (two more are down the road), a jazz café bar (see p44), a café (see p160) and a restaurant. The restaurant, with its glass waterfall feature, Venetian artworks and classical urns, seats over 150 people, but the way it's designed gives the place a rather intimate feel.

Zeffirellis is a vegetarian restaurant. Starters might be Gorgonzola, chicory and apple salad or goat's cheese and fresh chive soufflé. Main courses include Italian bean casserole (£7.75), butternut squash ravioli (£9.45), and Vesuvian red bean chilli. There are also the 'legendary' Zeffirellis wholemeal pizzas, a choice of nine which average out at £8.50. As Zeffirellis supports a botanical sanctuary in India, it donates 25p from every Rain Forest pizza sold.

Desserts – baked lemon and orange ricotta cheesecake, or warm pear and ginger pudding with chocolate and toffee sauce, for instance – are about £5–£5.25, while Zeffirellis 'double feature' offers a two-course dinner and reserved cinema seat for £16.95. The jazz café bar serves pizzas and pasta, with Saturday events mostly free.

Restaurant open: *Mon–Fri 18, Sat, Sun and high season weekdays 17.30. Last bookings are for 21.45.*

Bowness-on-Windermere
Fayrer Garden House Hotel

Lyth Valley Road, Bowness-on-Windermere LA23 3JP
Tel: 015394 88195
Website: www.fayrergarden.com

Three years after the nearby Arts and Crafts house of Blackwell was completed in 1901, Fayrer Garden was built for a wealthy businessman and his family. Like Blackwell's owner he knew a great spot when he saw one: Windermere gloriously stretching out below him and the woods creeping up the slopes on the fells beyond. This is the cracking view you get from the Terrace Restaurant which, like some of the other rooms at Fayrer Garden, has been added in the last 15 years.

The comfortable hotel is a much-liked establishment, plenty of returning visitors proving the point. It's got five acres of gardens and grounds, a helipad, a large outside terrace facing the lake, attractive shrubbery as you come down the drive, and a two-room restaurant with two AA Rosettes. Its grand piano is played on Saturday evenings.

Head chef Eddie Wilkinson has run the kitchens for 15 years and he and his team offer a daily changing, four-course dinner menu (£32.50 Sun–Thu, £40 Fri–Sat). Much produce is sourced locally, game and sausages, for example, coming from Cartmel Valley Game Supplies and Smokehouse, pork and bacon from

Richard Woodall and other meat from Hayton's butchers in Staveley.

For starters, expect dishes like wild mushroom mousse, tart of Thornby Moor goat's cheese and cherry tomato, confit of Pooley Bridge chicken leg, smoked Cartmel Valley duck, grilled tuna steak or tian of Cornish crab.

A soup or a sorbet comes next and then main courses could offer pan fried fillet of English beef, slow roasted pork belly, fillet of sea bass, fillet of hake, pan fried supreme of pheasant, or roasted loin of Cartmel Valley venison. Over 100 wines go from £11.50 to £69.50. Vegetarian and special diets are catered for. Lunch (soup and sandwiches) and afternoon tea are served in the lounges.

Lunch: *12–16. Dinner: 18.30–20.30. 29 bedrooms.*

Pictures of dishes opposite, clockwise from top left: from Rothay Manor (see p12), next two from Linthwaite House Hotel (see p16), next two from Fayrer Garden House Hotel

Bowness-on-Windermere
Linthwaite House Hotel

Crook Road, Windermere LA23 3JA
Tel: 015394 88600
Website: www.linthwaite.com

'Come up and see the view,' exhorts the sign at the end of the lane leading up to the hotel. You won't be disappointed. Built as a private house in 1901 and set in 14 acres of grounds, with a tarn for fishing, Linthwaite House stands high above Windermere, with exhilarating views of lake and fells.

Actually the first view you come across is one through the 'glass wall' into the new and considerably larger kitchen, built in 2008 with five bedrooms above it. Taken with the major refurbishment of one of two restaurant rooms in 2007, the conversion of the old kitchen into a bar and the arrival of a new head chef in late 2008, it was pretty busy here for a while. But Linthwaite House took it all in its stride. Nothing's going to rattle its place in the premier league of Lake District dining.

The head chef is Richard Kearsley who since working with Steven Doherty at the Punch Bowl Inn at Crosthwaite in 2000–2002 has been at the Waterside Inn and L'ortolan in Berkshire, Seaham Hall in County Durham, Mallory Court, Warwickshire and Lords of the Manor in the Cotswolds.

The 'unstuffy hotel' is how owner Mike Bevans describes Linthwaite House – there's even an 'unstuffy burger' on the open sandwich menu – and so there's a relaxed air about this well run and friendly place. An open fire burns on cooler days in the reception and the three public rooms (including a conservatory) have comfortable seats and sofas, pot plants and a collection of old travelling trunks. There's also a glassed-in veranda, and a large outside terrace.

The three-course lunch at £18.95 (two courses £15.95) might include roasted baby artichoke and fine bean salad with toasted hazelnut dressing; and ham hock and pea terrine with white grape chutney amongst the starters. Roasted chump of Cumbrian lamb, or pan fried fillet of brill, braised oxtail, truffle purée with red wine sauce may feature as main courses.

The four-course dinner (£50, includes canapés and petit fours) has a choice of six starters and six mains. Starters could offer diver scallops and Bury black pudding; roasted wood pigeon salad and celeriac remoulade; or risotto of roasted pumpkin with toasted pine nuts. Mains might include braised feather blade of Cumbrian beef; roasted fillet of pork, apple braised pork belly and cheek; or seared John Dory, fresh pasta with mussels, cockles and clams in a Vermouth sauce.

Six desserts might have hot chocolate fondant and chocolate mousse; apple Tarte Tatin and apple sorbet; and sticky toffee pudding. The 150 wines go from £15.50 to £135.

Lunch: *12–14. Dinner: 19–21. Afternoon tea: 15–17.30. Tea, coffee, hot chocolate, milkshakes and sandwiches available all day. 30 bedrooms.*
Directions: *from just outside Bowness-on-Windermere, take the B5284 road towards Crook. The hotel is on the right hand side, not far from Bowness.*

Brampton

Farlam Hall Hotel

Farlam, near Brampton CA8 2NG
Tel: 016977 46234
Website: www.farlamhall.co.uk

The hotel had been shut for almost two years when the Quinions took it over, so some locals wondered whether they could really make a go of it. That was in 1975 and the family is still here. Within two years of re-opening, Farlam Hall was in the *Good Food Guide* – it's now one of the 20 longest-serving restaurants in the guide – and in 1984 the hotel became a member of Relais & Châteaux. In 2001 it was named *Country House Hotel of the Year* by the *Good Hotel Guide.*

The chef proprietor is Barry Quinion (parents Alan and Joan retired in 2008) and his wife Lynne and sister Helen are in the business as well. The welcome, the old fashioned charm and the level of comfort is the same as ever. This from someone who's been coming here for over 25 years.

Barry learnt his trade at an inn in Buckinghamshire where the likes of Richard Burton, Elizabeth Taylor, Mick Jagger and Jackie Stewart were customers. Later, he went to the Waterside Inn at Bray with Michel and Albert Roux and Pierre Koffmann.

Sweep up the drive, past the lawn, the lake and the llamas, and you'll arrive at this handsome Victorian building. Through the front door is a large lounge, with sofas, antiques and paintings, and a log fire on chilly evenings. Guests assemble here or in the other lounge before being taken through to dinner, the 40-seat dining room sparkling with polished glass and silverware.

The daily changing menu is a four-course affair (five on Saturday nights), with three starters that always include a soup, and dishes like smoked duck and orange salad, or terrine of guinea fowl, herb and pistachio. Three main courses – 'a fish, a fowl and a flesh' – might see breast of local pheasant, loin of Cumbrian lamb or pan fried calf's liver. Vegetables, in the long established tradition, are served separately.

Vegetarians can make special arrangements and will have a choice of three mains as well. An English cheese board has eight–ten cheeses and there's a choice of five desserts (homemade ice creams, white chocolate cheese cake, spiced apple flan are three possibilities). A sorbet is the extra on Saturdays. About 60 wines go from £16.95 to £59.50.

Dinner: *19.30 for 20. Four-course dinner is £41.50, five-course dinner Sat £43. Lunch is served on Mothering Sunday and Easter Sunday but Farlam Hall will open the restaurant at other times for parties of ten or more. Two very popular brunches are held every year in May and Oct.*
Directions: *the hotel is about two miles (3.2km) south east of Brampton on the A689 to Alston.*

Below: Barry Quinion, Farlam Hall Hotel

Cartmel

L'enclume

Cavendish Street, Cartmel LA11 6PZ
Tel: 015395 36362
Website: www.lenclume.co.uk

When Simon Rogan and his partner Penny Tapsell opened L'enclume in late 2002 few could have imagined how far, in terms of food and reputation, this restaurant would come. But Simon's promise back then of 'modern, innovative cooking' has certainly struck a resounding chord.

The Michelin starred restaurant is in a 14th century smithy - L'enclume is French for anvil - but only the white stone walls and old beams smack of antiquity. 'Stretching boundaries with unusual flavour combinations, looking for tastes, textures and fragrances to surprise and excite,' is the philosophy here, so expect something of an adventure when you sit down.

Such exploration of new territory comes with its own culinary lexicon. Re-hydration, de-hydration, for instance, on the ten-course 'Introduction' menu in 2008, was fresh fig extract, soda syphoned at the table into shot glasses, accompanied by a pineapple tuile, set in a silver serviette holder. Egg drop hot and sour soup was pasteurised egg, syringed – once again at the table – onto hot and sour soup, in order to poach. Glazed pork cheeks, cacao, date, cassia; and confit lamb, hummus, tomato, molasses spoke for themselves.

Each course arrives with a little flourish and a simple explanation while at the same time going through an impressive range of tableware. It's all eagerly anticipated and provides a great talking point around the dark wood table. 'Superb, a real event,' says one visitor in 2008. Wines go from £22.

Lunch: Wed–Sun 12–13.30. Dinner (every night): 18.30–21. L'enclume offers three choices for the evening: Menu 1 (£50), Menu 2 (£70) and Menu 3 (£90). 12 bedrooms.

Rogan and Company: Simon Rogan and Penny Tapsell opened this eatery in The Square at Cartmel in 2008 (015395 35917, www.roganandcompany.co.uk). It's in a 16th-century building, with a bar, informal eating area and private dining room downstairs and a bar and restaurant upstairs. Sandwiches are available at lunchtime but for more substantial meals, starters (£5.25–£6.50) might include sausage of confit guinea fowl with white bean stew and watercress while main courses could offer herb crusted halibut and anchovy fritter (£15.50), or braised lamb shoulder and red cabbage (£13.95). Desserts are priced £5.50–£5.95. Wines go from £12 to £22. Lunch is 12–14, dinner from 18.30 to 21.00.

Cockermouth

Quince and Medlar

13 Castlegate, Cockermouth CA13 9EU
Tel: 01900 823579
Website: www.quinceandmedlar.co.uk

Colin and Louisa Le Voi were working at Sharrow Bay in the days of Francis Coulson and Brian Sack – he in the kitchens, she front of house – when they got the tip that Quince and Medlar was for sale. They saw out the 1988 season at the Ullswater hotel and then in January 1989 moved into this three-storey Georgian property, close to the castle in William Wordsworth's birthplace.

In the 20 years they've run Quince and Medlar it's been the Vegetarian Society's *Vegetarian Restaurant of the Year* on two occasions, 'never failing to impress,' as one non-vegetarian put it. There's a lounge area to the left while the restaurant is wood-panelled and candlelit and has an open fire.

Starters might take in balsamic baked red onion and Allerdale goats' cheese tartlet (£6.95) or leek and watercress terrine (£6.95). Main courses, with seasonal vegetables, are all £13.95 and could include crusted cashew nut ring; wild mushroom and aduki bean cassoulet or parsnip and crushed garden pea roulade.

Desserts (£5.25) run to dishes like blackberry and apple granola, Benedictine parfait and pumpkin pie. Organic wines go from £11.90.

Dinner: Tue–Sat from 19.00.

Pictures of dishes opposite, clockwise from top left: from L'enclume, from the Jumble Room (see p20), from Sharrow Bay (see p26) and from the Lakeside Hotel (see p23). Below: Quince and Medlar

Grasmere
The Jumble Room

Langdale Road, Grasmere LA22 9SU
Tel: 015394 35188
Website: www.thejumbleroom.co.uk

There's no doubt that the popularity of the Jumble Room lies with the food but the joyful nature of the place comes a close second: such a lovely atmosphere it almost sings, as one diner told owners Chrissy and Andy Hill. Once a building used for storage, the couple considered naming their venture the Junk Room when they opened in 1996. Jumble Room got the vote and anyway junk and food are never mentioned in the same breath here. Chrissy and Andy are keen supporters of local and, where possible, organic produce. That said they draw on considerably wider influences for their food, created in a kitchen that's barely big enough to swing a truffle in.

The two dining rooms – one upstairs, one down – are small too, but big enough to seat about 60 diners between them. Paintings and jazz photographs adorn the walls, there are books to read and, in the ladies and gents, album covers which may keep you a few seconds longer than you anticipated. Music's part of the thing here, so if you want to check out Andy and Chrissy's taste, look at the website. The review section's longer than most Sunday paper reviews put together.

And now the food. 'From Lakeland to Laos' is how Chrissy describes the influences so, for starters at dinner, expect dishes like Hyderabad chicken (chicken breast marinated in yoghurt and spices and baked in cashew, ginger and cardamom, £7.95), west coast scallops (£9.50), cullen skink (£5.95) or Thai tiger prawns, pan-seared in a gremolata of fresh parsley, garlic, preserved lemon and a little chilli, then served on a bed of Asian greens and juicy papaya (£8.50).

Main courses might include roast Galloway sirloin (£22.95), Romesco de peix (Catalan fish stew, £17.50), roast breast of Gressingham duck (£17.95), cod and chips (the cod fried in organic beer batter, £10.95), Graythwaite game pie (£16.95) and asparagus and mushroom potato rosti (£13.95). The menu changes regularly and seasonally. Cutlery comes wrapped in a white napkin like a tool kit.

Coffee, tea, cakes and scones are served during the day and so are soups and dishes like fresh haddock goujons, home cured bacon, topped with Brie on organic toast, homemade lamb sausages with sticky onion marmalade, and Thai chicken and Szechuan chilli beef with stir fried noodles.

Open: *Wed–Sun 11.30–15.30 and Wed–Sun 18.00 until the food runs out. Chrissy and Andy also run a B&B just outside Ambleside called Randy Pike (www.randypike.co.uk).*

Below: Chrissy and Andy Hill, the Jumble Room

Kendal

Bridge Street Restaurant

1 Bridge Street, Kendal LA9 7DD
Tel: 01539 738855
Website: www.bridgestreetkendal.co.uk

If you need evidence of diners' liking for Julian and Elizabeth Ankers' restaurant, simply thumb through the guest book in the downstairs lounge. 'Amazing food, amazing atmosphere, amazing service' is one comment about this small eatery, which is located in a double fronted Georgian property beside the River Kent. You can see the river from both upstairs restaurants.

Julian and Elizabeth have taken some pains to source produce from local suppliers: Peter Gott at Sillfield Farm, for example, Staff of Life (bakery), Richard Woodall, Mansergh Hall Organic Farm, Hawkshead Brewery and Hayton's butchers in Staveley.

Amongst seven starters, you might find dishes like crispy Mansergh Hall Saddleback pork belly, with apple cider fritter, golden sultana relish and watercress leaves while a similar number of main courses could include saddle of Kentmere fell venison, with roasted golden beetroot, curly kale and a port wine sauce; short loin of Kentmere spring lamb, with thyme fondant potato, buttered baby spinach and port shallot sauce.

To finish off, expect desserts like hot chocolate fondant with warm chocolate sauce and praline ice cream; and caramelised apple Tarte Tatin with vanilla ice cream and butterscotch sauce. Wines go from £12.50–£40.

Dinner: *Tue–Sat 18–21. A three course dinner costs £18–£27.*

Grain Store Restaurant

Brewery Arts Centre, Highgate, Kendal LA9 4HE
Tel: 01539 725133
Website: www.breweryarts.co.uk

As if three cinema screens, a theatre, a music venue, workshop space, two cafés and a bar aren't enough for the fortunate residents of Kendal, the Brewery also boasts this 80-seat restaurant. And you don't have to be one of 300,000 people a year who are drawn to the centre's excellent arts programme, to dine here.

The L-shaped eatery is on the first floor of Kendal's old brewery, with stained glass panels at one end and artwork by Cumbrian artist Ian Walton hanging on the walls. There's an informal feel about the place which offers both lunch and dinner. Lunch has soups (£3.95), sandwiches (£3.95–£4.45), char grilled wraps, pizzas (£6.50–£7.95) and other dishes like duo of Cumbrian fellbred pork and black pudding (£7.25) and sliced chicken and smoked bacon with dressed salad.

In the evening starters might be oak-smoked Cumbrian chicken and Woodall's Cumbrian pancetta (£5.50), haddock and spring onion fishcake or Grain Store assiette, with Westmorland ham, Mozzarella, mixed olives and warm focaccia (£5.95). Main courses could include Eden Valley roast chicken breast (£10.75), fellbred chump of lamb (£13.95), oven baked monkfish (£14.50) and Grizedale venison steak.

Raspberry crème brûlée, lime cheese cake and homemade sticky toffee pudding are three choices for dessert (all £4.95). About 25 wines are priced £11.95–£24.95.

Lunch: *11.30–14.30. Dinner: 17.30–21.00.*

Kendal
Greenhouse Restaurant

Castle Green Hotel, Kendal LA9 6BH
Tel: 01539 734000
Website: www.castlegreen.co.uk

There must have been a great surge of excitement when James and Catherine Alexander opened this hotel in 1997. Not only had they seen the possibilities of converting former electricity board offices into a hotel but the site was perfect as well: high on a hill to the east of Kendal, with panoramic views of the town and of Kendal Castle. The castle once belonged to the Parr family whose most famous member, Catherine, became the sixth and last wife of Henry VIII.

The two AA-rosetted Greenhouse Restaurant capitalises on the view, so when you're sitting at your table you've got a choice of looking west to Kendal or north, through a large 'theatre window', into the kitchens. The chefs in there are big supporters of local produce, something that's evident from the evening Cumbrian Tasting Menu. Not only is the producer named but – very unusually – so is the distance from producer to restaurant.

Various styles of Maurice Wharton's pork (fillet, loin, cheek, belly and trotter), for example, travel 48 miles; a slate of locally smoked produce (chicken, duck, trout, salmon and cheese) is smoked 15 miles away.

The inviting Cumbrian Tasting Menu (three courses £24, five courses £30) sits alongside an equally appealing à la carte menu, which also has daily specials. Dishes from both are interchangeable; the young, friendly staff will explain exactly what's what. Between the menus you might see starters like Cumbrian squirrel risotto, roasted quail or spiced scallops and main courses such as roasted sea bass, braised beef cheeks, monkfish with Cumbrian pancetta or cuts of Cumbrian lamb. Desserts generally offer a choice between a chocolate or a fruit selection. Some 50 wines go from £14.50 to £40.

Dinner: 18–21.30. The à la carte menu is £29.95 for three courses, £25.95 for two, with daily specials. The hotel has 99 bedrooms. Sun eve dinner, bed and breakfast for two people, £100 per night, subject to availability. The hotel also has a pub called Alexanders.

Low Lorton
Winder Hall Country House

Low Lorton, Cockermouth CA13 9UP
Tel: 01900 85107
Website: www.winderhall.co.uk

Nick Lawler's small Jacobean hotel is as historic as any you'll find in Cumbria, and there's a distinctly traditional way that this Slow Food enthusiast (see p106) sources his produce too. He breeds Saddleback pigs and keeps bees and chickens, and looks no further than two farms in his village near Buttermere for native lamb, Herdwick and Swaledale to serve in the restaurant. Beef is bought at W Lindsay & Sons in the nearby Cittaslow town of Cockermouth (see *www.cittaslow.org.uk* for more information about the Cittaslow movement). Much of the cheese comes from either Thornby Moor Dairy or Wardhall Dairy, both in Cumbria.

Winder Hall was originally built as a manor house for the Winder family and remained their home for over 300 years. Nick took it over in 2002 and has built up a good reputation for the food that's served in the 24-seat, 17th-century restaurant. The dinner menu changes daily and offers a choice of three starters, three mains and three desserts.

Starters might include warm, spicy Solway shrimps, served with Melba toast; or carpaccio of beef fillet, with pickled Lorton beetroot, garden leaves and Parmesan shavings. Main courses could see slow cooked Lorton lamb shoulder with aromatic jus and minty pesto; or fillet of chicken breast stuffed with roast black pudding and served with a grainy mustard sauce. Desserts offer possibilities of Cumbrian ginger sponge pudding with thick custard; or orange and Cointreau pannacotta with ruby grapefruit compote. More than 50 wines (including a selection of organic wines) go from £17 to £40.

Dinner: served at 19/19.30 in the week, 19/20.00 at weekends. Two courses £27.50, three courses £39. Morning coffee, afternoon tea, and sandwiches and snacks (11–16) also served. 7 bedrooms. Winder Hall appears at Cockermouth farmers' market as well (see p116).
Directions: Low Lorton is just over 3 miles (4.8km) south east of Cockermouth on the B5292.

Although the examples from menus – and the prices – were correct at the time of going to print, please be aware that they can change over the months.

Newby Bridge

Lakeside Hotel

Newby Bridge LA12 8AT
Tel: 015395 30001
Website: www.lakesidehotel.co.uk

'We overlook nothing but the lake,' goes the neat strapline on the front of the Lakeside Hotel's brochure. For nearly 400 years this former coaching inn – now a four-star, 76-bedroom hotel – has attracted countless visitors to its enviable location at the southern end of Windermere lake. Steamers, boats and swans pass by its large conservatory, the fells lie across the lake and behind the hotel and steam trains from Haverthwaite decant their jocular passengers at Lakeside station nearby.

The privately owned hotel, with its strong reputation for food, has a choice of two venues in which to eat. More formal is the fine dining, two AA-rosetted Lakeview Restaurant. Less formal is John Ruskin's Brasserie, just off the oak panelled bar – the oldest part of the hotel – and given a major makeover in 2008.

Refreshments and light meals are served throughout the day in the conservatory and on the terrace overlooking the lake. Open sandwiches (£12) at lunch might give you a choice between rare sirloin of beef, honey baked ham, smoked salmon, goat's cheese with red onion and basil and more. Lunch is also served every day in the wood panelled Lakeview Restaurant, with three courses for £29, two courses for £24. Traditional Sunday lunch is £29.

Dinner in the Lakeview Restaurant (flowers and Rosenthal candlesticks on the tables) offers a six-course gourmet menu

(£49) that includes several 'mystery' courses. Starters might be slow poached pigeon breast, west coast crab ravioli, seared hand dived scallops or pan fried Perigord foie gras.

Main courses could include loin of Lakeland lamb, fillet of Cumbrian beef, loin of Cumbrian pork, fillet of wild seabass and Holker Hall venison. About 150 wines on the *Cellarman's Choice* go from £19 to £195 while just under 30 wines on the *Directors' Wine List* are priced £42.50–£267.50.

Meanwhile John Ruskin's Brasserie has starters like smoked haddock and Gruyère fishcake, three year aged Iberico ham, confit of duck, grilled west coast sardines and arborio risotto. Main courses see dishes such as grilled lemon sole, artichoke tortelli, pan fried salmon, pork belly and rump of Lakeland lamb. Price for dinner here is £37.

On Thursday, Friday and Saturday evenings and Sunday lunch the sound of the hotel's Bechstein piano, played for some years by Peter Brown, can be heard drifting through the rooms. It's an elegant touch in a hotel, well known for its friendliness and old world courtesies.

Lunch: *12.30–14. Dinner: 18.30–22 (Ruskin's Brasserie), 19–21.30 (Lakeview). Afternoon tea is also served. 76 bedrooms.*
Directions: *the hotel is about 1 mile (1.6km) from Newby Bridge on the south west side of Windermere lake.*

Penrith
North Lakes Hotel and Spa

Ullswater Road, Penrith CA11 8QT
Tel: 01768 868111
Website: www.northlakeshotel.com

A crackling fire in a large hearth on chilly days, mighty beams in the reception's high ceiling, a general buzz of activity and sofas to sit and relax on. Such is the welcoming introduction to this well known hotel on the outskirts of Penrith, at the crossroads of routes east and west, north and south.

The keeper of the log fires is kept pretty busy because there's one in the bar and in each of the two rooms that make up the inviting, AA-rosetted Martindale Restaurant. One room is flagstoned with rugs, the other has an oak floor, and once again there are those impressive beams in the ceiling. A pianist plays in the restaurant on Friday and Saturday evenings.

The four star North Lakes is one of eight Shire Hotels owned by brewer Daniel Thwaites, the head chef, Mike Haddow, also being executive chef of the whole group. He's big on local suppliers so right from the word go – in the selection of possible starters for dinner – you might come across Cumbrian names: The Old Smokehouse oak smoked salmon blinis, Thornby Moor goat's cheese stumpies, or a speciality hors d'oeuvres selection that includes Cumbrian salamis. Starters can be taken as main courses as well, which is something you don't see that often.

Generously portioned mains might offer herb roasted Saddleback porchetta (£17.50), char-grilled 31 day aged fellside sirloin steak (£22) or baked smoked fillet of Shetland salmon (£17.25). Daily specials could include pan-roasted cod cheeks and tiger prawns Provençale or oriental duck stir fry. Lemon posset, double chocolate mousse, hot apple tart or crème brûlée are possible desserts, all at £6.75. The 70–80 wines on the list – photographs and recommendations make for added interest – go from £15.95 to £65.

Lunch: Mon–Fri (weekends and Bank Holidays closed) 12.15–13.30. Dinner: Mon–Thu 19–21.15, Fri–Sat 18.30–21.15, Sun and Bank Holidays 19–20.45. All day menu available in the Martindale Café. 84 bedrooms.

Ravenglass
The Estuary Restaurant

Pennington Hotel, Ravenglass CA18 1SD
Tel: 01229 717222
Website: www.thepennington.co.uk

Once people get to Ravenglass, it seems, they don't want to leave. The Romans were here for 250 years, the Penningtons have been at nearby Muncaster Castle for 800 years. You can still see the ruins of the Roman bath house, while Muncaster Castle and its gardens offer a wide sweep of attractions. The Penningtons also own this hotel, completely refurbished in 2007, a few steps from the sea and the terminus of the Ravenglass to Eskdale railway, and a short distance from glorious countryside.

The hotel bar has a light stone floor, detailed black and white photographs of Ravenglass on the wall and a light oak counter. Three beers – two Jennings, one Marstons – are on handpump. Sandwiches and baguettes are served in this room (12–14.30 only), as are Thai fish cakes, chicken liver parfait, black pudding fritter, smoked salmon platter, trio of Cumberland sausages, fillet steak, beef lasagne, broccoli and cauliflower creamy bake and more.

Next door is the AA-rosetted restaurant which has a similar sunny feel to it as the bar. For starters, expect dishes like coriander and garlic marinated scallops (£8.25), aubergine parcels (£5.50), cognac crêpes filled with fresh crab (£6.95), and pan fried chicken livers (£4.95). Main courses might include Herdwick loin of lamb (£15.50), medallion of Galloway beef (£18.50), rocket and baby beetroot risotto (£9.95), classic bouillabaisse (£16.95) and roasted peppers, courgettes, onions and chick pea casserole (£13.95).

Finish off with possibilities such as passion fruit pannacotta, bread and butter pudding or white chocolate and raspberry parfait (all £5.50–£5.95). The hotel's kitchen makes as much use as possible of fruit, herbs and vegetables from Muncaster Castle. Wines go from £15 to £45.

Lunch: 12–14.30. Dinner: 19–21 (21.30 Fri–Sun). 20 bedrooms. The Penningtons also run Sella Park House Hotel (see p38).

Pictures opposite, clockwise from top left: restaurant at the North Lakes Hotel and Spa, roaring fire at the North Lakes Hotel and Spa, the Estuary Restaurant at the Pennington Hotel, the restaurant at Winder Hall (see p22), a dish from the Greenhouse Restaurant at the Castle Green Hotel (see p22), the Greenhouse Restaurant (see p22), dish from Winder Hall (see p22)

Ullswater
Sharrow Bay

Pooley Bridge, Penrith CA10 2LZ
Tel: 017684 86301
Website: www.sharrowbay.co.uk

This famous Lakeland hotel, generally reckoned to be the first country house hotel in Britain, stands beside the shores of Ullswater, the views down the lake pretty well the same as those which captivated Francis Coulson when he first set eyes on the place in June 1948. The following Easter he opened Sharrow Bay, with five rooms and a price of just over £1 for bed, breakfast, tea, dinner and hot chocolate (before guests went to bed).

In 1952 he was joined by Brian Sack and for many years they ran the business together, gaining all manner of accolades for the high standard of food, comfort and hospitality. In 1967 the hotel became a member of Relais & Châteaux, in 1997 the restaurant gained its Michelin star.

Surrounded by 12 acres of gardens and grounds, Sharrow Bay these days is part of von Essen hotels. Downstairs in the main house are two lounges, a conservatory and two dining rooms, one overlooking the lake. There's a three-course local lunch (£32) or a five-course lunch costing £43.

In the evening, the six-course dinner (£70) might have starters of braised belly pork with homemade black pudding; or sautéed scallops with roasted asparagus, pancetta and scallop velouté. Soup or fish comes next, followed by a sorbet. Main courses could then include fillet of lamb, rolled in fresh herbs with lamb sweetbread; tournedos of Scottish fillet steak with braised shin; or fried fillet of turbot with shrimp risotto.

Desserts, traditionally displayed as guests go in for dinner, offer possibilities like passion fruit tart with pineapple sorbet; raspberry trifle with raspberry compote; or – something the hotel is very well known for – its sticky toffee pudding. A vegetarian menu is also £70. About 700 wines on the list range in price from £15.95 to £595.

Lunch: *13. Dinner: 20. Morning coffee and afternoon tea are also available.*
Directions: *Sharrow Bay is about 2 miles (3.2km) from Pooley Bridge on the south east side of Ullswater.*

Below: Sharrow Bay – the bay – at Ullswater. Below far right: Bea Grice, Temple Thai

Ulverston

Temple Thai

1 Cavendish Street, Ulverston LA12 7AD
Tel: 01229 580566
Website: www.thetemplethai.com

After 11 years living in Hong Kong and Thailand, Bea and Matthew Grice moved to England and to Ulverston where, a couple of years ago, they opened this restaurant. In a relatively short time it's picked up plenty of fans, of both the food and the service. Matthew is front of house in the two sided restaurant and Bea – born in Thailand – is the chef.

She'll happily come out of the kitchen to explain the menu and then cheerfully adapt dishes to suit your taste. Those main dishes include 25 vegetarian options, red curry with coconut milk, tofu, mushrooms, green beans, bamboo and chillies being one.

There are starters, soups and salads and, for the non-vegetarian, nearly 15 main courses, marked with a sign either indicating mildly spicy, medium spicy, very spicy and 'are you sure?' These might be yellow curry with coconut milk, tiger prawns, potatoes, onions and sliced bell peppers; stir fried pork in a peppery, garlic sauce with a touch of coriander; or stir fried chicken with onions, tomatoes, spring onions and chillies, all three priced £8.85–£9.85. Restaurant specials offer dishes like fillet of haddock, wok fried and topped with a sweet and spicy sauce (£10.10).

There's a children's menu (£2.95–£3.25 per dish), 15 wines, including a red and a white from Thailand and with prices £10.95–£25.75 and Thai beer. Happy hour is 17.30–18.30 when all dishes are £5.75. A loyalty card gives you the chance to buy seven lunches and then have the eighth one free. Vouchers for meals are also available.

Lunch: *daily except Wed and Sun 12–14.* **Dinner:** *daily 17.30–22 (23 on Fri and Sat).*

1973 Menu from Rothay Manor

Bronwen Nixon bought Rothay Manor (see p12) as a guest house in 1966 and then opened the place as a hotel a year later. It's still in the hands of the same family. This was the menu offered on Saturday, 6th October 1973. The price was £3.00

Chicken liver pâté and toast fingers
Melon boats
Carrot and orange soup
Beef sherry consommé

Roast venison marinated in red wine and cooked in huff puff pastry with fresh herbs
Stuffed leg of lamb; stuffed with kidneys, bacon, onion and herbs
Poulet L'estragon. Chicken casseroled with tarragon and chopped bacon in white wine sauce, enriched with cream

Parsley potatoes, croquettes, courgettes, broad beans

Coffee Bavarois
Strawberry gâteaux
Sherry trifle
Vanilla slice
Fruit salad
Fresh pineapple and cream

Cheese

1975 Menu from Farlam Hall

The Quinion family came to Farlam Hall, near Brampton in 1975 (see p17) and have been there ever since. This was the menu offered on Thursday, 12th June 1975, their opening night. The price was £3.

Potato soup
Hot fish pâté
Homemade cannelloni

Poached salmon and Hollandaise sauce
Grilled pork cutlets with Bercy sauce
Fillet of beef Wellington

Cheese

Food of the Gods (something akin to Eton mess, with crushed digestive biscuits) Cheese cake

Whitehaven

Zest Restaurant

Low Road, Whitehaven CA28 9HS
Tel: 01946 692848
Website: www.zestwhitehaven.com

After a year long search Ricky and Emma Andalcio were on the verge of going back to London when they found the premises in Whitehaven they wanted. Family and friends helped gut and refurbish the former pub and Zest opened in February 2000.

The couple were no strangers to the business. Ricky had started his career as a 16 year old in a gentlemen's club in St James, London, following that with spells at Langan's Brasserie and for the Roux Brothers. Emma had worked in contract catering in London, cooking her way round film studios, banks and record companies.

A visit for dinner in 2001 by the then Prime Minister Tony Blair gave the restaurant considerable publicity and Ricky has brought the Zest and Zest Harbourside names – and his enthusiasm – to a wider audience, as well, through numerous TV appearances over the last four to five years.

Zest is the more formal of the two eateries, a bar/reception area giving way to a 60-seat restaurant. Pan roasted seabass fillet (£7), char-grilled asparagus, wrapped in Cumbrian air dried ham (£6.95) and roasted garlic mushrooms (£5.50) might be amongst the starters while main courses could include chicken breast, stuffed with roasted vegetables (£14), griddled rump of lamb (£16), Thai squash and vegetable curry, grilled duck breast and grilled ribeye steak (£16). There are also weekly specials. Desserts are all priced about £4.95 and offer possibilities such as sticky toffee pudding, homemade cheesecake and Champagne sorbet with fresh fruit. Wines go from £12.75 to £21.50.

Open: *Wed–Sat 18.30–21.30 (22 on Sat).*

Zest Harbourside

8 West Strand, Whitehaven CA28 7LR
Tel: 01946 66981
Website: www.zestwhitehaven.com

Ten days after Zest Harbourside opened in 2002, Ricky and Emma Andalcio had to close the front doors. The bar/restaurant couldn't cope with the number of diners, so the kitchens had to be enlarged. Seven years later it's still a popular and lively venue, converted from an old warehouse and located on the quayside at Whitehaven which in the mid-18th century was one of the busiest harbours in Britain. The many Georgian buildings in the town are reminders of those days.

There are two small rooms upstairs with good views of the harbour but the main room is downstairs, where a bar counter runs along one side. It's more informal than Zest at Low Road and the food reflects that. 'The ultimate snacking menu,' is how Ricky describes the offering where 'blinding butties' list about ten choices: the bacon one, the egg one, the sausage one, the burger, the chip one and so on (£4.25–£6.95).

There's pasta, salads and dishes like mini Cumberland sausages (£6.25), wok chicken (£7.95), roast turkey slices (£7.25), fish stew (£7.95), Thai spiced crab cakes, and butternut squash and pineapple curry. Sweet treats include sticky toffee pudding, hot chocolate and raspberry pudding, and lemon curd cheesecake. Wines go from £12.75 to £21.50.

Open: *Mon–Thu 11–21.30, Fri– Sat 11–22, Sun 12–21.*
No reservations.

Below left: Zest Restaurant. Below: Emma and Ricky Andalcio, Zest
Below far left and right: views of the World Marmalade Festival at Dalemain

Food Festivals
(Please check websites for specific dates)

February: *World Marmalade Festival*, Dalemain, near Ullswater. This is a bi-annual event, which celebrates the taste, tradition and varieties of this preserve, with cookery demonstrations, stalls selling local produce and marmalade, tastings and an advisory service. But the day revolves around a marmalade competition, its different categories including ones for Seville orange, organic marmalade, the clergy, politicians and peers of the realm, B&Bs, children and commercial producers. When it's not festival year there's still a February marmalade competition.
Website: www.marmaladefestival.com

Easter: *Kendal College Food Festival*. This annual three-day festival coincides with Easter and gives students at the Lakes Hotel School the opportunity to show off their talent, and learn from some of the leading chefs in Cumbria. The hotel school has 350 students on its roll and does training all over the country, from colleges at Cambridge University to five-star hotels in London. Check website for festival details.
Website: www.kendal.ac.uk

April: *Damson Day*, Low Farm, near Gilpin Bridge, Lyth Valley. The one-day event takes place just as the blossom appears on damson trees in the Lyth and Winster valleys, an area of Cumbria where the fruit's been picked for generations. Organised by the Westmorland Damson Association (see p98), the event sees tastings of all things damson: jam, jelly, chutney, pickles, wine, beer, gin, syrups, vinegars, cake, bread, chocolate, ice cream, sorbets, cheese, pies, pickled damsons and more. Stallholders sell local produce, and there's music, crafts and cookery demonstrations.
Website: www.lythdamsons.org.uk

August: *Lakes Chilli Fest*, Levens Hall near Kendal. It's billed as one of the hottest annual events in the Lake District and nobody can dispute that. This inspired weekend takes place at one of the finest Elizabethan mansions in the north of England where the famous topiary gardens date from the 17th century. Cookery demonstrations, salsa dancing, children's activities and stalls selling all manner of chilli related produce and items (jams, jellies, chocolate, sauces, seeds, powders, chutneys) are the main attractions.
Website: www.levenshall.co.uk

October: *Apple Day*, Acorn Bank near Temple Sowerby. The popular celebration of the English apple at this National Trust property encompasses advice on growing apples, pruning demonstrations, tastings and sales of different apple varieties, traditional games, cookery demonstrations, local food producers' market and children's workshops. The sheltered orchards at Acorn Bank grow both local and traditional varieties of fruit.
Website: www.nationaltrust.org.uk

November: *Waterhead Hotel Food Week*. Waterhead Hotel, Ambleside. 'Inspirational lunch and dinner menus,' are promised for this annual event in the hotel's Bay Café Bar and Restaurant. English Lakes Hotels, owners of the Waterhead, say chefs showcase some of the finest local produce 'with unusual and innovative twists'.
Website: www.elh.co.uk/restaurants

Beer festivals are on page 71

Windermere

Gilpin Lodge

Crook Road, Windermere LA23 3NE
Tel 015394 88818
Website: www.gilpinlodge.co.uk

Built as a private house in 1901, this was a bed and breakfast when John and Christine Cunliffe bought it in 1987. John was no stranger to the property because his grandmother Harriet had lived here between 1919 and 1961.

The couple's collective experience, including that at the Waldorf-Astoria in New York and at Grosvenor House in London, did wonders for the place as they turned Gilpin Lodge into a luxurious hotel, with a lofty standing in the ranks of Lakeland hotels and restaurants. These days, two generations of the Cunliffe family run Gilpin Lodge because in 2001 John and Christine were joined by their son Barney and daughter-in-law Zoë. Barney's younger brother Ben carries out all the architectural work.

Downstairs at this Relais & Châteaux hotel, there are two lounges with fires in each room, and a stylish and spacious bar, with walk-in wine cellar, which was added in 2008. The garden area outside the bar was completely re-designed at the same time while two years earlier, six glass-fronted garden suites, all with cedar wood hot tubs and individual gardens, were built in the 22 acres of grounds. A bar menu is available (12–17) in the bar, lounges and gardens, with prices £5–£20.

Four very smart dining rooms, all slightly different in size and character, seat 60–70 people between them. The head chef (from January 2009) is Russell Plowman whose pedigree includes two and a half years at the Berkshire restaurant L'ortolan, and three years (before that) at the Waterside Inn

in Bray. He stepped into a kitchen at Gilpin Lodge which itself has a top reputation: 'exceptional food', 'as good as we've eaten anywhere in the world', as two visitors said in 2008.

Lunch might offer dishes like ballotine of oxtail with parsnip purée and horseradish foam; or poached and roasted breast of Goosnargh chicken, with truffled cream sauce and wild mushrooms.

At dinner, starters could include confit of organic salmon with beetroot salad and potato mousse; or velouté of Jerusalem artichoke with a mushroom croque monsieur. Roasted loin of Grizedale venison, with Wellington and Cumberland sauce; and roasted breast and confit leg of Goosnargh duck, with celeriac fondant and Bramley apple purée are possibilities for main courses while desserts might see pistachio crème brûlée with vanilla ice cream and candied pistachios; and dark chocolate soufflé with white chocolate ice cream.

There is a vegan and vegetarian menu offered as well (£47). 200–250 wines range in price from £20 to £300.

Lunch: 12–14. Two courses £20, three courses £25. Dinner: 18.30–21.15. Price: £47. Morning coffee and afternoon tea are also available. 20 bedrooms, including six garden suites.
Directions: Gilpin Lodge is about 2 miles (3.2km) east of Bowness-on-Windermere on the B5284.

Below far right: the Champagne Bar at Gilpin Lodge

1983 Menu from Michael's Nook

Michael's Nook near Grasmere was built in 1859 for a Victorian industrialist and was opened as a hotel in 1969 by Reg and Elizabeth Gifford. The couple ran it for over 30 years, winning, and then retaining a Michelin star for a number of them. Chefs who worked there included David McLaughlin (now at Holbeck Ghyll, Windermere), Andrew McGeorge (now at the Rampsbeck Country House Hotel, Ullswater), Kevin Mangeolles, Mark Treasure, William Drabble and Michael Wignall. William Drabble later took over from Gordon Ramsay at Aubergine in London. The hotel was closed in 2002 but Reg Gifford still runs the Wordsworth Hotel in Grasmere (see p39).

This was the menu offered on Saturday, 17th December 1983.

A gently poached galantine of duck, studded with pistachio nuts and presented upon a golden duck jelly enriched with port and thyme.

Cream of parsnip soup

Fresh Scottish salmon, oven baked and filled with a fine mushroom duxelle with tarragon, enclosed in a crispy pancake and wrapped in flaky pastry, served on a fish cream sauce with salmon caviar, mangetout Julienne and Parisienne potatoes

------

Crispy filo pastry parcel filled with stewed apple, flambéed with Calvados, presented upon sauce Anglaise and garnished with a brandy snap basket, filled with vanilla ice cream and strawberries.

Alternatively

Fresh orange juice
Thinly sliced, marinated gravadlax, flavoured with coriander, served with a sweet mustard sauce and a salad
Crispy spring rolls, filled with young vegetables with a hint of soya, presented upon a tomato coulis
A salad of warm chicken livers, sautéed and deglaced with port, served on a bed of salad with haricot vert, garlic croutons and fried quail eggs

------

French onion soup with Parmesan croutons

Pan-fried loin of Lakeland lamb, garnished with an aubergine cake and gratin potatoes, accompanied by a garlic and rosemary lamb jus
Half an oven roasted duck, set upon a bed of spinach and galette potatoes, served with a port and cassis duck jus and a garnish of blackcurrants
Sautéed calf's liver, presented with a veal jus with mustard and Madeira, served with sweetcorn and tomato and a garnish of roast potatoes

A selection of fresh vegetables

Your choice from our dessert menu

English cheeses with fresh fruit

Windermere
Holbeck Ghyll

Holbeck Lane, Windermere LA23 1LU
Tel: 015394 32375
Website: www.holbeckghyll.com

'Outstanding food', 'wonderful chef'. Those two comments no doubt echo the thoughts of many who have dined at David and Patricia Nicholson's luxury hotel, where a light touch, top notch ingredients and unswerving attention to detail are the hallmarks of David McLaughlin's craftsmanship as head chef.

Perched high above Windermere, with its magnificent views to the lake and the Langdale fells, Michelin starred Holbeck Ghyll has been in the hands of the Nicholsons since 1988. That was exactly 100 years after the Fifth Earl of Lonsdale acquired the property for use as a hunting lodge. The 'Yellow Earl', as he was known, was first president of the Automobile Association and gave his name to boxing's Lonsdale Belt.

Come in through the front door and you're in the oak panelled entrance hall with its inglenook fireplace and hefty carved oak table. More panelling is evident in one of two dining rooms, the one that looks out over the lake.

Two inviting lounges complete the picture downstairs while bedrooms include the Miss Potter Suite, named after Beatrix Potter. Actress Renée Zellwegger stayed at Holbeck Ghyll – a member of Small Luxury Hotels of the World – in 2006 during the filming of *Miss Potter*.

Lunch at Holbeck Ghyll can either be a two or three-course affair (£22.50 and £29.50), with starters such as salad of warm Scottish langoustines with lobster and celeriac remoulade; or terrine of confit duck, pear, foie gras and toasted brioche. Main courses could see braised daube of beef with pomme purée and root vegetables; or best end of Cumbrian lamb with Puy lentils, swede purée and haggis beignets. Try the likes of lemon tart with raspberry sorbet or crème brûlée with apple sorbet cider sauce for dessert.

A three-course dinner (£52.50) may include – for starters – salad of warm Perigord quail with white grape and Sauternes dressing; or rillette of rabbit with crostini and truffle cream vinaigrette. Mains offer possibilities such as roasted seabass with aubergine caviar and red pepper sauce; roasted loin of Lakeland venison with celeriac and juniper; and breast of Goosnargh duck with pickled beetroot and choucroute. A six-course gourmet menu (£72.50) is available as well.

Holbeck Ghyll's wine list, *Wine List of the Year* in the 2009 *Good Food Guide*, includes a selection called 'Fantastic Finds' and a big range of half bottles. Prices for full bottles – the list runs to over 300 – go from £19.50 to £610.

Lunch: *12–14. Dinner: 19–21.30. The gourmet menu is available up to 21.00. A well priced, three-course set dinner is offered Sun–Thu at quieter times of the year. Morning coffee and afternoon tea are served all year. The hotel has 23 bedrooms and a health spa.*
Directions: *the hotel is just off the A591 between Windermere and Ambleside.*

Above far right: a small ferry on Windermere. Below far right: the restaurant at Holbeck Ghyll and the view from the Miss Potter Suite at Holbeck Ghyll

Windermere
Jerichos at the Waverley

College Road, Windermere LA23 1BX
Tel: 015394 42522
Website: www.jerichos.co.uk

Just when Jerichos upped sticks from its former premises on Birch Street, hundreds of cars were being re-directed past its new front door on College Road. It became a lot quieter once the redevelopment of Windermere town centre was complete but the first few months of 2008 gave Chris and Jo Blaydes a golden opportunity to advertise their move. Good job too: this is somewhere most certainly worth coming to.

Self-taught – through reading cook books, watching chefs and eating out – Chris became head chef at Miller Howe under proprietor John Tovey, before opening Jerichos in March 1998. Birch Street was a restaurant only but the Victorian property the couple bought in 2008, originally built as a temperance hotel with tiled entrance hall and plenty of pitch pine, has 11 bedrooms plus the restaurant.

Artwork on the walls in the restaurant has a music and dance theme and there's seating for 26 people. That's less than at Birch Street, and you can't see into the kitchen either. But the food's as good as ever, simplicity being a key ingredient of the offering.

Five or so starters might include confit of organic guinea fowl leg on sweet and sour onions with onion purée, warm emulsion vinaigrette and pancetta (£7.75); pan fried king prawn, local west coast crab, vine tomato risotto with balsamic reduction and crispy ginger (£8.50) or roasted local pheasant broth with Madeira glazed sliced mushrooms (£4.50).

Of four to five mains expect dishes such as seared fillet of brill (£17.50), pan seared loin of Lune Valley lamb (£17.50), glazed egg pasta noodles with mushroom truffle cream sauce (£15.25) and a regular on the menu – char-grilled, mature, première Scotch beef (rib eye, £20.50, fillet £22.50) with grilled tomatoes, mushrooms, reduced Cabernet wine sauce, well done salted homemade French fries and Dijon butter.

Desserts (£6.25) take in the likes of dark chocolate, coffee fudge cake with homemade ice cream and mocha sauce, or organic apricot, honey and cinnamon sticky sponge pudding. Over 80 wines go from £14 to £39.50.

Dinner: *Fri–Wed from 19.00.*

Miller Howe Hotel

Rayrigg Road, Windermere LA23 1EY
Tel: 015394 42536
Website: www.millerhowe.com

Eat out at Miller Howe and you'll dine out on one of the best views from any restaurant in the Lake District. The grandstand panorama of Windermere (the lake) and the Langdale fells is the perfect introduction to lunch and dinner at this well known hotel.

Inside, things look pretty good too, thanks to a very tasteful refurbishment of the restaurant, lounges, conservatory and entrance hall over several months in 2008 by owners Martin and Helen Ainscough. At the same time the two-tiered restaurant was enlarged to take in one of the old lounges and the kitchen got a makeover as well.

Built in 1916 as a private home for a wealthy industrialist, Miller Howe was turned into a hotel in 1971 by John Tovey who, through his cooking, books and television appearances, helped put the Lake District on the culinary map of Britain. These days daytime offers lunch in the two AA-rosetted restaurant, or 'simply lunch' in the two lounges (one with wood burning stove), or in the conservatory with its slate topped tables and wonderful view. In summer you can dine on the terrace as well.

Lunch proper embraces starters like Cumbrian ham hock and foie gras ballotine (£6), main courses such as Farmer Sharp's Herdwick mutton rump or braised Cumbrian feather beef (both £12.95) and desserts like sticky toffee pudding or vanilla egg custard. If you take all three courses it'll be £23.50. 'Simply lunch' might involve Caesar salad (£7.50), pan roasted fish of the day (£12.95), or grilled Cumberland sausage (£12.95).

Dinner is a choice of either a set menu (£40) or à la carte. Between them you could see starters of risotto of Morecambe Bay shrimps; seared calf's liver (£9.50), or seared curry scented scallops, green pea purée, smoked pancetta, baby caper and poultry reduction. Holker Hall venison, roast Goosnargh mallard breast, oven roasted cod, and roast pheasant breast are possibilities for mains, most priced at £22. Wines go from £17.

Lunch: *12.30–13.45. Dinner: 18.45–20.45. Morning coffee and afternoon tea are also available.*

Windermere
Storrs Hall Hotel

Storrs Park, Windermere LA23 3LG
Tel: 015394 47111
Website: www.elh.co.uk/hotels/storrshall

Of all the grand properties and great locations on the shores of Windermere, Storrs Hall is up there with the best. Built in the 1790s by a Yorkshire landowner, it was advertised as 'one of the most desirable properties in the kingdom' when he put it on the market in 1804. Further enhancement came under the ownership of a wealthy Liverpool merchant, so that the Storrs Hall of today, set in 17 acres of woodland and landscaped gardens, bears the stamp of both these characters.

A cupola in the large reception hall is its most distinctive feature. Fortunately for diners the ornate Terrace Restaurant (two AA Rosettes) bags pride of place in the hotel, which means that while tucking into the good food here you can gaze at the boats going past at the end of the lawn.

Lunch and dinner are both served, lunch (£19.75) offering three starters (ham hock terrine on a slate board might be one), three mains and three desserts. Mains could include truffle risotto or grilled fillet of salmon.

For dinner there's a choice between an à la carte menu and a five-course gourmet menu (£42.50). A ballotine of wild rabbit (£11.50) or seared hand dived scallops with cep risotto (£13.50) are possible à la carte starters, followed by line caught halibut (£21.50), Holker Estate venison or 'a tasting of Gloucester Old Spot pork' (£18). Desserts might be banana and passion fruit soufflé or 'a sample of all things apple'. Some of these dishes could also be found on the gourmet menu.

Around 160 wines are priced £16.50–£355 while a bin end list has about 30 wines, with prices up to £165. Wine tastings sometimes take place in the original kitchen area in the cellars, so you can sample the wine at the same time as soaking up the history.

Lunch: *12.30–13.45. Dinner: 19–20.45. 30 bedrooms and 9 self-catering lodges on site. Morning coffee and cream tea/afternoon tea are available.*

What better way to start the day than have a full breakfast at one of Cumbria's country house hotels? A number of them offer breakfasts to non-residents so all you have to do is contact them and book a table. It'll give you a good meal and a great flavour of what to expect, if and when you go back for lunch or dinner. Many of them also offer morning coffee and afternoon tea, but once again, please check first.

More Restaurants

Ambleside

Doi Intanon

Market Place, Ambleside LA22 9BU
Tel: 015394 32119
Doi Intanon is the highest mountain in Thailand, so when Chris Knight and his Thai born wife, Busara, opened this restaurant – in a mountainous area of England – in July 2000, Doi Intanon seemed a fitting name for it. The two main chefs are also from Thailand, as are a number of other staff.

Well known locally, the restaurant has received plenty of favourable comments from visitors. One diner in 2006 was actress Renée Zellweger who popped in three or four times when she was filming *Miss Potter* in the Lake District.

The 32-seat restaurant is open 18–22 Mon–Thu (also 18–22 Sun in high season) and 18–22.30 Fri–Sat. 'Traditional Thai food, served in a relaxed, friendly atmosphere,' is how Chris describes the restaurant's offering, where starters include lamb satay (£5.75) and marinated chicken in pandan leaves (£5.65).

Main courses see the likes of salmon fillet in red curry and coconut sauce, with kaffir lime leaf (£13.50), king scallops, stir-fried with ginger, chilli and lemon (£12.95) and duck breast with sticky tamarind sauce (£11.50). There's a take-away service as well.

Carlisle

Crosby Lodge Country House Hotel

Crosby-on-Eden, near Carlisle CA6 4QZ
Tel: 01228 573618
Website: www.crosbylodge.co.uk
The Sedgwick family has been running Crosby Lodge for almost 40 years. The country house hotel is not far from Carlisle and only a few minutes from the M6. Much of the produce used is Cumbrian and the hotel makes its own breads, pastries, ice creams and preserves, the latter for sale as well.

Crosby Lodge is open for breakfast, lunch and dinner seven days a week, with a sandwich menu, light menu and not so light menu available at lunchtime, and a 'classical' and table d'hôte menu (£38) offered in the evenings. Sunday lunch is £28. The table d'hôte dinner menu might have pork loin with mini black puddings, the classical menu dishes like grilled Dover sole meunière (£25) and fillet steak (£29.75). Sandwiches start at £3.50.

The Spice Enterprise

Briar Bank, Carlisle CA3 9SN
Tel: 01228 599888
Website: www.thespiceenterprise.co.uk
Converted from the Enterprise pub and opened in 2007, Urvesh Bhagudia and Mansingh Rana's spacious Indian restaurant is in Belah, to the north of Carlisle city centre. It's open every night, offering kebab and curry specials (£9.95) all evening on Monday and Tuesday, and 17–19 on Wednesday, Thursday and Sunday nights.

Those specials have a pre-starter, starter, main course, rice or bread and side dish. On the menu itself, prices for main courses (including vegetarian dishes) and house specials range from £6.95 to £10.95. There's a takeaway service, with 25 per cent discount on collection only, and free home delivery Sun–Thu on orders over £20 and within a three mile radius.

Right: Crosby Lodge Country House Hotel

Gosforth

Sella Park House Hotel

Calder Bridge, Gosforth CA20 1DW
Tel: 01946 841601
Website: www.penningtonhotels.com
Set in six acres of gardens that fringe the River Calder, the property dates back over 500 years and may well have once belonged to nearby Calder Abbey.

The Penningtons of Muncaster Castle at Ravenglass, who also have the Pennington Hotel and Estuary Restaurant in Ravenglass (see p24), opened Sella Park as a hotel in 2008. The Priory Restaurant here is open every day for lunch and dinner, with most herbs, some fruit and many vegetables grown in the gardens at Muncaster.

The menu is similar for lunch and dinner, with starters including warm tea-smoked duck breast salad, with wild mushrooms, pak choi, soy ginger dressing and pancetta crisps (£7.95) or home cured Scottish gravadlax and potted shrimps with horseradish potatoes, wild leaf salad and dill and whole grain mustard sauce (£8.95).

Main courses might involve roast rump of Herdwick lamb and gratin potato cake (£18.95), slow roast belly pork with sage and shallot potato rosti (£14.95) or seared sea bass on a warm Niçoise salad. Sticky toffee pudding with Chantilly cream and vanilla pod ice cream is one of a number of possible desserts.

The restaurants on these last few pages are grouped around the nearest biggest place. Opening days and times vary, so it's best to check first if travelling far.

Grasmere

Lancrigg Vegetarian Country House Hotel

Easedale, Grasmere LA22 9QN
Tel: 015394 35317
Website: www.lancrigg.co.uk
Plenty of history is woven into the fabric of this former Westmorland farmhouse, peacefully located a few minutes from Grasmere and not far from Easedale Tarn.

It was once the home of naturalist Sir John Richardson, and a place where William Wordsworth used to wander through the grounds and write poetry. Robert and Janet Whittington have been here since 1985, their Green Valley Organic Café and Vegetarian Restaurant offering breakfast, morning coffee, lunch, afternoon tea and dinner.

An all-day menu has pizzas, sandwiches, salads and hot dishes, while dinner main courses (£12.80–£13.75) might include walnut, rosemary and pumpkin croquettes on sauté potatoes. Fig and almond pudding with an orange liqueur sauce is a possibility for dessert. Many dishes are either gluten free or vegan. Organic wines, beers and spirits are served as well.

White Moss House

Rydal Water, near Grasmere LA22 9SE
Tel: 015394 35295
Website: www.whitemoss.com
This is the place that William Wordsworth bought for his son 200 years ago and where the poet used to rest his weary legs when out walking around Grasmere. 'Never, ever, leave this vale because it's so beautiful,' a garden designer once told Sue and Peter Dixon. So although they're winding down after 35 years, they're not ready to leave yet. That said, five-bedroom White Moss House now only caters for house parties and three night dining weekends (£270–£300 per person, dinner, bed and breakfast). Check website for dates and details.

Peter's cooking got the hotel into the *Good Food Guide* in 1974 and it was still there in the 2009 edition. His five-course meals include mains like roast fillet of Cumbrian air dried Galloway beef, marinated in Coniston real ale, with woodland mushroom sauce; and free range, maize-fed Vale of Lune guinea fowl, braised with dry cider and infused with tarragon on a bed of Puy lentils. Desserts could be bread and butter pudding with Calvados; or guardsman's pudding with raspberry sauce.

Right: Lancrigg Vegetarian Country House Hotel

Kendal

Wordsworth Hotel

Grasmere LA22 9SW
Tel: 015394 35592
Website:
www.thewordsworthhotel.co.uk
For over 30 years Reg Gifford owned the famous, Lakeland restaurant Michael's Nook, just outside Grasmere. The hotel closed in 2002 but he still has the Wordsworth Hotel in the village itself, with its two AA-rosetted Prelude Restaurant (named after Wordsworth's poem *The Prelude*) and a bar/bistro called the Dove and Olive Branch. The restaurant – the food is really good, enthuses a diner – is open for lunch and dinner.

A five-course dinner costs £39.50 and may include starters like seared scallops with cauliflower risotto and lemon purée or ballotine of foie gras, salad of fine beans and truffle dressing. Main courses could be crispy belly of pork, pomme purée, confit cabbage and sherry vinegar jus; or roast turbot with a crab and ginger tortellini and sweetcorn velouté. In the Dove and Olive Branch, mains take in pan-fried breast of Goosnargh chicken, with bubble and squeak and red wine jus (£11.95) and traditional sausage and mash with onion compote (£9.95).

Bistro Déjà Vu

124 Stricklandgate, Kendal LA9 4QG
Tel: 01539 724843
Website: www.dejavukendal.co.uk
Painters, grocers, tailors, fishmongers, solicitors and picture framers have all inhabited this building at one time or another over three centuries. For the last few years it's been a restaurant and, since 2002, owned by Ian and Fran Wood. It's open every evening except on Tuesdays, offering a three-course à la carte menu for £9.95.

The menu is available Sun–Thu (all evening) and Fri–Sat (last orders 19.30). Starters take in avocado and red pepper terrine; and goats' cheese salad while main courses include the likes of pan roasted Toulouse sausage, with a chorizo sauce and garlic mash; and braised Holker Hall beef steak in a rich red wine, carrot, mushroom and onion sauce (£4 supplement). Some dishes are vegetarian and gluten free.

The Restaurant

Kendal College, Milnthorpe Road,
Kendal LA9 5AY
Tel: 01539 814700
Website: www.kendal.ac.uk
You won't find the Lakes Hotel School at Kendal College in many restaurant guides but this is where you'll get a flavour of the future of British cooking. The hotel school, with its production kitchen, pastry kitchen and a demonstration kitchen incorporating a 40-seat cinema, has already produced a number of chefs who've gone on to work in some of Cumbria's finest restaurants.

'Kendal's best kept secret,' is how the school's head Mike Mounfield describes the 54-seat restaurant, which is only open during term times: three times a week for lunch (three courses from £9.95) and every Wednesday evening for dinner (six-course tasting menu from £19.25).

Some lunches are themed, and there are occasional guest chefs. Check the website for events and openings. Giving students real experience and promoting local producers are two principle aims of The Restaurant where starters might be purée of cauliflower soup with a scorched queen scallop; ham hock terrine, warm new potatoes and sweetcorn essence; or deep fried quail's egg, poached salmon and pickled plum tomato.

Main courses could take in rump of Cumbrian lamb, red wine glaze, fondant potato and carrot purée; and pan-fried beef, braised oxtail purée potato and white onion sauce.

Left: the demonstration and private dining kitchen at the Lakes Hotel School, Kendal College

Kirkby Stephen

Augill Castle

South Stainmore, Kirkby Stephen
CA17 4DE
Tel: 01768 341937
Website: www.stayinacastle.com
It was a Victorian eccentric who built
this folly in the Eden Valley, and quirky
is still a word that springs to mind
when you step into its large entrance
hall. *Guest Accommodation of the Year*
at the Cumbria Tourism Awards 2008
and *Bed and Breakfast of the Year* at
England's Northwest Tourism Awards
2008, Simon and Wendy Bennett's 12-
room castle hosts house parties, private
dining parties (minimum six people) and
weddings, as well as offering B&B and
children's cookery courses (see p151).

As far as dinner goes, it's open to
non-residents on Friday and Saturdays
(private dinner parties can be held any
time) when a four-course meal (£35) is
eaten communally around one big table.
Warm salad of wood pigeon with lentils
and bacon; and pan fried scallops with
Muscat and honey might be amongst
the starters while roasted shoulder of
venison with red wine; baked halibut
with cockle broth; and pork loin stuffed
with garden herbs and garlic are three
possible main courses.

Cumbrian suppliers include
Mansergh Hall Organic Farm, Haigh's
butchers (Kirkby Stephen), Sillfield Farm
and Richard Woodall.

Maryport

McMenamins

Irish Street, Maryport CA15 8AD
Tel: 01900 819777
Website: www.mcmenamins.co.uk
Of all the sons of Maryport, Thomas
Henry Ismay is probably the most
famous. He was one of the founders
of the Oceanic Steam Navigation
Company, the official title of the White
Star Line whose best-known liner was
the Titanic.

As a child Ismay spent many hours
at the harbour and that's where you'll
find this 60-cover restaurant, opened in
2006 by Matty Todd and named after his
grandfather Patrick.

It's open for lunch and dinner
Wed–Sun, its menu taking in scallops
(£5.95) and king prawn linguine (£6.50)
for starters at lunch and dinner, and
steak and ale pudding (£9.95); rump
steak (£10.95), and Cumbrian lamb
chump for mains. Desserts (all under £5)
might be sticky toffee pudding; lemon
cheesecake; or syrup sponge.

Ullswater

Rampsbeck Country House Hotel

Watermillock, Penrith CA11 0LP
Tel: 017684 86442
Website: www.rampsbeck.co.uk
For many people Ullswater is their
favourite lake and you couldn't get
much closer to it than the Rampsbeck.
An 18th-century property in 18 acres
of gardens and parkland, the hotel has
lovely views across the water to Barton
Fell and High Street. Head chef Andrew
McGeorge has been here for nearly
20 years, the restaurant — completely
refurbished in the last two years —
having three AA Rosettes.

Lunch and dinner are both served,
dinner, for instance, offering a soup, and
then appetisers like roast loin of hare,
confit and purée of beetroot, grilled
chanterelles and hare jus; or pan fried
John Dory with shrimp risotto and a
lemon grass foam.

Main courses might include roast loin
of venison with braised red cabbage,
spiced blackberries, swede fondants
and a natural jus; and pan fried turbot
with caramelised apple, langoustine
tortellini and a cider emulsion. Hot
Bramley apple soufflé with toffee apple
ice cream; and hot Valrhona chocolate
fondant with Amaretto ice cream are
two possible desserts. Four-course
dinner is £49.50, soup, starter and main
course are £43.

Ulverston

Rustique

Brogden Street, Ulverston LA12 7AJ
Tel: 01229 587373
Website: www.eatatrustique.co.uk
'Excellent food', 'good value for lunch'
are two comments on the 40-seat
restaurant which Jason and Alison
Bright have run for six years. They are
open Tue–Sat, offering a table d'hôte
menu for lunch and dinner Tue–Thu
and for lunch only Fri–Sat (two courses
£15.50, three courses £19.50).

In the evening there's also an à la
carte menu which, for starters, might
offer venison, smoked ham and wild
mushroom terrine (£7.50) or pan-fried
duck salad, with soy, honey, ginger and
coriander marinade (£8.50).

Dinner main courses could see roast
lamb rump with truffle mash (£19),
roast monkfish (£20), or roast chicken
breast with wild mushroom, shallot and
smoked bacon confit (£18.50). Local
suppliers include Irvings (butchers) in
Ulverston, Cornvale Foods at Kirkby
Lonsdale and Cartmel Valley Game
Supplies and Smokehouse. Breads,
ice cream and pasta are made in the
restaurant's kitchen.

Windermere

The Hideaway at Windermere

Phoenix Way, Windermere LA23 1DB
Tel: 015394 43070
Website:
www.thehideawayatwindermere.co.uk
Richard and Lisa Gornall – he a former
catering student at Kendal College
– took over this 11-bedroom hotel in
2004. Four years later came an AA
Rosette for their two-room restaurant,
which is open for dinner Wed–Sun, and
for Sunday lunch. Richard is the chef
and for starters he offers dishes like
tempura king prawns; salmon and cod
tartare fishcake; and Welsh rarebit.

Main courses might include
Cumbrian lamb shank with rosemary
and garlic (£15.95); Reg Johnson's
Goosnargh chicken breast (£13.95);
poached lemon sole or Lancashire hot
pot. Round off the meal with the likes of
chocolate brownie sundae or hot sticky
toffee pudding.

Two-course dinner is £19.50, three
courses are £23.50. Sunday lunch is
£15.50 (three courses), £12.50 for two.
Afternoon tea is also served. You'll
notice evidence of their days at Virgin
Atlantic in one of the restaurant rooms.

Page 42
Above left: Blacksmiths Arms, Broughton Mills (see p47). Above right: Pheasant Inn, Bassenthwaite Lake (see p46). Below: Punch Bowl Inn and Restaurant, Crosthwaite (see p55)
Pictures by Helen Whitaker

Below left: Water Cut by Mary Bourne, one of the Eden Benchmarks. The sculpture is close to the source of the River Eden, above the Mallerstang Valley and a few miles from Augill Castle

Below: daffodils beside Ullswater, the lake where you'll find the Rampsbeck Country House Hotel Above right: cakes and desserts at The Hideaway at Windermere

Pubs, Inns and Bars

Ambleside

Langdale Bar

Low Wood Hotel, Ambleside LA23 1LP
Tel: 015394 33338
Website: www.elh.co.uk/hotels

It could have been called the Windermere Bar, so close is the lake to the hotel, but the restaurant got there first, and anyway the Langdales are in the distance across the water. The bar's just off the big lounge area, with globe lights, mirrors and part wooden, part black and white tiled floor. Two beers are on handpump and one of them is usually a Hawkshead.

Soup and sandwiches are served 12–19.30, the sandwiches £6.50–£7.95 and including prawn, rocket and lemon zest mayonnaise, Westmorland Cheddar and roast sirloin of beef. There are ciabattas, salads and light meals like confit of duck leg, and corned beef hash, black pudding and Woodall's streaky bacon (both £10.25). Wines, cocktails, mocktails (non-alcoholic cocktails) and a big range of coffees are available too.

Bar open: *daily 10–23. Food served 12–19.30. The Windermere Restaurant (booking advisable) serves dinner 19.30–21.30.*

Zeffirellis Café/Jazz Bar

Compston Road, Ambleside LA22 9AD
Tel: 015394 33845
Website: www.zeffirellis.com

'Great relaxed atmosphere and an intimate venue to see some amazing musicians'. So says one visitor to this bar on the first floor of Zeffirellis cinema/café/restaurant complex in Ambleside (see p13 and p160). The music evenings are usually on a Saturday and are generally free; paid for contemporary jazz concerts are occasionally held in the main auditorium.

The jazz bar is still open on other evenings of the week for coffee, drinks and food, with Jennings and Hawkshead beers on handpump and wines from £11.95–£21.50. A choice of about ten pizzas go from £7.25–£8.95 and there are snacks like green salad, garlic bread with cheese (£3.45) and goats' cheese and cherry tomato lasagne (£9.45). There's a small outside terrace.

Bar open: *daily 16.30–23.00.*

Although the examples from menus – and the prices – were correct at the time of going to print, please be aware that they can change over the months.

Below: the Langdale Bar
Below right: the Drunken Duck Inn

Drunken Duck Inn

Barngates, near Ambleside LA22 0NG
Tel: 015394 36347
Website: www.drunkenduckinn.co.uk

The legend of the drunken duck has almost become the legendary Drunken Duck. Solitarily perched at a crossroads on the back road between Ambleside and Coniston, this 400-year old coaching inn is very well known and a great favourite with many people. The cracking views, AA-rosetted food (two rosettes), cosy public rooms and beers from the pub's own Barngates Brewery all add to the attraction. And if you're staying the night, so do the 17 stylish bedrooms. Stephanie Barton, who's been here for over 30 years, has the perfect knack of mixing the new and the traditional.

For all that there's a relaxed atmosphere about the place. Hunting prints, photographs of Lakeland scenes, cartoons, and hops hanging from the beams adorn the oak-floored bar area where the counter is of Brathay Black slate. Wines are chalked up behind it while a range of Barngates ales – the choice may include Westmorland Gold, Tag Lag, Chesters Strong and Ugly, Red Bull Terrier, Cracker and so on – are on handpump. A more contemporary looking dining space is off the bar; two other dining areas – with beams in the ceiling – have white linen on the tables. As for the legend of the drunken duck, that's told above the fireplace in the main bar.

The bar menu (12–16) might have soup, cheese ploughman's (£7.50), Cumberland sausage, mash and onion gravy (£8.50) or lamb hotpot with pickled red cabbage. Cob sandwiches come wrapped in greaseproof paper and can be eaten in the bar, outside or taken away. A changing lunch menu offers two courses for £15.95, three for £19.95. Expect starters like carpaccio of beef fillet, horseradish and Parmesan shavings, or marinated salmon tartare. Main courses might be roasted loin of lamb, roasted sirloin of beef, pan fried fillet of sea bass or pan roasted monkfish, wrapped in prosciutto.

For dinner, eight to ten starters could include seared scallops and Jerusalem artichoke purée (£13.95) and salad of crab claw meat, asparagus soup, white asparagus and truffle jelly (£9.25). Main courses might have dishes like roasted loin of venison and pickled red cabbage (£24.95), fillet of sea bass, crab potato cake and confit tomato (£18.95), wild mushroom and spinach risotto (£12.95) or confit pork belly, stuffed trotter, Puy lentils and black pudding (£17.95).

Leave space at the end for puddings like dark chocolate pannacotta and pistachio ice cream or iced honey parfait and grapefruit stem ginger sauce (both £7.25). The 236 wines go from £16.95 to £175. Food suppliers are listed at the back of the menu. Barngates' Tag Lag and Red Bull Terrier are bottled, Chesters Strong and Ugly is next on the list for bottling (website: *www.barngatesbrewery.co.uk*).

Open: 11.30–23. Lunch 12–14.30, dinner 18–21. 17 bedrooms.
Directions: from Ambleside head towards Coniston on the A593. About a mile out of Ambleside at Clappersgate turn left on the B5286 towards Hawkshead. Less than 2 miles (3.2km) from that turning you'll see a road to the right signposted the Drunken Duck. The pub is about a mile up the hill.

Bassenthwaite Lake
Pheasant Inn

Bassenthwaite CA13 9YE
Tel: 017687 76234
Website: www.the-pheasant.co.uk

It says much for the Pheasant Inn that a local who first had a drink here in 1937 was still popping in almost daily 65 years later. Time and changing staff had clearly not diminished his enthusiasm for the place, and the same goes for many, many other people. This is a charming, friendly and very comfortable establishment, run in the best traditions of British inns.

The wooded slopes of Sale Fell lie right behind the Pheasant while Bassenthwaite Lake is the other way. Originally a farmhouse, it became a pub in 1778. Huntsman John Peel was a familiar face in the tap room, which is now the hotel bar. Prints and paintings of hunting scenes hang on its mellow, varnished walls and a photograph records the day in 1972 when North Western Counties beat the All Blacks at Workington.

Jennings and Coniston (Bluebird Bitter) are amongst the beers on handpump and there are over 50 malt whiskies. Soups, sandwiches and snacks are served in the bar at lunchtime, but not at night. Formal lunches can be taken in the dining room.

Lounges have comfy chairs and sofas, antiques, rugs (on parquet flooring) and log fires in winter. Fresh flowers – some picked from the inn's secret garden – are everywhere. The dining room is beamed, like the lounges, and seats about 45 people. Evening diners have a choice of either the chef's daily menu or the seasonal menu, the two being interchangeable. Three courses are £33.95, four courses £37.75, with supplements for certain dishes.

Starters might be seared hand-dived scallops or pheasant, partridge, pigeon and venison terrine. Main courses could include grilled fillet of sea bass; roast cannon of Lakeland lamb; pan fried pavé of halibut; or seared loin of local wild venison. Desserts include hot sticky toffee pudding; baked vanilla cheesecake or white and dark chocolate bombe. The 25 white wines go from £17 to £50 and the 30 reds from £17 to £76. 'An inviting menu and very good food,' enthuses one diner. Cumbrian afternoon tea is also served.

Bar open: *daily 11–14.30, 17.30–23. Lunch 12–13.30, dinner 19–21. 15 bedrooms.*
Directions: *6 miles (9.6km) west of Keswick, just off the A66 (signposted).*

Bouth

White Hart Inn

Bouth LA12 8JB
Tel: 01229 861229
Website: www.bed-and-breakfast-cumbria.co.uk

Just off the road between Newby Bridge and Ulverston – and well worth the short detour – this atmospheric 17th-century inn was Furness CAMRA's *Pub of the Season* (summer) in 2008.

Step into the partially flagstoned and horseshoe-shaped bar and you can easily envisage all those generations who've preceeded you. Old clay pipes, photographs, maps and prints, beer barrel collars and long outdated farming implements adorn the walls, as does the odd stuffed animal. Another flagstoned area is to the right of the main bar (both have woodburning stoves), there's a big games room, and upstairs a 40 seat restaurant.

The White Hart has been run by Nigel and Kathryn Barton for 10 years. Nigel won the Manx Grand Prix (senior 500) in 1989. Six beers are on handpump (Nigel and Kathryn have a Cask Marque) and there's a choice of 35–40 malt whiskies.

Lunch offers soup, sandwiches (£4.95–£5.25) and soft baguettes (£5.95–£6.25). Main courses might include rare breed sirloin steak (£15.75), gammon steak (£10.95), Cumberland sausage and halibut steak, while vegetarian options take in five bean chilli, vegetable korma, and spinach and ricotta cannelloni. Wines go from £10.75 to £16.75.

Open: Mon–Sat 12–23, Sun 12–22.30. Lunch Mon–Sat 12–14, dinner Mon–Sat 18–20.45, Sun 12–20.45. 5 bedrooms.
Directions: from Newby Bridge head west along the A590 and shortly after Haverthwaite station on right you'll see the sign for Bouth, also on right.

Broughton Mills

Blacksmiths Arms

Broughton Mills, near Broughton-in-Furness LA20 6AX
Tel: 01229 716824
Website: www.theblacksmithsarms.com

This is an enchanting old pub where the interiors are much the same as they were 200 years ago. No wonder it's one of only 250 or so places on CAMRA's National Inventory of pubs and bars with important historic interiors. Four small rooms, huge, uneven flagstones, ancient timbers, a cast iron range, open fires, original oak partitioning, gas lights, a large old table in the main bar – around which the locals gather to drink – are what Michael and Sophie Lane inherited in 2004 when they took ownership. The couple have done their legacy proud. The main bar is used for drinking only, the three beers on handpump rotating between Jennings, Dent, Barngates and others.

Starters and main courses are the same for lunch and dinner, the menu including slow braised steak, ale and mushroom pie (£9.25), vegetarian puff pastry parcel, filled with mushrooms, spinach, sun-dried tomatoes and red onion (£8.95), roasted halibut steak with crème fraîche and chive potatoes, duo of crisp belly pork and apricot and forcemeat stuffed loin of pork, and char-grilled fillet steak (£17.45). Wines go from £10.95 to £27.65.

Open: Jul–Sep, Mon 17–23, Tue–Sat 12–23, Sun 12–22.30; Oct–Jun Mon 17–23, Tue–Fri 12–14.30 and 17–23, Sat 12–23, Sun 12–22.30. Lunch 12–14, dinner 18–21. The Blacksmiths Arms takes part in the Broughton Festival of Beer in Nov (see p71).
Directions: from Broughton-in-Furness, take the A593 towards Torver and Coniston. About 2 miles (3.2km) from Broughton, fork left for Broughton Mills and it's not far down the minor road.

The Carlisle and District State Management Scheme

For more than half of the 20th century the pubs in Carlisle and the surrounding area were under government control. A scheme which was introduced during the First World War to control the drinking habits of a population was eventually brought to an end by Ted Heath's Conservative government in the early 1970s. Pubs, which for years had been run by 'civil servants', were sold off and Carlisle came back into line with the rest of the country.

The origins of the Carlisle and District State Management Scheme lay in a vast munitions factory – 9 miles (14.4km) long – built in 1915–16 across the Scottish border from Carlisle, between Dornock and Longtown. As many as 15,000 navvies descended on the area to help in the construction and when they were finished, up to 30,000 people were employed in the manufacture of munitions for the war effort.

The influx of such numbers had an alarming effect on Carlisle's night life. Many came to the city to drink, and incidences of drunkenness and violence rose enormously in the space of a short time. In 1916 the Government's Central Control Board (Liquor Traffic) and the local authorities decided that the state should take action.

The number of pubs in Carlisle and the surrounding area was drastically reduced and those that did remain open – often very plain inside – had to adhere to strict rules. Buying rounds was banned (the 'no treating' rule), prices of drinks were fixed, opening hours were cut, people under 18 were refused alcohol and advertising was outlawed. As employees of the government, landlords were paid a standard wage, so there was no incentive to sell as many drinks as possible.

With the ending of the war there was every expectation that state control of pubs should cease as well. No such thing. Drunkenness had been reduced at the same time as state ownership had brought in money for the government. In 1919 control was extended for another two years and then in 1921 the Carlisle and District State Management Scheme

was set up, its headquarters in a building in Castle Street, Carlisle which is now home to the Bookcase bookshop. Bookcase, incidentally, are publishers of Olive Seabury's comprehensive history of State Management.

In the next few years a number of restrictions were lifted and pubs themselves became more attractive, with greater emphasis on food and comfort. In the 1920s and 1930s, the chief architect of the SMS, Harry Redfern, designed a number of pubs in Carlisle – some in the Arts and Crafts style – which attracted interest from all over the country. Pub gardens and bowling greens were often a feature.

By the time the State Management Scheme came to an end in the early 1970s, many people had grown rather fond of it, in particular the beer produced by the state-controlled brewery in Caldewgate. Part of that brewery building is now used as accommodation for students, while most Carlisle pubs have changed beyond recognition. But The Redfern still stands in Etterby, Carlisle and the Silloth-based Derwent Brewery produces a beer called Carlisle State Bitter in tribute to the old scheme.

The Carlisle State Management Scheme by Olive Seabury and *Gretna's Secret War* by Gordon L Routledge are both published by Bookcase, Carlisle. An exhibition called *The Devil's Porridge*, charting the story of the huge munitions factory, built in the First World War between Dornock and Longtown, is based at Daleside, Butterdales Road, Eastriggs, just across the Scottish border.

Exhibition open: daily Easter–end October (check for details of opening times). Tel: 01461 700021.
Website: www.devilsporridge.co.uk

The pictures below come from Tullie House Museum and Art Gallery in Carlisle where numerous State Management objects are displayed in Carlisle Life, a permanent gallery which explores the modern evolution of the city.

SWEET STOUT

BREWED & BOTTLED BY
CARLISLE & DISTRICT
STATE MANAGEMENT
BREWERY
CARLISLE

CARLISLE LIGHT ALE

BREWED & BOTTLED BY
CARLISLE & DISTRICT
STATE MANAGEMENT SCHEME
OLD BREWERY · CARLISLE

CARLISLE AND DISTRICT
STATE MANAGEMENT SCHEME
19 CASTLE STREET, CARLISLE

CHOICE
DEMERARA
RUM

70° PROOF
26⅔ FL. OZS.

PRODUCE OF
THE BRITISH WEST INDIES

Cartmel

Cavendish Arms

Cartmel LA11 6QA
Tel: 015395 36240
Website: www.thecavendisharms.co.uk

The flower tubs and flower baskets lend a wonderful splash of colour to this narrow street in Cartmel, and when you step through the front door, past the old block for mounting horses, things are just as cheery and welcoming inside. Run by Richard and Donna English, the Cavendish Arms is about 450 years old and was once a coaching inn. The former stables are now the bar, the low beams and uneven floor offering evidence of age.

That bar is to the left as you come in (a separate restaurant is to the right), a biggish room where a pianist plays on Thursday nights and local food suppliers like Higginsons and Daughter of Grange-over-Sands, Cartmel Valley Game Supplies and Grange Bakery are thoughtfully chalked up on a blackboard by the fireplace. The four beers on handpump are usually Jennings Cumberland Ale, Theakstons Best Bitter and Dark Mild, and Charles Wells Bombardier.

Lighter bites and sandwiches – available from Monday to Saturday (12–14) and Sunday (12–18) – include hot rib of beef bap with chips and sautéed onions (£4.95), potted Morecambe Bay shrimps (£5.50), Cheddar cheese with tomato relish, and tuna and lemon with ground black pepper (both sandwiches, £4.95). Appetisers include fresh crab with a lime and ginger dressing. Main courses offer dishes such as roasted vegetable moussaka and Greek salad (£9.95) or braised lamb shank (£14.50). A children's menu has six choices, all under £5. Wines go from £14.95 to £27.50. Whether you're in the bar for a meal or in the restaurant, white linen tablecloths and napkins are provided.

Open: *9–23. Lunch: Mon–Fri 11.45–14.15. Dinner: Mon–Fri 18–21. At weekends food is served 11.45–21. Hours may vary slightly in winter. 10 bedrooms.*

Cartmel Fell

Masons Arms

Strawberry Bank, Cartmel Fell LA11 6NW
Tel: 015395 68486
Website: www.strawberrybank.com

Such is the commanding position of the Masons Arms that this would have been a perfect place for a castle in days gone by. Fortunately they built a coaching inn instead, in the 17th century, and the amazing views towards Whitbarrow Scar and the Lyth and Winster Valleys are here for all to enjoy.

Inside, the place has the cosy feel of less hurried times when country folk might have sat for hours and talked of this and that. Over the years countless pubs have been knocked around inside into bigger, often less intimate, rooms, but not this one. A fire burns in the hearth to your right as you enter, the floor is flagstoned and there are black beams in the ceiling. A little carpeted area is tucked round to the left while a door leads into a small, panelled room on the right. Another room, also with a range, is just past the bar. The bar itself has five ales on handpump, including Hawkshead Gold and Bitter, and about 40 bottled continental and American beers.

Upstairs is the restaurant: three different rooms which were redecorated in old fashioned paint colours in 2008. Those who sit at the oval table in the front room should pay another kind of VAT – view added tax – because of the glorious sight out of the windows. The same view is available from the outside terrace where you can sit on warmer days.

'It's always lovely, with good beer,' says one visitor. 'Great food,' says another. And that food puts a strong emphasis on the beef, lamb and cheese which Cumbria has to offer. Diane and John Taylor, who run the Masons Arms, are big supporters of what is produced in the county.

For meals, starters might include brie and tomato tart (£6.45), and chilli garlic king prawns (£7.50). Main courses could be Masons Arms steak and ale pie (£12.25), rib eye steak (£14.99), Mediterranean vegetable spaghetti (£9.99), beef and venison casserole or honey and mustard chicken (£11.95). Desserts include jam roly poly, bread and butter pudding and the Cartmel sticky puddings. Sandwiches and baguettes are also available (served Mon–Fri 12–14.30 and 12–18 on Sat and Sun). Wines go from £13.50 to £32.95.

Open: *12–23. Lunch: Mon–Fri 12–14.30. Dinner: Mon–Fri 18–21. On Sat and Sun food is available 12–21. 5 guest suites. There are also two holiday cottages available for letting.*
Directions: *from Bowness-on-Windermere head south on the A5074, through Winster and after 2 miles (3.2km) turn right on a minor road towards Bowland Bridge. The pub is up the hill on the other side of Bowland Bridge.*

Cautley, near Sedbergh
Cross Keys Temperance Inn

Cautley, Sedbergh LA10 5NE
Tel: 015396 20284
Website: www.cautleyspout.co.uk

If you take the lovely drive from Kirkby Stephen to Sedbergh, you'll come across the Cross Keys, just as the Howgill Fells come into view. It's a temperance inn which makes up in location, welcome, history and real country cooking what it can't serve in beer, wine and whisky.

Built originally as a farmhouse in the early 1600s, it was run as a coaching inn until 1903. In 1949 it was left to the National Trust by the then owner on the understanding that it never again sold alcohol. That doesn't stop you bringing your own, and tenants Alan and Christine Clowes will charge you no extra for doing so. They'll also offer you soft drinks like elderflower pressé, sarsaparilla, ginger beer, orange jigger, nettle cordial and dandelion and burdock.

Inside, the Cross Keys feels almost untouched in 200 years. The low beamed, flagstoned parlour has an 18th-century Yorkshire settle, a range, old copper scales, a piano, grandfather clock and wind-up gramaphone. Next door is the dining room, with its wooden floor and 17th century Westmorland settle, and off that is a glassed-in verandah where the tables have ringside views of Cautley Spout (waterfall).

On certain days of the week you can get tea, coffee, homemade cakes, scones and snacks and then on three nights of the week the restaurant is open. Daytime offerings might be English breakfast or vegetarian breakfast (both £7.95), toasted sandwiches, jacket potatoes, and the very popular Wensleydale gammon and two eggs. The latter is also available at night, along with steak and ale pie (£10.95), venison casserole (£13.50), rabbit pie (£10.95) and vegetable curry. Starters might be smoked salmon, black pudding or butternut risotto. Crundle (a sponge cake with milk) and lemon and meringue pie are two desserts.

Open: *Wed–Sun 10–16.30, Wed–Sat from 19. Alan and Christine will open on other nights for parties of 10 and more. A tiny shop sells drinks, cakes and biscuits. 2 bedrooms.*
Directions: *Cautley is about 4 miles (6.4km) north east of Sedbergh on the A683.*

Clifton
George and Dragon

Clifton, Penrith CA10 2ER
Tel: 01768 865381
Website: www.georgeanddragonclifton.co.uk

'Great food from the Lowther estate,' proclaims the blackboard in the sizeable car park of this former coaching inn. This is a major selling point for the George and Dragon where three months of tasteful renovation in mid-2008 put a real sparkle into an 18th-century building.

The George and Dragon is the business of two members of the Lowther family: Charles, the eighth and youngest child of the late Earl of Lonsdale, and his mother, Caroline, the Countess of Lonsdale. The estate they can call on for a lot of the produce – chickens (see p82), eggs, beef, lamb, mutton, pork, venison, game, vegetables and salmon – takes in 4,000 acres of home farm, another 65,000 acres after that and an ever expanding kitchen garden.

There's a reception straight ahead when you enter and on the left is the 90–100 seat, oak-floored restaurant where specials, such as a half pint of shell on prawns (£6), pan fried Shorthorn rib eye steak (£15.95), and oven roasted salmon and white fir apple potatoes (£13.50), are chalked up on a large board.

Starters (£4.50–£6.50) might include Brougham Hall smoked salmon with soft boiled egg or Paul's twice baked cheese soufflé. A choice of five or six main courses could have Nord Vue sausage, bubble and squeak and Yorkshire pudding (£9.50), slow cooked shoulder of pork and black pudding mash (£12.50), chicken linguini and tarragon (£12.50) and courgette and tomato penne pasta (£7.95). Wines go from £11.50 to £42.

Open: *12–23 (slightly later Fri and Sat). Lunch: 12–14.30. Dinner: 18–21.30. 10 bedrooms.*
Directions: *Clifton is just over 2 miles (3.2km) south of Penrith on the A6.*

Cockermouth
Bitter End

15 Kirkgate, Cockermouth CA13 9PJ
Tel: 01900 828993
Website: www.bitterend.co.uk

Not only did Sue and Mike Askey transform this run down, long-empty building in 1995 into a much liked local but they added a small brewery for good measure. Five years after the opening, the Bitter End was named CAMRA's *Cumbria Pub of the Year* and it's been the West Cumbrian branch's *Pub of the Year* a number of times as well.

The Bitter End's beers – take your pick from Lakeland Bitter (ABV 3.8%), Lakeland Best Gold (ABV 4.3%), Lakeland Pale Ale (4%) or seasonal ones like Cuddy Lugs (4.3%), Dark Mild (3.6%) and Wild Honey (5.5%) – are usually four of the eight ales on handpump. Others might include those from Jennings, Hawkshead or Coniston (check *www.bitterendbeer.blogspot. com*). There's a Cask Marque here too.

Quiz nights are held every Tuesday but make sure you know your Van Morrison from your Van Halen because there's usually the odd question about the former, Sue and Mike's favourite singer. The couple also have the Royal Yew pub at nearby Dean (see p56).

The lunch menu takes in soup (£3.25), sandwiches, baked potatoes, tomato and feta salad (£4.25) and main courses, all £8–£9, like bangers and mash, scampi, steak and ale pie, spinach and ricotta cannelloni, handmade fishcakes and Bitter End burger. In the evening, main courses could include fillet of haddock (£9.25), trio of lamb chops, gammon and egg, Cumbria cheese ploughman's and rump (£12.95) and sirloin (£13.95) steaks. All bottles of wine are £11.75.

Open: *Mon–Thu 12–14.30, 18–23.30. Fri 11.30–15, 17–24. Sat (summer) 11.30–24. Sat (winter) 11.30–15, 18–24. Sun 11.30–15, 18–23.30. Lunch 12–14, dinner Sun–Thu 18–21, Fri–Sat 18–21.30.*

Although the examples from menus – and the prices – were correct at the time of going to print, please be aware that they can change over the months.

Opposite above left: the bar at the George and Dragon
Above right: Charles Lowther
Right: the Bitter End
Pictures by Helen Whitaker

Coniston

Black Bull Inn and Hotel

1 Yewdale Road, Coniston LA21 8DU
Tel: 015394 41335
Website: www.conistonbrewery.com

You can't get any closer to the brewery that produces Coniston Bluebird Bitter than this 400 year old former coaching inn. Ronald and Sue Bradley have owned the Black Bull for many years while their son Ian runs the Coniston Brewery immediately behind (see p100).

Understandably, Ian's beers – Bluebird Bitter, Blacksmiths Ale, Oliver's Light Ale – are on handpump while a collection of newspaper articles about Bluebird Bitter being *Champion Beer of Britain* are on the wall of the beamed bar.

Bluebird Bitter also finds its way into the Richard Woodall Cumberland sausage which is one of the dishes on offer (£8.10), along with grilled gammon and two eggs, slow roasted English lamb (£13.95), deep fried scampi (£9.50), beef chilli, and fillet of haddock in Bluebird Bitter batter (£8.25). Vegetarian options, salads, sandwiches, toasted sandwiches, ploughman's lunch and jacket potatoes are served and there's a children's menu too.

Pub open: *10–23. Food served: 12–21. 15 bedrooms.*

Crook

The Famous Wild Boar Hotel

Crook, near Windermere LA23 3NF
Tel: 015394 45225
Website: www.elh.co.uk/hotels/wildboar

'Bend or bump', says a sign on the padded beam as you step into the small bar area at the Wild Boar. The bar is old but nowhere near as old as the 18th-century reception area, with its flagstoned floor, cooking range and display of wine.

Sandwiches (£4.95) and hot sandwiches (£8.95) are served 12–18 in two lounge areas and in the bar, where three beers, including Hawkshead Bitter, are on handpump. A malt whisky and a brandy of the month are promoted as well. Most of the food, though, is taken in the restaurant, the chef's daily specials (like smoked haddock risotto or deli platter of dried beef, ham, salami and goats' cheese) chalked up on small boards in the bar.

Starters might include bubble and squeak with ham, cheese and fried egg (£5.75), smoked salmon parcel or tomato and curd cheese salad (£4.95). Mains offer dishes such as deep fried hake and chips (£9.95), shank of Lakeland lamb (£15.50), slow cooked haunch of wild boar, and creamy vegetable pie in filo pastry (£8.95). Wines go from £13.95 to £40.95. 'Delicious food and well presented,' says one visitor.

Open: *bar, 11–24 with food served until 18.30. Lunch: 12–14. Dinner: 18.30–21.30. 36 bedrooms.*
Directions: *the Famous Wild Boar is about 4 miles (6.4km) east of Bowness-on-Windermere on the B5284.*

Crosthwaite

Punch Bowl Inn and Restaurant

Crosthwaite, Lyth Valley LA8 8HR
Tel: 015395 68237
Website: www.the-punchbowl.co.uk

This is damson country where, towards the end of April, the orchards of the Lyth Valley are ablaze with blossom. At the heart of the valley lies Crosthwaite and at the edge of the village, beside St Mary's Church, is this 300 year old inn. It certainly looks great for its age. Six months of refurbishment in 2005 put a real zing into the old timbers and the Punchbowl today is a very smart, comfortable country inn, serving much praised food. It was *Pub of the Year* in Michelin's *Eating out in Pubs* 2009.

Wander through reception (which acts as a post office on five mornings a week), into the bar and then into the two rooms off it and you'll note the subdued paint colours on the walls, the beams and the two wood burning stoves, the slate on the bar room floor (recycled from the old dining room), the long chunk of Brathay slate on the bar counter, and the chalkboards with menus, and choices of beers and wines.

The L-shaped restaurant has a low, beamed ceiling and a sweep of burnished oak floor, with a rug here and there. Tables are simple, the leather chairs high-backed and very comfortable.

Dinner at the Punch Bowl is a 6/7 starter, 7/8 main course and dessert affair, drawing heavily on Cumbrian produce. Starters might include baked Cumbrian Cheddar cheese and spring onion soufflé, wilted spinach and Parmesan cream

(£6.25); or braised pig's trotter with seared scallops and quail egg (£8.50). Main courses offer braised daube of beef, garlic mash and pot roast of seasonal vegetables (£16.95), slow cooked belly pork, served with confit root vegetables and apple jus (£14.50), or roast fillet of hake with a wild mushroom and garlic risotto. Desserts could be pear poached in red wine with vanilla cheesecake (£5.25), or apple, rhubarb and raisin crumble with honey ice cream. The 80 wines on the list go from £16.25 to £185.00.

Lunch has soups, sandwiches, baguettes, and dishes like lamb hot pot and red cabbage (£9.95), and grilled queenie scallops with Gruyère and garlic (£8). Four handpumps on the bar dispense mainly Barngates beers and there's a good choice of wine and Champagnes by the glass.

Outside is a large terrace, while upstairs the bedrooms take their names from former vicars of Crosthwaite church: Heelis, Hebblewhite, Peake, Danson and so on. For once in this part of Cumbria it's Danson, not damson.

Bar open: *12–23. Lunch: 12–18. Dinner: 18–21.30. 9 bedrooms.*
Directions: *from Bowness-on-Windermere take the A5074 south towards Winster. About 6 miles (9.6km) from Bowness turn left into Crosthwaite village and the Punch Bowl Inn is at the far end.*

Cumwhitton

Pheasant Inn

Cumwhitton, Brampton CA8 9EX
Tel: 01228 560102
Website: www.thepheasantinncumwhitton.co.uk

Considering that Chris Marshall and her daughter Sara Pearson had no experience of running a pub before they took on the Pheasant Inn in 2005, they've done a great job. Pretty well everything you'd want from a traditional country local is distilled into this sandstone building, a few miles from Carlisle. That's why it was named *Pub of the Year* in 2007 and 2008 by the Solway branch of CAMRA.

To the left when you enter is the restaurant area and on the right is the bar, with its flagstoned floor, old beams, fire in a big hearth and flowers and lighted candles dotted around the room. A quiz night is held on the first and third Thursday of each month, there's a darts board, and space on the wall is given over to exhibitions of work by local artists.

Chris and Sara (recipients of a Cask Marque) are strong supporters of the nearby Geltsdale Brewery so there are always one or two of Fiona Deal's beers on handpump, along with the likes of Yates, Hesket Newmarket or Black Sheep. 'Try before you buy' gives you a chance to sample one of the ales first.

Food is home cooked, with garlic mushrooms (£4.25), king prawns, and salmon and haddock fishcakes amongst the starters. Main courses might include fish and chips (£7.95), fillet steak (£15.95), steak and ale pie (£8.95), roasted vegetable and goats' cheese tart, brazil nut roast or chicken and ham pie. Desserts (£3.95) offer chocolate mousse, crème brûlée, sticky toffee pudding, vanilla cheesecake and more. Children's meals have scampi, sausage or mini chicken fillets, with chips or new potatoes. Wines are £10.95–14.95. 'A delightful place,' says one of many admirers.

Open: *Tue–Sat 18–23; Sun 12–15 and 18–22.30. 2 bedrooms.*
Directions: *from Carlisle head east on the A69 towards Newcastle. About 4 miles (6.4km) from the city centre, just after crossing the River Eden, turn right for Great Corby. Go through Great Corby and Cumwhitton is almost 3 miles (4.8km) on from there and signposted.*

Above far left: the Britannia Inn
Above far right: the Royal Yew Inn
Below far left: Sara Pearson and Chris Marshall at the Pheasant Inn
Below far right: the bar at the Royal Yew Inn

Dean

Royal Yew Inn

Dean, Workington
CA14 4TJ
Tel: 01946 861342

It's a toss-up as to what's more impressive – the 800 year old yew tree that stands outside the front door or the job which Sue and Mike Askey did in a two week makeover of the pub in spring 2008. Out went the old bar counter, carpets and furniture. In came oak and slate floors, a new bar with Honister slate above, comfortable high-backed leather chairs, re-upholstered benches, tables with small slate insets for table numbers, a large ironwork chandelier, a pretty cylindrical stove, new curtains and more.

Refurbishment also revealed a fireplace and bread oven in the snug, one of five rooms in this attractive 300 year old building. Two rooms have high beamed ceilings, all have nooks, crannies and alcoves in the thick stone walls. Those who know the Bitter End at Cockermouth (Sue and Mike's other pub, see p52) will notice the same creative touch at work here.

The bar is deep and of the four beers on handpump, the Bitter End's brewery supplies two. One other is a changing Cumbrian ale (Whitehaven Brewing Company, Jennings, Coniston, Cumbrian Legendary Ales). 'Try before you buy,' it says. Bottled beers from China, Russia, Thailand, USA, Germany and so on are chalked up in the bar, as are the wines. Most wines are £11.75, some are £19.

For lunch, food goes from sandwiches (£3.95), baked potatoes, and mussels in white wine (£4.50) to Royal Yew 'pub favourites' like steak and ale pie (£7.95), chicken and leek pie, fish and chips, Cumberland sausage, scampi and roasted red pepper lasagne (£8.25). Small portions of most main dishes at lunch are available at almost half the price.

Dinner includes mains like guinea fowl breast braised in Yew Tree Ale, lamb and rosemary cobbler (both £8.95), gammon and egg, char-grilled steaks (T-bone, rib eye, sirloin and rump, £12.95–£18.95) and the 'pub favourites'. Meat, notes the menu, is supplied by local butchers and is 100% traceable to Cumbrian farms.

Open: *Mon–Fri 12–14.30, 18–23. Sat 12–15, 18–24. Sun 11.30–15, 18–22.30. Lunch: 12–14. Dinner: Sun–Thur 18–21, Fri and Sat 18–21.30.*
Directions: *from Cockermouth take the A5086 south towards Egremont. About 5 miles (8km) south of Cockermouth turn right to Dean (the pub is signposted from the road).*

Elterwater

Britannia Inn

Elterwater LA22 9HP
Tel: 015394 37210
Website: www.britinn.co.uk

There must have been thousands of walkers and climbers who've come off the Langdale fells over the years and been heartily relieved to walk into this centuries old inn. Not least because of the blazing fires in the small rooms on chilly days and the six handpumps dispensing the likes of Dent, Coniston and Jennings beers. There's a Cask Marque here for the quality of the ale served while a Champion Beer Festival takes place every November (see p71).

The building's full of character and in its bar areas – one with slate-flagged floor, two with oak beams, a hall with a rocking chair by the fire – homemade food is available from noon each day. There's also a dining room where tables can be booked for certain times. Outside, a large patio area has splendid views, beyond the village green, to Elterwater's tarns.

Bar lunches include hot and cold rolls such as hot roast beef and onion gravy, hot Cumberland sausage with onion marmalade, cheese and pickle, and roast ham (£3.90–£5). More substantial dishes offer lamb Henry, steak, ale and mushroom pie, and steak mince burgers (£6.30 with chips).

Evening meals might feature king prawn skewer with sweet chilli sauce (£5), local wild venison (£12), char-grilled ribeye steak (£16), and desserts such as the Britannia's own recipe sticky toffee pudding (£4.90) and blueberry brûlée. The 27 wines on the list go from £13 to £27.50. The wine list and the menus can be seen on the inn's website.

Open: *daily 10–23. Lunch: 12–14. Snacks: 14–17.30. Evening meals: 18.30–21.30 (summer), 18.30–21 (winter). 9 bedrooms. Champion Beer Festival takes place here in November (see p71).*
Directions: *from Ambleside take the A593 towards Coniston and at Skelwith Bridge turn right for Elterwater on the B5343.*

CAMRA. The Campaign for Real Ale
Website: www.camra.org.uk

CAMRA was founded in 1971 by a group of enthusiasts who were keen to push back the wave of keg beer that then seemed to be washing over the country. The post-war years had seen wholesale closure of small, independent breweries (some absorbed into bigger operations) and the loss of many breweries attached to local pubs. Their disappearance meant a sharp decline in the availability of cask conditioned ales, beers that CAMRA felt had real character and individuality.

In its own words the organisation campaigns for 'real ale, real pubs and consumer rights'. Real ale, sometimes called cask conditioned beer, cask beer or hand pulled beer, is a living, natural product, left to mature and develop flavour in the cask from which it's finally served in the pub or bar.

CAMRA's success can be measured by its more than 90,000 membership and by the 500 plus microbreweries now operating in Britain, about 25 of them in Cumbria alone. CAMRA has four branches in Cumbria: Furness, Solway, Westmorland and West Cumbria. All four branches have information on their websites and together they produce the *Cumbria Real Ale Guide* (£4.95).

Four pubs in Cumbria are on CAMRA's National Inventory, a list of pub interiors which the organisation regards as being at the top of 'national pub preservation priorities'. The pubs are the Blacksmiths Arms at Broughton Mills near Broughton-in-Furness, the Cumberland Inn in Carlisle, the Pheasant Inn at Bassenthwaite Lake and the King's Head in Bootle.

Every summer the organisation holds the Great British Beer Festival in London and every year a *Champion Beer of Britain* is announced. In 1998 that was Coniston Bluebird Bitter. In 2008 at the same festival, Black Dog Freddy from Beckstones Brewery near Millom won gold in the 'mild section' of the *Champion Beer of Britain* awards and silver (second) in the overall competition.

Furness branch: www.furnesscamra.co.uk
Solway branch: www.solwaycamra.org.uk
Westmorland branch: www.camrawestmorland.org
West Cumbria branch: www.westcumbriacamra.org.uk

Foxfield
Prince of Wales

Foxfield, near Broughton-in-Furness LA20 6BX
Tel: 01229 716238
Website: www.princeofwalesfoxfield.co.uk

Cumbria CAMRA's *Pub of the Year* in 2007, the Prince of Wales was built at a point on the Furness railway where the branch line turned north towards Coniston. Although the Coniston route closed many years ago, the main line to and from Barrow and Lancaster still serves the place well, especially on its well known beer weekends. As many as 1,000 people can descend on Stuart and Lynda Johnson's pub for these events – a brewers' weekend, for instance, or a stout, porter, mild and strong ale weekend.

Stuart describes the Prince of Wales as a niche destination for real ale enthusiasts. It's also home to the Foxfield Brewery which over the last 11 years has produced an ever changing range of beers, Giant's Foot, Hoad Ale, Brief Encounter, Flowers of Saaz and Foxfield Flyer to name five out of about

200. Most of the beers are destined for the bar at the Prince of Wales where there's always a mild, and often a beer from Tigertops, a small brewery in Wakefield which the couple also own. Scrumpy's normally available too. Dominoes, bar billiards and shove ha'penny are played, and on the second, third and fourth Wednesday of each month there's an open evening for musicians.

Open: *Wed and Thur 14.45–23. Fri and Sat 12–23. Sun 12–22.30. Closed Mon and Tue except Bank Holiday Mons 12–23. 4 bedrooms. The Prince of Wales takes part in the Broughton Festival of Beer in Nov (see p71).*
Directions: *the pub is opposite Foxfield Station, just over 1 mile (1.6km) from Broughton-in-Furness.*

Hawkshead

Queen's Head Hotel

Main Street, Hawkshead LA22 0NS
Tel: 015394 36271
Website: www.queensheadhotel.co.uk

The inn was here before Wordsworth came to study in Hawkshead and before Beatrix Potter met and married the local solicitor, so, if proof of age were needed, the Queen's Head has it all. Whitewashed and timbered on the outside, its L-shaped, partially flagstoned main bar has lovely, low oak beams, wood panelling on the walls, an open fire and a mix of paintings, prints, old photographs and plates above the panelling.

There's a terrace outside the 16th-century building and, as you come in, a small room to the left, a cosy window enclave to the right and a panelled dining room at the back. 'It's a very inviting place and worth the drive,' says one visitor.
The four handpumps generally offer Robinson's and Hartley's beers and a guest beer, and the food makes use of much local produce: hams and sausages from Richard Woodall, organic trout from nearby Esthwaite Water, pheasant from the Winster Estate and Herdwick lamb from the Lakeland hills.

Lunch can be taken in the bar or the AA-rosetted restaurant and includes light bites like fresh crevettes with chilli and garlic (£6.50) and mains such as the popular haddock and chips (a very large portion for £8.75) and Woodall's Cumberland sausage (£7.25). There are sandwiches, salads and vegetarian options as well.

For dinner, expect starters like fresh mussels (£6.75) or special dressed terrine of Cartmel pork fillet and rabbit. As fish gets a good showing here mains might have pan-fried hake fillet (£14.95), herb crust organic salmon or seafood medley (salmon, scallops, mussels and tiger prawns in a crab sauce, £16.75).

Meat dishes include lamb King Henry (£14.75), local organic chicken breast, roast belly of Winster Valley Saddleback pork (£14.95) and prime sirloin of Cumbrian beef (£19.50). Vegetarian options include wild mushroom and asparagus tagliatelle, served with a cream and chive sauce (£12.75). The 50 or so wines are £9.50–£45.

Pub open: *11–23.30. Lunch 12–14.30 (weekdays), 12–17 (weekends). Dinner: 18.15–21.30. 14 rooms.*

Hesket Newmarket

Old Crown

Hesket Newmarket CA7 8JG
Tel: 016974 78288
Website: www.theoldcrownpub.co.uk

'Britain's first co-operatively owned pub', it says on one of two slate plaques above the fireplace in the small main bar, the plaques commemorating visits here by Prince Charles in 2004 and 2007. When the Old Crown came up for sale in 2003, 120 people stumped up £1,500 each to buy shares in this famous 18th-century pub, a much lauded example of Pub is the Hub (below). Two things really motivated them. They didn't want their local to be taken over by a big brewer or a pub chain, and they certainly wanted to carry on drinking beer produced round the back of the building by the Hesket Newmarket Brewery (see p102), another co-operatively run venture.

All this means is that when you step into what seems like the lived-in front room of a seasoned traveller's house, with its books and walking boots, climbing equipment, mountaineering photographs, and tankards hanging from the beamed ceiling, the six beers on handpump are as local as you can get. A list of the Hesket Newmarket beers – Doris's 90th Birthday Ale,

Blencathra Bitter, Great Cockup Porter, Helvellyn Gold, Skiddaw Special Bitter and such like – are chalked up behind the bar. The Old Crown was Solway CAMRA's *Pub of the Season* in winter 2007 and there's a Cask Marque here too.

To the right of the front door is a games room, with darts and snooker table, and to the left, as you head towards the high ceilinged restaurant, is another small bar. You can get soups and sandwiches, while main dishes might include Cumberland sausage (£7.45), pepper pot beef (£8.45), rump steak (£12.50), lamb chops, steak and Hesket Newmarket ale, and breaded haddock.

Open: *daily 17.30–23, also Fri–Sun 12–14.30. Lunch Fri–Sun 12–14.30, dinner daily 18–21.*
Directions: *from Carlisle take the B5299 to Dalston and then on to Caldbeck. Carlisle to Caldbeck is about 13 miles (20.8km). Turn left in Caldbeck for Hesket Newmarket.*

Pub is the Hub
Website: www.pubisthehub.org.uk

Pub is the Hub was set up by the Prince of Wales in 2001 to help retain and improve rural services through these traditional centres of village life. By way of the Rural Action Programme of Business in the Community, the scheme aims to encourage publicans, breweries and local communities to work together to enhance those services, particularly in isolated areas. If additional uses can be found for a pub – incorporating a post office or a village shop, for instance, in places where they are threatened with closure – so much the better. Such a move would save a much valued facility and also make the pub more viable, in terms of its social and community role.

One good example in Cumbria is the Black Swan in Ravenstonedale (see p64), a place that Pub is the Hub has helped and which Prince Charles visited in spring 2008. Owners Alan and Louise Dinnes opened the Village Store in what was previously a ground floor bedroom of their inn.

The shop has given Ravenstonedale a facility which it hasn't had for some years, created a handful of full/part time jobs, cut down on the number of car journeys which locals have to make for their everyday shopping and supported local suppliers.

The Old Crown at Hesket Newmarket (above) is another business that fits the ethos of Pub is the Hub, with Prince Charles coming here twice over the last few years.

Pub is the Hub believes there are many ways in which rural pubs can diversify and improve their viability but taking on a retail or post office role, in circumstances where these facilities might be threatened, is probably the most important. The latter is what the Punch Bowl Inn at Crosthwaite did in 2006, its reception today doubling as a post office counter on five mornings of the week (see p55). In August 2008 a general store was opened at the Queen's Head Inn at Tirril near Penrith, Pub is the Hub once again giving support (see p75).

Above far right: Keith and Edna Graham who run the Old Crown
Middle far right: a sign at the Black Swan in Ravenstonedale (see p64)
Right: the bar at the White Hart Inn, Booth (see p47)

HESKET NEWMARKET BEERS

The Old Crown

The Black Swan Village Store

RAVENSTONEDALE

Ings

Watermill Inn & Brewing Co

Ings, near Windermere LA8 9PY
Tel: 01539 821309
Website: www.lakelandpub.co.uk

The Watermill Inn's not even 20 years old as a pub but the awards the Coulthwaite family have already picked up outnumber the very impressive selection of hand drawn beers which are served here. *Beer Pub of the Year* in the *Good Pub Guide* 2006, CAMRA's Westmorland branch *Pub of the Year* 13 times and finalist in the *Daily Telegraph's Perfect Pub Award* 2005, the Watermill has up to 16 ales on handpump at any one time, probably the biggest permanent number in any pub in Cumbria.

Amongst them are Coniston Bluebird Bitter, Hawkshead Bitter, Theakstons Old Peculier and four from its own brewery – Collie Wobbles (ABV 3.7%), A Bit'er Ruff (ABV 4.1%), Wruff Night (5%) and Dogth Vader (5.1%) - which was opened by Brian Coulthwaite in 2006. A Winter's Tail (4.3%), Paws for Thought (4.5%) and Ruff Justice (4.2%) are three other ales he has produced.

Food is served all day but baguettes, sandwiches and jacket potatoes are only available 12–17. For more substantial meals 12–21, main courses might be beef and Collie Wobbles ale pie (£10.25), Mediterranean pasta bake (£8.95), gammon steak, Thai fish cakes, Kentmere lamb steaks, Cumberland sausage (£9.50), minted lamb Henry (£13.25) or sirloin steak.

Open: *Mon–Sat 11.45–23, Sun 11.45–22.30. Food served 12–21. 8 bedrooms. Collie Wobbles, A Bit'er Ruff and Wruff Night are available in bottles.*
The Lakeland Beer Festival takes place here in April (see p71).
Directions: *Ings is just off the A591, about 3 miles (4.8km) east of Windermere town.*

Kendal

Burgundy's Wine Bar

Burgundy's Wine Bar
19 Lowther Street, Kendal LA9 4DH
Tel: 01539 733803
Website: www.burgundyswinebar.co.uk

Home of the Cumbrian Micro-Brewery Challenge, Burgundy's has been run since 1986 by Mike and Yvonne Pennington. Wines, beers, lagers and Champagnes are served from a tile-roofed bar just inside the front door, with four real ales always on tap. Hawkshead Bitter and Hesket Newmarket's Helvellyn Gold might be two of them.

Fruit wines, teas and coffees are also available, while soups, sandwiches and baguettes are offered at lunchtimes. The list of 24 wines goes from £10.50 to £30 and there's a separate Champagne list as well. Thursday nights here see live jazz.

Open: *Thu–Sat 11–15.30, Tue–Sat 18.30–24, Sun 19–24.*

Below: a choice of the Watermill Inn's own beers. Below right: Mike Pennington at Burgundy's Wine Bar.

Loweswater

Kirkstile Inn

Loweswater, near Cockermouth CA13 0RU
Tel: 01900 85219
Website: www.kirkstile.com

It's not hard to see why Londoners make the 14-hour round trip for a weekend stay at the Kirkstile Inn. The pub's habitat is pure, unadulterated Lakeland, with Melbreak, Grasmoor, Low Fell and others standing like sentinels around the 16th-century building. Crummock Water is a few minutes away down a track, and Loweswater and Buttermere are not that far either.

This very welcoming inn has been owned by Roger and Helen Humphreys since 2000, their aim of providing 'real ale, good food, a hospitable atmosphere and good service' bringing plenty of accolades. The Kirkstile has been West Cumbria CAMRA's *Pub of the Year* on four occasions, including 2008, and regional winner in 2006 and 2007 in the *Daily Telegraph's Perfect Pub Award*.

A small brewery adds to the attraction because its four beers – Kirkstile Gold (ABV 4.3%), Melbreak (ABV 3.7%), Grasmoor Dark (4.3%) and Loweswater Pale Ale – LPA (4%) – are only available here. Kirkstile Gold and Grasmoor are both bottle conditioned and sold at the Kirkstile only. The brewers are Matt Webster and Hayley Barton.

The beamed, L-shaped bar has a fire which never seems to go out (Yates and Coniston beers might be two of the six on handpump) and there are two other bar areas, a restaurant and a verandah overlooking the beer garden. For lunch the Kirkstile offers sandwiches, baguettes, jacket potatoes and such dishes as Cumberland tatie pot (£6.95), poached salmon fillet (£8.75) and penne pasta carbonara (£6.95).

Evening starters might be Brougham Hall smoked chicken or Crofton goats' cheese stumpie (both £4.95). Main courses could include roasted hake fillet (£9.95) and baked lamb shoulder (£12.25), with deserts like Cumberland rum nicky (£4.75). The Old Smokehouse at Brougham Hall, near Penrith and Thornby Moor Dairy near Carlisle are amongst the suppliers. Wines are £13.95–19.50.

Open: *11–23 (coffees available earlier). Lunch: 12–14. Dinner: 18–21. 8 bedrooms including a family suite. Morning coffees, afternoon teas and snacks available. Beer and Tatie Pot Festival here in April (see p71).*

Directions: *from Cockermouth take the B5292 south east out of the town and then after about 4 miles (6.4km) keep straight ahead on the B5289. 3 miles (4.8km) after Low Lorton fork right for Loweswater and then look out for signs for the Kirkstile.*

Right: Loweswater, not far from the Kirkstile Inn

Ravenstonedale

Black Swan Hotel

Ravenstonedale, near Kirkby Stephen CA17 4NG
Tel: 015396 23204
Website: www.blackswanhotel.com

Such has been the transformation effected by Alan and Louise Dinnes at the Black Swan that Prince Charles paid a visit here in spring 2008. What particularly interested him was how his vision for Pub is the Hub (see p60) had thrown up such a good example in this lovely part of Cumbria. Not only do Alan and Louise offer four real ales on handpump, food in the bar and restaurant, newspapers to read and internet access, but their creation of the Village Store out of a ground floor bedroom has provided locals with the chance to buy groceries, gifts, newspapers, stamps, stationery and such like without leaving the village.

The Black Swan is a late Victorian building with a biggish bar area, a smaller bar/restaurant with fireplace off to the left, and another restaurant. Light refreshments are available all day and include soups, sandwiches, panini and jacket potatoes.

The same menu is available in the bar and restaurant. Starters might include homemade trout or salmon fish cake (£4.95), black pudding with apple, bacon and creamy pepper sauce (£4.75) and soup of the day. Main courses could be grilled whole Borrowdale trout (£8.95), Ravenstonedale rump steak (£13.95) or a seasonal pie with game and rabbit (£9.95). Wines go from £11.95 to £49.95.

Open: *Sun–Thur 8–24, Fri and Sat 8–1am. Lunch: 12–14. Dinner 18–21. 11 bedrooms. Riverside garden.*
Directions: *from the M6 at Tebay take the A685 east towards Kirkby Stephen. Ravenstonedale is about 8 miles (12.8km) along there, just off the main road.*

Seathwaite

Newfield Inn

Seathwaite, near Ulpha LA20 6ED
Tel: 01229 716208
Website: www.seathwaite.freeserve.co.uk

The Duddon Valley was one of William Wordsworth's favourite places, a sliver of the Lake District about which he wrote over 30 sonnets. It's no surprise then that 17th-century Newfield Inn, which he also visited, stands in glorious countryside, not far from Walna Scar where the floor slate in the pub's round table bar was originally quarried. Next door to the bar is the snug, with a 1904 photograph of the inn hanging on the wall. There are two other rooms (for games and eating) and a garden, with a children's play area.

You'll come across quite a few of the Batten family in the Duddon Valley but it's Paul and Alwyn Batten who run the pub, as Paul's parents, John and Gail, did before them. They're cheerful and very welcoming people and the pub is extremely popular with walkers and climbers. The four beers on handpump could include those from Jennings, Cumbrian Legendary Ales, Dent and Barngates but well over 200 guest ales have also been served in the last seven years or so. It's not unknown for big groups visiting the pub from elsewhere in the country to order up a particular beer before their arrival.

Expect to find soup and sandwiches on the menu along with dishes like ham and eggs, steak pie, sirloin steak, T-bone steak (£15.95), spicy bean casserole (£7.95), beef lasagne and Cumberland sausage (£8.45). Most wines are £10.95.

Open: *11–23. Food served 12–21. 2 self-catering flats (next door).*
Directions: *from Duddon Bridge (near Broughton-in-Furness) on the A595 head north on a minor road to Ulpha and then fork right for Seathwaite. Duddon Bridge to Seathwaite is about 6 miles (9.6km).*

Sizergh
Strickland Arms

Sizergh, near Kendal LA8 8DZ
Tel: 015395 61010
Website: www.ainscoughs.co.uk

Handsome is as handsome does. For several years this fine looking pub lay empty, before Martin Ainscough took on the lease from the National Trust and did the place up. He scoured the auction houses and antique shops of Cumbria and Lancashire to find tables, chairs, settles, prints, rugs, paintings and other objects, aiming to do justice to the work of George Webster, believed to have been the pub's 19th-century architect.

There's an outside terrace, a quiz night on Wednesdays, and four beers on handpump. 'Staff are really welcoming,' says one visitor. 'Excellent bar menu for lunch and dinner. Fish evening on Thursday. Huge Sunday lunches (too huge). Great wine by the glass,' comments another.

The lunchtime menu includes baguettes (smoked salmon and cream cheese; roast chicken, mustard mayonnaise and fresh rosemary, for example, at £5) and salads at £8.95.

In the evening there might be lamb hot pot, topped with sliced potato and served with pickled red cabbage and warm crusty bread (£10.95) or mixed game casserole (venison, rabbit, guinea fowl and pheasant), with brandy and autumn berries (£11.95). Wines (including organic wines) go from £12.65. Martin Ainscough owns the well-known Miller Howe Hotel at Windermere (see p35).

Open: *winter, Mon–Fri 11.30–15, 17.30–23, food served 12–14, 18–21. Sat 11.30–23, food served 12–14.30, 18–21. Sun 12–22.30, food served 12–20.30. Jun–end Sep bar is open all day, every day with food service as above. Food served all day on Bank Holidays.*
Directions: *about 4 miles (6.4 km) south of Kendal, just off the A591.*

Staveley
The Beer Hall

Staveley Mill Yard, Staveley, Kendal LA8 9LR
Tel: 01539 822644
Website: www.hawksheadbrewery.co.uk

Hawkshead Brewery's move to Staveley in 2006 not only gave it expanded brewing capacity but also space for The Beer Hall, an increasingly popular destination by day, and by night when it's privately hired for parties and other events. The long bar offers Hawkshead Bitter, Red and Lakeland Gold, Brodie's Prime (named after owner Alex Brodie) and Lakeland Lager. The handpumped beer is fed from the cold cellar directly below.

There's a growing range of bottled beers from Europe and the United States, and a wine list, which specialises in organic wines (Organico is next door, see p144), with a changing choice of organic wine by the glass. Bottles of Hawkshead beers and gift packs are for sale too.

The hall is a large, oak-floored space with four sofas, and chunky tables and chairs, which were made by Out of the Woods in Staveley. Peer through a large internal window and you'll see the brew house below (see p102), while the brewing process itself is clearly explained on one of the walls. You can take your beer through to Wilf's Café next door or have a Wilf's meal served in the bar. There are two beer festivals a year here showcasing SIBA (Society of Independent Brewers) gold medal winners.

Open: *Mon and Tue 12–17, Wed–Sun 12–18. Brewery tours by arrangement. Beer festivals take place here in February and July (see p71).*
Directions: *Staveley is about 4 miles (6.4km) east of Windermere, just off the A591.*

Staveley
Eagle and Child

Kendal Road, Staveley LA8 9LP
Tel: 01539 821320
Website: www.eaglechildinn.co.uk

'If you're sitting in an office in London your view of a Lakeland pub will be of a place that has a real fire, a decent pint of Cumbrian beer and food made from local produce'. If Richard Coleman's right then the Eagle and Child, which he runs with his wife Denise, fits the bill perfectly. Westmorland CAMRA's *Pub of the Year* 2007 has two fires in its main room, five beers on handpump (which might include those from Hawkshead, Coniston, Hesket Newmarket and Yates), and a food suppliers' list which takes in Lakes Speciality Foods and Hayton's butchers. Both are in Staveley.

It's a part-flagstoned and vaguely L-shaped room which you step into, with the bar counter to the left and a mildly eccentric mix of bits and bobs either hanging from the ceiling or fixed to the wall. Roller skates, truncheons, fishing rods, a rope ladder, bottles, mirrors, bellows, tennis rackets, football boots, helmets, lamps and beer mats are amongst them. Newspapers are available, candles are on the tables and a live music quiz is held every Thursday night. A great sense of well-being hangs in the air. The beer garden, which lies across the road, beside the River Kent, was runner-up in 2007 in The Guardian newspaper's *Top 10 Pub Gardens*.

'Lunch for a fiver' (Mon–Sat 12–14.30) could have vegetarian chilli, beef chilli, battered cod and chips or Cumberland sausage and mash. Sandwiches and baguettes are available as well. Desserts might be apple crumble or a trio of chocolate terrine (£4.50). There are changing specials, a Junior Eagles menu and a two course Sunday lunch for £9.95. Look forward to roast silverside of fellbred beef or cod loin, oven roasted with garlic and herb butter, as two of numerous possibilities. The dinner menu has main courses like lamb Henry (£12.95), Hawkshead ale pie, vegetarian paella (£8.50), vegetable lasagne and sirloin steak (£16.95). Wines go from £11.50–£29.50.

Open: *Mon–Sat 11–23, Sun 12–22.30. Lunch: 12–15. Dinner: 18–21. The Taste of Cumbria Beer Festival is held here in May (see p71).*
Directions: *Staveley is about 4 miles (6.4km) east of Windermere, just off the A591.*

Opposite, clockwise from top left: the bar at the Church House Inn, Torver (see p68), the restaurant at the George and Dragon, Clifton (see p52), one of the bars at the Strickland Arms, Sizergh (see p65), a restaurant area at the Masons Arms, Cartmel Fell (see p50), a roaring fire at the Pheasant Inn, Cumwhitton (see p56) and the Strickland Arms, Sizergh.

Talkin

Blacksmiths Arms

Talkin, near Brampton CA8 1LE
Tel: 016977 3452
Website: www.blacksmithstalkin.co.uk

Even on a Monday or Tuesday evening in winter this fellside pub can buzz with the sound of conversation, such is its popularity. Close to lovely Talkin Tarn, the Blacksmiths has been very cheerfully and efficiently run by Anne and Donald Jackson for over ten years. The bar areas are straight ahead and to the right as you enter, the room on the right having an open fire which is assiduously tended by Donald (after putting on his big gloves). The Old Forge restaurant is to the left and there's a garden room at the back.

Four handpumps offer a revolving choice of beer, including Yates, Jennings, Hawkshead, Geltsdale (its bottled beers are also sold to take away), Black Sheep and Copper Dragon, while there are over ten house red wines and ten whites, chalked up on a board. Generously portioned food is home cooked and traditional, the head chef being Emma, Anne and Donald's daughter.

Starters could include black pudding (£4.65), or deep fried brie with cranberry sauce (£4.75), mains might have duck breast fillet with port and plum sauce (£11.95), smoked haddock pasta, vegetable curry (£7.25), mushroom stroganoff, breast of pheasant, venison casserole and lamb shank (the last two £11.95). Desserts, like lemon crunch, hot chocolate fudge cake and ginger sponge pudding, go from £3.45. Wines start at £11.95.

Open: *12–15 and 18–23. Lunch: 12–14. Dinner 18–21. 8 bedrooms, and a former chapel which is available for self-catering or B&B.*
Directions: *from Brampton head south on the B6413 towards Castle Carrock and after about 2 miles (3.2km) turn left for Talkin.*

Torver

Church House Inn

Torver, near Coniston LA21 8AZ
Tel: 015394 41282
Website: www.churchhouseinntorver.com

I didn't expect to see David Bowie in Torver but there he was, on the corridor wall of this pub, which lies in quiet countryside near Coniston Water. For six years owner Mike Beaty was chef on the musician's private yacht in the south of France, then later he was the first head chef of The Samling at Windermere. Renowned Michael's Nook at Grasmere (no longer a restaurant) is on his CV as well, so lots of experience lies behind the food here.

There's an immediately welcoming feel to the Church House Inn which Mike, a keen fisherman, took over three years ago with partner Mandy Groves. Low beams, a bar incorporating old beer barrels, a big fire with slate surround, and tables and benches dotted about give the place plenty of character. On the other side of the bar is the snug and at the end of the corridor a large, high ceilinged room, the restaurant.

Light lunches include sandwiches (£4.95), served on white or granary bread with a seasonal salad. In the evening starters might be crispy confit duck (£5.25) or seared scallops and Bury black pudding, while mains offer possibilities like rib eye Belted Galloway beef (£16.95), cassoulet (in winter, £13.25,) steamed steak, ale and kidney pudding, or Church House fish pie. 'The cooking certainly lives up to the reputation. It's great,' says one visitor. 'Wonderful, food ten out of ten,' another told me just before I arrived.

Open: *summer, daily 12–24; winter, daily 12–24 but closed Mon and Tue lunchtimes. Lunch: 12–15. Dinner: 18–21.*
Directions: *Torver is just over 2 miles (3.2km) south of Coniston on the A593.*

Ulverston

Bay Horse Inn

Canal Foot, Ulverston LA12 9EL
Tel: 01229 583972
Website: www.thebayhorsehotel.co.uk

Past the auction mart, past the building supplies firm, the kitchen and bathroom showroom and the complex that is GlaxoSmithKline, and the world finally opens up. You've arrived at one of the best eating pubs in Cumbria, with views across the Levens Estuary thrown in free. Former Miller Howe head chef Robert Lyons and Lesley Wheeler have been at the helm for 20 years, creating food at this hotel and restaurant that elicits praise from far and wide. In the 2009 edition of the Good Hotel Guide the Bay Horse received a César Award as *Cumbrian Inn of the Year.*

Go in the main door and there's a small pubby room which leads into a bigger bar area, traditional, beamed and cosy, with an open fire in an attractive green surround. Three handpumps serve beers from the likes of Jennings and Marstons and there's a Cask Marque here as well. Off the main bar is the conservatory restaurant, with its views across the water. In the 18th century the Bay Horse was a collection of fishermen's cottages, then later a coaching inn, used by people waiting to get across the treacherous sands of Morecambe Bay to Lancaster.

Lunch offers soup (£3.95), sandwiches and baked potatoes. Sandwiches include roast beef with grain mustard and a horseradish cream (£4.85) or smoked chicken with curry mayonnaise and toasted coconut (£4.60). Hot sandwiches are available on toasted ciabatta or multigrain baguette. For bigger meals the lunch menu has about six starters and seven or eight main courses. The latter might include Lakeland lamb shank, braised, with orange, ginger and red wine, or fresh crab and salmon fish cakes on a white wine and fresh herb cream sauce (both £13.95). The chunky chips are the 'best in England' says one visitor.

For dinner, a monthly changing à la carte menu could offer main courses of rack of saltmarsh lamb, roasted with honey, lemon and crushed coriander (£23.50), fresh fillets of sea bass, lightly poached with a Noilly Prat and chive cream sauce (£22.50) or Aberdeen Angus fillet steak (£25.50). Plenty of vegetarian options are available, including hazelnut pancake, filled with fresh wild mushrooms and served with a garlic and chive cream sauce. 'Great wines as well as food,' says one visitor. Those wines generally go from £16.50 to £40 although a Wine of the Month is £12.50.

Pub open: *daily 9–23. Lunch: 12–14 (lite bite menu offered 12–16 on Monday, 12–18 every other day). Dinner: 19.30 for 20. 9 bedrooms with names like Curlew, Sandpiper and Heron. Robert Lyons holds cookery courses here every November (see p150).*
Directions: *as you come into Ulverston on the A590 from Newby Bridge, turn left at the cattle market into North Lonsdale Road and the Bay Horse is just over 1 mile (1.6km) down there.*

Yanwath

Yanwath Gate Inn

Yanwath, near Penrith CA10 2LF
Tel: 01768 862386
Website: www.yanwathgate.com

Right from the word go Matt Edwards had a very clear idea of what he wanted to offer at this friendly 17th-century inn, a few minutes from Ullswater: top quality, informal dining with Cumbrian producers at the heart of his suppliers' list. Well, the producers are listed at the back of the menu. They include Lowther Park Farms, Saddleback Foods and Smokerie, Lakes Speciality Foods, Cumbrian Fellbred, Thornby Moor Dairy and Frank Stainton Wines, and in the *Good Pub Guide* 2007 and 2009 the Yanwath Gate was named *Cumbria Dining Pub of the Year*.

There's a rather smart feel to the bar area, with its old beams, mix of chairs and tables (church candles in the centre), small paintings on the walls, newspapers and magazines to enjoy and an open fireplace, dated 1687. Three handpumps offer beers from the likes of Tirril, Keswick and Hesket Newmarket breweries. Nearer the garden at the back there are two oak-floored dining areas, one of them with panelled walls.

Matt Edwards, who 'champions Cumbrian food and ales', as one visitor enthuses, took over the pub in 2004 and with him came head chef Matt Lucas. The two Matts have proved a winning combination. For lunch, appetisers might be a bowl of mussels (£7.95), soup (£4.50) or ham terrine (£6.95). Main courses offer choices such as fisherman's pie, venison burger and chips (both £9.95) or Cumberland sausage and Yanwath Gate black pudding (£9.95).

Dinners include mains like red bream (£15.95), crispy pork belly, smoked venison loin (£18.95) and open lasagne of mushrooms and summer vegetables (£15.95). A selection of desserts might have chilled chocolate timbale or sticky date pudding.

Open: *12–23. Lunch: 12–14.30. Dinner: 18–21.*
Directions: *from Penrith head south on the A6 and just out of town (after crossing the River Eamont), turn right towards Pooley Bridge on the B5320. Yanwath is about 1 mile (1.6km) along that road on the right.*

Beer Festivals

Here are a number of the beer festivals that take place in Cumbria every year. Please check websites for specific dates. You can also look at the websites of the four different CAMRA branches in the county (see page 58) for dates and news of other beer festivals.

February: *Beer Festival.* The Beer Hall, Staveley.
Website: www.hawksheadbrewery.co.uk

April: *Cumbrian Micro-Brewery Challenge.*
Burgundy's Wine Bar, Kendal.
Website: www.burgundyswinebar.co.uk

April: *The Lakeland Beer Festival.* Watermill Inn, Ings.
Website: www.lakelandpub.co.uk

April: *Beer and Tatie Pot Festival.* Kirkstile Inn,
Loweswater, near Cockermouth.
Website www.kirkstile.com Tel: 01900 85219.

May: *Taste of Cumbria Beer Festival.*
Eagle and Child, Staveley.
Website: www.eaglechildinn.co.uk

June: *Keswick Beer Festival.*
Keswick Rugby Club.
Website: www.keswickbeerfestival.co.uk

June: *Boot Beer Festival.* The Boot Inn, Brook House Inn and Woolpack Inn, Eskdale.
Website: www.bootbeer.co.uk

July: *Eden Valley Beer Festival.*
The White Horse at Kings Meaburn near Penrith.
Tel: 01931 714256.

July: *Beer Festival.* The Beer Hall, Staveley.
Website: www.hawksheadbrewery.co.uk

August: *Cumbrian Beer and Sausage Festival.*
Queen's Head Inn, Tirril, near Penrith.
Website: www.queeensheadinn.co.uk

August: *Rheged Annual Beer Festival.*
Rheged near Penrith.
Website: www.rheged.com

September: *Furness CAMRA Ulverston Beer Festival.*
Coronation Hall, Ulverston.
Website: www.furnesscamra.co.uk

September: *Silloth Beer and Music Festival.*
Takes place in a marquee on the green.
Website: www.sillothbeerfestival.co.uk

October: *Solway Beer Festival.* In 2008 the festival was held at the Lakes Court Hotel in Carlisle.
Website: www.solwaycamra.org.uk

October: *Westmorland Beer and Cider Festival.*
Town Hall, Highgate, Kendal.
Website: www.camrawestmorland.org

November: *Broughton Festival of Beer.*
8 pubs in the Broughton area participate.
Website: www.broughtonfestivalofbeer.org.uk

November: *Champion Beer Festival.* Britannia Inn,
Elterwater. *Website: www.britinn.co.uk*

November: *West Cumbria CAMRA Beer Festival.*
Civic Hall, Whitehaven.
Website: www.westcumbriacamra.org.uk

December: *Cockermouth Beer Festival.*
Kirkgate Centre, Cockermouth.
Website: www.cockermouthbeerfestival.co.uk

The Cask Marque Trust
Website: www.cask-marque.co.uk

The Cask Marque Trust was set up in 1997 to raise the standards of cask ale being offered in pubs and bars, after a survey of more than a 1000 pubs found that one in every five pints then sold was of poor or inconsistent quality. Since 1997 almost 5000 licensees have been presented with the familiar looking Cask Marque plaque, 50–60 of them in Cumbria. In order to qualify, each licensee has to pass two unannounced visits by an assessor who checks every cask ale on the premises for temperature, appearance, taste and aroma. Regular inspections, says the Trust, continue from then on. The award is made to the licensee, for his or her good cellar management, not the pub.

More Pubs, Inns and Bars

Ambleside

Golden Rule

Smithy Brow, Ambleside LA22 9AS
Tel: 015394 32257
Up a side street at the northern end of town, the Golden Rule is a well known beer pub. Four bitters and a mild are on handpump (Robinson's and Hartley's) while food is confined to rolls, pork pies and pickled eggs. Photographs in the darts room show what a jolly time can be had here.

Lucy4 Wine Bar and Bistro

2 St Mary's Lane, Ambleside LA22 9DG
Tel: 015394 34666
Website: www.lucy4.co.uk
This is one of two Lucy4 wine bars, the other being in Bowness-on-Windermere. A range of 70–80 wines and beers are offered and food includes antipasto nibbles, grilled sardines and feta stuffed peppers. Lucy4 at the Porthole is at 3 Ash Street, Bowness-on-Windermere (*015394 42793*).

The pubs, inns and bars on these pages are grouped around the nearest biggest place. Opening days and times vary, so it's best to check first if travelling far.

Old Dungeon Ghyll Hotel

Great Langdale, near Ambleside LA22 9JY
Tel: 015394 37272
Website: www.odg.co.uk
The sloping, flagstoned floor of the Hikers' Bar – with great views outside – has been well trodden by walkers and climbers over the years, which explains the climbing photographs and equipment on the walls. There are eight handpumps, a blazing fire in the big range on chilly days and two lots of seats built into old cow stalls. Music nights are held on the first Wednesday of every month.

Other pubs in the Langdales include Wainwrights at Chapel Stile, Three Shires Inn, Little Langdale (*www.threeshiresinn.co.uk*) and the New Dungeon Ghyll Hotel, Great Langdale (*www.dungeon-ghyll.com*).

Appleby

Royal Oak

Bongate, Appleby CA16 6UN
Tel: 017683 51463
Website: www.royaloakappleby.co.uk
Major refurbishment has taken place at this warm and welcoming 17th-century inn since Kyle Macrae and Janice Hunter took over in 2006. New oak panelling has gone into the tap room and lounge bar (Alan Stones prints on the wall), but an 18th-century presence remains with two settles in the lounge. There are fires in both rooms. A comfortable restaurant seats about 60. Good use is made of local suppliers and up to three beers are on handpump. There's a Cask Marque and a Beautiful Beer Award (gold).

Barrow-in-Furness

Duke of Edinburgh Hotel

Abbey Road, Barrow-in-Furness LA14 5QR
Tel: 01229 821039
Website: www.thedukehotelandbar.co.uk
Major refurbishment of this grand Victorian hotel has brought a new look to the Consort Bar, with walls back to bare brick, fireplaces exposed, and cornicing and wooden floors spruced up too. The high-ceilinged bar offers eight hand drawn beers and some 50 bottled beers. There's regular live music.

Stagger Inn

Long Lane, Stainton-with-Adgarley, near Barrow LA13 0NN
Tel: 01229 462504
Website: www.wormall-leisure.co.uk
The original part of the pub has old beams, exposed stone, decorative ironwork and leather tub chairs huddling near the fire. Another area has a part oak, part slate floor, artwork on the walls and a TV above a leather sofa. Four handpumps dispense the likes of Hawkshead and Coniston beers.

Beetham

The Wheatsheaf

Beetham, Milnthorpe LA7 7AL
Tel: 015395 62123
Website: www.wheatsheafbeetham.com
The Wheatsheaf, which has been welcoming guests since 1609, has a lounge bar as you come in and another bar at the back, with open fire and attractive horse prints on the wall. A 'Feast of Fish' is offered every Friday while 'A Taste of Cumbria' speciality food board is available all day.

Bowness-on-Windermere

The Angel Inn

Helm Road, Bowness-on-Windermere
LA23 3BU
Tel: 015394 44080
Website: www.the-angelinn.com
Built originally as a private home, it's been the Angel Inn since 2005. There are various areas in which to eat and drink, including two lounges at the front and a conservatory. The inn has a stated commitment on its menu to Cumbrian suppliers. The chocolate torte is 'divine', says one visitor.

Brown Horse Inn

Winster, near Bowness-on-Windermere
LA23 3NR
Tel: 015394 43443
Website: www.thebrownhorseinn.co.uk
A few minutes from Bowness-on-Windermere is this 1850s inn, with farm shop attached. Both make good use of produce – beef, lamb, game, vegetables and such like – from the local Brown Horse Estate. One side of the pub is the bar area, with Coniston, Dent and Hawkshead amongst the three or four changing hand drawn beers, and the other side is a 50 seat restaurant.

Below: the sign of the Cask Marque (see p71)

Broughton-in-Furness

Manor Arms

The Square, Broughton-in-Furness
LA20 6HY
Tel: 01229 716286
Website:
www.manorarmsthesquare.co.uk
Cumbria CAMRA's *Pub of the Year* and West Pennines *Regional Pub of the Year* 2008 lies on the pretty main square of Broughton-in-Furness. Numerous other awards are dotted around the bar, which has eight beers on handpump, including those from Yates and Coniston. About 200 guest ales are served every year. There's a pool table, bay windows and photographs of old Broughton on the walls.

Carlisle

The Plough

Wreay, near Carlisle CA4 0RL
Tel: 016974 75770
A few steps from one of the most extraordinary churches in Cumbria lies this pub, completely refurbished in 2006 with flagstoned floor, underfloor heating, chunky furniture and sofas. Two hand-pumps regularly serve Hawkshead and Hesket Newmarket beers. Chef Melanie Dixon, who runs the pub, used to work at Sharrow Bay and makes great use of local produce.

Queen Inn

Great Corby, near Carlisle CA4 8LR
Tel: 01228 562088
Website:
www.queeninngreatcorby.co.uk
This whitewashed village pub has two bar areas, upstairs and downstairs dining rooms and a coffee lounge at the back. Cumbrian breweries provide the changing beers for two handpumps. There are occasional quiz nights (with generous prizes) and wine tastings. Beer festivals are held in spring and autumn.

Cockermouth

Wheatsheaf Inn

Low Lorton, near Cockermouth
CA13 9UW
Tel: 01900 85199
Website:
www.wheatsheafinnlorton.co.uk
This cosy 17th-century inn has a small bar area to the left, with fishing rods, old books and a stove, and a bigger wood panelled bar area (including open fire) to the right. Four to six Jennings beers are on handpump but almost 100 guest ales are also served over the year. Fish nights take place on Thursdays and Fridays.

Coniston

The Sun Hotel

Coniston LA21 8HQ
Tel: 015394 41248
Website: www.thesunconiston.com
The hotel was finished in 1902 but the inn precedes it by over 250 years. With stone floors, old beams and a big old range, the pub offers eight beers on handpump (from 2009). That's because of a new bar area upstairs. The Sun has strong associations with water speed ace Donald Campbell.

Eskdale

Bower House Inn

Eskdale, Holmrook CA19 1TD
Tel: 019467 23244
Website: www.bowerhouseinn.co.uk
The 17th-century inn, with its beamed ceilings, log fires and well kept pub garden, lies in wonderful countryside in western Lakeland. The oldest parts of the building include the restaurant and part of the bar where five handpumps offer Theakston's Best Bitter (on permanently) and guest beers, most of which are Cumbrian.

Three other pubs/inns in Eskdale are the Woolpack Inn (*www.woolpack. co.uk*), Brook House Inn (*www. brookhouseinn.co.uk*) and Boot Inn (*www.bootinn.co.uk*). The Woolpack Inn has its own Hardknott Brewery.

Grange-over-Sands

Derby Arms

Witherslack, Grange-over-Sands
LA11 6RH
Tel: 015395 52207
Website: www.ainscoughs.co.uk
This 19th-century pub, just off the A590, was totally refurbished in late 2008. There's a bar area, a games room, two snugs and a larger room. Owner Martin Ainscough, leaseholder of the Strickland Arms at Sizergh (see p65) and owner of Miller Howe (see p35), promises the same standard and style of interiors and food as at the Strickland Arms.

Page 76: Above left: The Watermill,
Little Salkeld (see p97)
Above right: cheeses at Thornby Moor Dairy,
near Carlisle (see p88)
Below left: hams at Richard Woodall,
Waberthwaite (see p85)
Below right: Solway brown shrimps, landed
by Ray's Shrimps in Silloth (see p109)

Grasmere

Tweedies Bar

Dale Lodge Hotel, Grasmere LA22 9SW
Tel: 015394 35300
Website: www.dalelodgehotel.co.uk
Part of Dale Lodge Hotel, the stone-flagged bar has a good choice of hand drawn beers, including a revolving selection of Cumbrian ales. The popular 'bat of beer', enables you to sample three beers – in small glasses – for the price of one pint. There's a dining area off the bar and another restaurant in the hotel itself.

Kendal

The Sun Inn

Main Road, Crook, near Kendal
LA8 8LA
Tel: 01539 821351
The pub is mid-way between Kendal and Bowness, the original building dating back to 1710. Low beams, a partially flagstoned floor, an open fire and country prints on the wall welcome you as you come into the bar, where four beers are on handpump. Coniston Bluebird is usually one of them. There are two restaurant areas to the left.

The Wheatsheaf

Brigsteer, near Kendal LA8 8AN
Tel: 015395 68254
Website:
www.thewheatsheafbrigsteer.co.uk
Close to the Lyth Valley, the Wheatsheaf underwent major refurbishment in 2007, leaving it with an oak and flagstoned floor in the bar, an oak floor in the main dining area and light oak furniture throughout. 'Our menus are truly seasonal and proudly Cumbrian,' says the pub, which gained an AA Rosette in 2008. Two handpumps serve Cumbrian beers.

Keswick

Horse and Farrier

Threlkeld, near Keswick CA12 4SQ
Tel: 017687 79688
Website: www.horseandfarrier.com
The date above the main door of this Cask Marqued pub, located at the foot of Blencathra, is 1688. Beams, fires and flagstones all add to the character, as do the 'Wilk' cartoons on the wall. There's a main bar, a smaller bar area to the left and a restaurant to the right. Beers are mainly Jennings.

Langstrath Country Inn

Stonethwaite, near Keswick CA12 5XG
Tel: 017687 77239
Website: www.thelangstrath.com
A favourite with walkers, there's a restaurant and a small bar, offering the likes of Jennings, Hawkshead and other beers. Part of the building dates from the 16th century. Local produce includes Herdwick lamb from Rosthwaite. Please note: the pub is closed in winter, from the end of November till the beginning of March.

Kirkby Lonsdale

Barbon Inn

Barbon, near Kirkby Lonsdale LA6 2LJ
Tel: 015242 76233
Website: www.barbon-inn.co.uk
This 17th-century, former coaching inn is just off the scenic drive between Kirkby Lonsdale and Sedbergh. There's the Coach Lamp Bar with a Yorkshire range as you come in and, at the back, the bigger Oak Room Restaurant with 17th-century oak settles and chairs, and a log fire. The two beers on handpump are nearly always local. There's a beer garden here too.

Sun Inn

*6 Market Street, Kirkby Lonsdale
LA6 2AU
Tel: 015242 71965
Website: www.sun-inn.info*
Not far from the view that John Ruskin described as the 'one of the loveliest in England, therefore in the world' is the Sun Inn, tastefully refurbished in the last couple of years. The flagstones, wooden floors, beams and log fire, though, are still much in evidence. Sofas and two armchairs are tucked inside the main door. Four cask ales are served at the long bar while its AA-rosetted restaurant draws heavily on local produce: cheese from next door, for instance, meat, sausages and bacon from next door but one.

Penrith

Black Swan Inn

*Culgaith, near Penrith CA10 1QW
Tel: 01768 88223
Website: www.blackswanculgaith.co.uk*
This is a cheerful pub in a village just north of Temple Sowerby, off the A66. There's a games room at one end, a central bar area with tables, chairs, and tub chairs near an open fire, and then a restaurant to the right. They hold occasional gourmet evenings and the Mucky Duck Smokehouse here smokes food for the pub and to sell.

Mardale Inn

*Bampton, near Penrith CA10 2RQ
Tel: 01931 713244
Website: www.mardaleinn.co.uk*
Close to Haweswater and in a delightful part of Cumbria that's not overly busy, is this 18th-century inn, completely refurbished in 2007. Neatly laid flagstoned floors, solid furniture and two bar areas, both with log fires, greet the visitor. Local beef and lamb are well used in the food, two to four beers (mainly Cumbrian) are offered on handpump. Dogs are very welcome.

Queen's Head Inn

*Tirril, near Penrith CA10 2JF
Tel: 01768 863219
Website: www.queensheadinn.co.uk*
Once the property of the Wordsworth family, this was *Pub of the Year* in the *Good Pub Guide* 2003. The atmospheric main bar has flagstones, beams and an inglenook fireplace (dated 1719) with a few hooks up the chimney for smoking meat. Up to four handpumps serve Robinsons beers. There's a bar at the back (games room), three restaurant areas and a village shop. A beer and sausage festival is held in August (see p71).

The pubs, inns and bars on these pages are grouped around the nearest biggest place. Opening days and times vary, so it's best to check first if travelling far.

Troutbeck

Queen's Head Hotel

*Townhead, Troutbeck LA23 1PW
Tel: 015394 32174
Website: www.queensheadhotel.com*
A well known pub, with bags of character, two fires in the bar and a good reputation for food, the Queen's Head incorporates a wonderfully carved, 17th-century, four-poster bed into its bar counter. There are different eating and drinking areas, some flagstoned and beamed, and you get great views of Garburn Pass from the outside terrace. The children's menu includes mussels. Five Robinson's beers are usually on handpump.

Wasdale

Wasdale Head Inn

*Wasdale CA20 1EX
Tel: 019467 26229
Website: www.wasdale.com*
Close to England's deepest lake (Wastwater) and highest mountain (Scafell Pike), the pub is well patronised by climbers and walkers. There's the Ritson's Bar, the Residents' Bar (for residents) and a restaurant where residents take priority. Many of the ales are from the pub's own Great Gable Brewing Company.

Below: Wastwater, England's deepest lake, close to the Wasdale Head Inn.

Food
and Drink
Producers

Meat

Askerton Castle Estate

near Brampton CA8 2BD
Tel: 016977 3332
Website: www.askertoncastle.co.uk

In what was once lawless border country stands Askerton Castle, a fortified manor house dating back to the 14th century. This is the home of Jane Eden and Chris Evans, organic farmers and producers of beef, lamb, mutton and pork. They breed Belted Galloway cattle, Kerry Hill and Scottish Blackface sheep, and Tamworth and Berkshire pigs. Free range chickens provide organic eggs. The couple, members of the Rare Breed Survival Trust, also keep alpacas, whose fibre is for sale.

Outlets include: *online from the website; farmers' markets in Carlisle, Greenhead and Hexham. Jane and Chris deliver every Friday to Brampton and the surrounding area, and elsewhere in Cumbria at other times.*

Croft Farm Meats

The Croft, Houghton, Carlisle CA3 0LD
Tel: 01228 549628
Website: www.hadrianorganics.co.uk

Two-hundred and fifty years ago Longhorn cattle were a familiar sight in the British countryside but now they're on the watchlist of the Rare Breeds Survival Trust. Susan Aglionby (below left) has been keeping pedigree Longhorns at her small farm near Carlisle since 1990 'because they're a northern breed and they taste delicious,' she says. Celebrated chef Heston Blumenthal is amongst those who agree with her.

Alongside the organic beef, Susan produces organic lamb, and geese for Christmas, growing her own organic cereal to feed the animals. She is a member of Hadrian Organics, a co-operative of organic producers.

Outlets include: *Croft Farm itself; farmers' markets at Brampton, Carlisle's Borderway Mart and Greenhead in Northumberland.*

Deer 'n Dexter

Old Stoddah Farm, Penruddock, Penrith CA11 0RY
Tel: 01768 480069
Website: www.deer-n-dexter.co.uk

Jane Emerson (below right) and Peter Stoeken breed red deer and Dexter cattle, their Dexter beef sirloin steak being voted *Best Beef* at the North West Fine Food Awards 2008. The first deer arrived in 1987 (the breeding herd now numbers over 150) and the Dexters, the smallest native breed of cattle, in 2003. The organically reared deer are slaughtered at the farm's own small slaughter house.

Outlets include: *online from the website; farmers' markets at Brampton, Brough, Cockermouth, Kendal, Orton, Penrith and Pooley Bridge; Westmorland Farm Shops on the M6; the Farm Shop at Rheged; Low Sizergh Barn Farm Shop near Kendal; and Carleton Farm Shop just outside Penrith; you can buy from the farm itself but please phone first.*

Herdwick sheep

In its own small, hardy way the Herdwick (below at Ennerdale Water) is as much a Lakeland icon as, say, Scafell Pike and Windermere. The breed's not been around here for quite as long, but long enough. Some say that it came over with the Vikings, a few recount the tale of Herdwick sheep being washed up on the west Cumbrian coast after a shipwreck and deciding to stay. They've got a lot of sense, these Herdwick, a breed beloved of Beatrix Potter.

Go anywhere in the Lake District, particularly the central and western parts, and you'll see them grazing the heather and grasses of the rougher terrain, shaping the landscape as they eat, maintaining the open fells, which are so loved by walkers. As lambs, their mothers imbue them with a lifelong sense of place, so they rarely stray from the area of Lakeland to which they have been 'heft'.

When young they're mainly black in colour but as they get older they turn to brown and then grey. Diet and slow maturity gives their meat a distinct flavour, 'rich and tender, with a superb depth of flavour and high in beneficial Omega 3 fatty acid', say Jon and Caroline Watson at Yew Tree Farm Heritage Meats (see p86), one of a number of farmers, producers and butchers who sell Herdwick lamb.

Farmer Sharp

Diamond Buildings, Pennington Lane,
Lindal-in-Furness LA12 0LA
Tel: 01229 588299
Website: www.farmersharp.co.uk

Andrew 'Farmer' Sharp is the genial
public face of a co-operative of more
than 50 small farmers in the Lake
District who between them produce
lamb and mutton from Herdwick sheep,
beef from Galloway and other native
breed cattle and 'naturally reared
pink veal'. Farmer Sharp was *Cumbria
Producer of the Year* at the North West
Fine Food Awards 2007, winning *Best
Cured or Cooked Meat* for his three
month air dried mutton. At the same
awards in 2008 he won *Best Air-Dried
Meat* for his air-dried beef.

Andrew's father, John, was a
farmer and so were another eight or
nine generations of Sharps before
that. His great uncle on his mother's
side, Tom Storey, was a shepherd for
Beatrix Potter, a noted champion of
the Herdwick breed. Andrew's own
promotion of Herdwick lamb and
mutton has made him a very well
known Cumbrian producer.

On Fridays at Borough Market in
London, where he has a stall (see
p122), Andrew runs 'mastering meat'
courses (husbandry, butchery and
cookery) for lamb and mutton, and beef
and veal. He runs them at Lindal-in-
Furness as well (check for details).
Farmer Sharp's products – as well
as those mentioned above – include
pastrami and Herdwick prosciutto.

Outlets include: *online from the website;
pre-booked orders from the premises at
Lindal-in-Furness; Westmorland Farm Shops
on the M6; and Borough Market in London
(Thu–Sat).*

Hallsford Farm Produce

Hethersgill, Carlisle CA6 6JD
Tel: 01228 577329
Website: www.hallsford.co.uk

This is a family business, located in
unspoilt countryside, close to Hadrian's
Wall and the Scottish border. Andrew
and Helen Tomkins, who run Hallsford
Farm on an extensive as opposed to an
intensive basis, breed pedigree Beef
Shorthorn cattle, Llanwenog sheep and
Saddleback pigs.

The meat and meat products are
produced at their farm and include
Shorthorn beef, lamb and mutton, pork,
dry cured bacon, hams, and homemade
pies, sausages and burgers. The beef
is hung for a minimum of three and a
half weeks.

Outlets include: *online from the website;
Carlisle farmers' market; county shows and
events such as the Cumberland Show and
Westmorland Show.*

Below: Saddleback pig at Hallsford Farm

High Borrow Bridge Farm

Selside, Kendal LA8 9LG
Tel: 01539 823270

There was a time when Jayne Knowles
thought a Rough Fell was a 'rough fella'
who came out of the hills. Not any
longer. Moving to a farm where these
sheep have been stocked for several
generations quickly turned her into an
enthusiastic promoter of the breed.
'As the animals spend most of the year
up on the fells, grazing on grass, they
have a good diet. So the meat is full of
flavour and it's also high in Omega 3
fatty acid which is good for you,' says
Jayne who with her husband Brian sells
half or full Rough Fell lambs or mutton,
fresh or frozen.

Rough Fell sheep (*www.
roughfellsheep.co.uk*) have distinctive
black and white faces, are bigger than
Herdwicks and have longer fleeces.
They're traditionally associated with an
area that takes in Kendal, Tebay, Kirkby
Stephen and Sedbergh.

Outlets: *direct from Jayne and Brian's High
Borrow Bridge Farm.*

Cumberland sausage

By 2009/2010 there are high hopes that 'traditional Cumberland sausage' will join the likes of Cornish clotted cream, Parma ham, Whitstable oysters and the Melton Mowbray pork pie in the ranks of those foods that are protected by the European Union. If the application under the EU's Protected Food Name Scheme is successful then there will be strict criteria as to what constitutes a 'traditional Cumberland sausage'.

The sausage, wider in diameter than the average sausage, will most certainly have to be produced within the county of Cumbria and contain at least 80 per cent pork meat – 'no skin, gristle, rind, offal or any form of mechanically recovered meat' – and be encased in natural pig intestines. The meat must be coarsely chopped, and so, where a mincer is used, the application specifies that the mincing holes of the plate should be no smaller than 4.5mm in diameter, to ensure a rough texture.

The sausage has to be produced in one continuous coil – in other words, unlinked – and sold by weight. The continual length of Cumberland sausage is one of its 'key features', says the application.

The Cumberland sausage has been around for a long time, but quite how long is a matter of debate. Some people believe it originated with German miners who came to work in Cumberland in the 16th century. Missing the 'wurst' they ate at home, they set about producing a thicker sausage

here. Whitehaven's subsequent trade in spices with the West Indies in the 18th century may account for the often spicier flavour of the Cumberland sausage.

In Cumbria, recipes for Cumberland sausage are often passed down from one generation of butchers to another, so there's a proud tradition wrapped up with the making of this regional speciality.

Go anywhere in the country, though, and you'll come across a product calling itself a Cumberland sausage that falls far short of the criteria mentioned above. Meat content can be nearer 45 per cent, the meat itself emulsified rather than coarse cut and the sausage sold in thin links rather than thick continuous lengths, according to the Cumberland Sausage Association.

The association was formed in 2005 to promote the quality of traditionally made Cumberland sausage and to push on with the application for protected status. Its members include Colin Woodall of Richard Woodall, Philip Cranston of Cranstons, Stuart Higginson of Higginsons, Austen Davies of Border County Foods, Peter Gott (Sillfield Farm) and Andrew Tomkins of Hallsford Farm. The application for protected status, which in the first place went to the Department for the Environment, Food and Rural Affairs (Defra), was facilitated by Made in Cumbria (www.madeincumbria.co.uk).

Website: www.traditionalcumberlandsausage.com

Lowther Park Farms

Lowther, Penrith CA10 2HG
Tel: 01931 712407
Website: www.lowtherparkfarms.co.uk

The first documented reference to the Lowther Estate near Penrith was made in 1283, which gives some idea of how long the Lowther family has been in Cumberland and Westmorland. These days some 3,000 acres of the estate produce beef, lamb, free range eggs and the well known Lowther free range chicken. These chicken are sold at a number of shops and farm shops in Cumbria and supplied to restaurants as well. Bronze turkeys are available at Christmas time. A good showcase for much Lowther produce is the George and Dragon pub at Clifton, near Penrith (see p52), owned by two members of the Lowther family, Charles, the eighth and youngest child of the late Earl of Lonsdale, and his mother, Caroline, the Countess of Lonsdale.

Outlets include: *online from the website; Westmorland Farm Shops on the M6, Low Sizergh Barn Farm Shop near Kendal and Cranstons Cumbrian Food Hall, Penrith.*

Matson Ground Farm

Matson Ground, Windermere LA23 2NH
Tel: 015394 45756
Website: www.matsongroundorganic.co.uk

Ten minutes from the shores of Windermere, Matson Ground Farm has been in family ownership since the 1920s. The farm, which became fully organic in 2002, produces beef from Beef Shorthorn cattle and lamb from Texel cross and Swaledale sheep.

Individual cuts of organic meat, such as steak (rump, sirloin, fillet), rib of beef, topside, braising steak, leg and shoulder of lamb, chops and cutlets, are popular and so are Shorthorn quarter pounder beef burgers, seasonal meat boxes and a sausage box. Sausage varieties might include lamb and rosemary. At the moment much of the meat is supplied frozen although an increasing amount of fresh lamb and beef is available. Matson Ground also supplies cafés and restaurants in the area.

Outlets: *direct from the farm, with orders by email or telephone. Free local delivery or customers can collect themselves.*

Mansergh Hall Organic Farm

Kirkby Lonsdale LA6 2EN
Tel: 015242 71397
Website: www.manserghhall.co.uk

The Hadwin family is now on its fourth and fifth generations at Mansergh Hall which became fully organic in 2004. Jim and his son James breed Aberdeen Angus cross cattle, Texel cross (with North Country Cheviot) sheep and pigs that include Saddleback, Large Black and Gloucester Old Spot. 'If we can't meet demand from our own cattle we source from an organic producer nearby,' says Jim's daughter Amanda.

Check out the website and you can see the range which Mansergh Hall offers: from legs of lamb, organic mutton, lamb burgers, fillets of beef, braising steak, loins of pork and belly pork to award winning dry-cured bacon (North West Fine Food Awards 2003), pancetta and a variety of organic sausages. The latter include pork; pork and sun dried tomatoes; and Granny's recipe sausage which is based on a recipe used by Jim's grandmother, Elizabeth.

'We're keen to support other local producers,' says Amanda and so the family operates an organic box scheme, offering Mansergh Hall meat, milk from Low Sizergh Farm near Kendal, organic vegetables from Howbarrow Farm near Cartmel, bread from Grange Bakery and cheese from Churchmouse Cheeses at Kirkby Lonsdale.

Outlets include: *online from the website; their own farm butchery (by appointment); Wednesday market in Lancaster; Thursday market in Kirkby Lonsdale; Carleton Farm Shop near Penrith; Low Sizergh Barn Farm Shop near Kendal; the Village Bakery at Melmerby; the Farm Shop at Rheged near Penrith; and the Westmorland Farm Shops on the M6.*

Opposite above far left: chicken at Lowther Park Farms
Above far right: Mansergh Hall Organic Farm
Below far left: Shorthorn cattle at Matson Ground Farm
Below far right: organically reared deer at Deer 'n Dexter (see p78)

Cumbria Organics

Now ten years old, Cumbria Organics encompasses some 70–75 businesses and other bodies, which between them produce lamb, pork, beef, poultry, venison, eggs, cheese, milk, bakery products, flour and dried goods, and fruit and vegetables.

The businesses include Askerton Castle, Croft Farm Meats, Deer 'n Dexter, Eva's Organics, Howbarrow Farm, Low Sizergh Farm, Mansergh Hall, Matson Ground, Slack House Farm, South Lakes Organic Milk, The Village Bakery and The Watermill. Details of all these suppliers can be found elsewhere in this chapter.

Originally set up to offer support for the increasing number of farmers converting to organic production, Cumbria Organics also aims to raise consumer awareness about organic food, help develop supply chains for the producers and provide technical information to anyone interested in organic farming.

A leaflet called *Organic Origins* gives details of where you can buy organic food directly from Cumbrian producers. For more information contact Kate Gascoyne on 01768 881462 or visit the website: *www.cumbriaorganics.org*.

Millbeck Farm

Great Langdale, near Ambleside LA22 9JU
Tel: 015394 37364
Website: www.millbeckfarm.co.uk

There's a chance that if you're walking in the Langdale fells you might come across some of Sue and Eric Taylforth's Herdwick sheep. The couple stock about 2500 of these hardy creatures on their National Trust farm, along with a herd of Aberdeen Angus cattle. 'The stress-free upbringing, traditional Angus qualities and high standards of animal husbandry produces beef like you remember: tender, tasty and with old fashioned marbling that gives it a superior flavour. Likewise Herdwick lamb, slow matured with a fuller flavour and succulent texture,' say Sue and Eric. The lamb and beef are sold fresh, not frozen.

Outlets: *People can order the meat from Millbeck Farm and then either collect it from there or at Airey's butchers in Ayside on the A590 near Newby Bridge. Alternatively the meat can be delivered to your door. Millbeck Farm is a B&B and has two self-catering cottages.*

The Old Smokehouse

Brougham Hall, Brougham, Penrith CA10 2DE
Tel: 01900 815757
Website: www.tasteofthelakes.com

Based at Brougham Hall, which in the 19th century was described as the 'Windsor of the North', the Old Smokehouse produces a range of cold and hot smoked foods – meat, game, sausages, bacon, poultry, fish, vegetables and cheeses – which between them have won over 30 Great Taste Awards. Golds have come the way of the smoked duck breast, the Penrith pepperpot sausage, smoked Fellman sausage, honey roasted smoked salmon and more.

About 85 per cent of the produce that goes through the Old Smokehouse, says smoker Neil Harrison, comes from Cumbria. That includes the bacon, sausage and pancetta, made with pork from local, free range, Saddleback pigs. The business, in partnership with the Maryport fresh and frozen seafood supplier Brookside Taste of the Lakes, supplies numerous hotels, restaurants and shops.

Outlets include: *Low Sizergh Barn Farm Shop near Kendal; Westmorland Farm Shops on the M6; the Holker Food Hall at Holker Hall; Fortnum and Mason in London; and Harvey Nichols in London, Manchester, Leeds and Edinburgh.*

Saltmarsh lamb

Well known in France, particularly in Normanny and Britanny, as *l'agneau pré-salé* (salt meadow), Saltmarsh lamb has become increasingly popular in this country. In Cumbria the two main areas associated with the delicacy are the marshlands around Morecambe Bay and those around the Solway coast.

Wild grasses and herbs like sea beet, samphire and sea lavender are washed regularly by the tide – this also helps clear the areas of parasitic worms – and that gives the meat its sweetish, tender taste, a 'uniquely delicate flavour,' says Philip Cranston, managing director of Cranstons butchers (see p136).

The meat itself is slightly darker in colour than other lamb but has none of the saltiness that one might expect. Saltmarsh lamb is a seasonal product, generally available from early summer to late autumn. Higginsons and Daughter in Grange-over-Sands (see p124) sell Saltmarsh lamb from the Holker Estate and from other nearby farms, Cranstons sells Anthorn Farm Saltmarsh lamb from the shores of the Solway coast.

Sillfield Farm

Endmoor, Kendal LA8 0HZ
Tel: 015395 67609
Website: www.sillfield.co.uk

It comes as no surprise that Peter Gott's holiday reading once included *A History of the British Pig*, *Handy Guide for Pork Butchers* and *Pigs, Breed and Management*. He is one of Cumbria's highest profile food producers, breeding wild boar, Herdwick and Rough Fell sheep, and Saddleback, Tamworth, Middle White and Gloucester Old Spot pigs. The wild boar herd started as a present of four sows from his brother, Walter.

Jamie Oliver is a big fan of Sillfield Farm's pork products – he has sent students from his London restaurant Fifteen to see how the animals are reared – and Clarissa Dickson Wright once described its wild boar prosciutto as 'utterly fabulous'.

Peter's range of produce is extensive, from air dried salami and dry cured pancetta (both made with wild boar meat), to pies, pork haslet (seasoned meatloaf), Cumberland speck, Cumberland roast ham, dry cured bacons, cheeses, and over 20 varieties of sausage. The latter include a traditional Cumberland sausage, as well as a pork and apple, Herdwick minty lamb, and a pheasant, venison and red wine sausage.

Outlets include: *online from the website; the Sillfield Farm Shop; Westmorland Farm Shops on the M6; Holker Food Hall; Borough Market in London and other markets (see p123 for details of the farm shop, and the markets which Sillfield attends).*

Below: Peter Gott

Richard Woodall

Lane End, Waberthwaite, near Millom LA19 5YJ
Tel: 01229 717237
Website: www.richardwoodall.co.uk

Richard Woodall is a great name in Cumbrian food, eight generations of one family producing hams, bacon and sausages since the Duke of Wellington became Prime Minister in 1828. The business, which holds a Royal Warrant to supply the Queen with Cumberland sausage, bacon and hams, is based in a small village in Cumbria's delightful south west corner (see p146). It was started by Hannah Woodall as a way of feeding her family of five children and by the early 1900s was sending hams all over the country, including the House of Commons in London.

Richard Woodall prides itself on traditional ways of production for most of its range: 'the identical curing method', for instance, used by Hannah Woodall for its Cumbrian ham; salt, unrefined brown sugar and a dash of saltpetre 'the only ingredients' in its dry cured Cumberland bacon; an adaptation of a recipe from 1843 – with a 'rich pickle of old ale, molasses and brown sugar, followed by a light smoke over oak' – for the Cumbria mature royal ham.

Other products include Cumbria air-dried ham, pancetta, Cumberland sausage (95 per cent meat), smoked Cumberland sausage, ham shanks and black pudding rings. There's also a cured snack sausage and a 'country cure' range of bacon and gammon.

Outlets include: *online from the website; Booths stores in Cumbria, Tesco in Carlisle, Workington and Whitehaven, Cranstons Cumbrian Food Hall in Penrith; Cartmel Village Shop; and The Honeypot, Hawkshead.*

Yew Tree Farm Heritage Meats

Yew Tree Farm, Coniston LA21 8DP
Tel: 015394 41433
Website: www.yewtree-farm.com

There's certainly a lot of history about Heritage Meats. Jon and Caroline Watson's business is based at a farm, once owned by Beatrix Potter (see p166) and one that doubled as the writer's home of Hill Top in the 2006 film *Miss Potter*. Herdwick sheep and Belted Galloway cattle (belties) graze on the nearby fells, a 'stress free way of life which produces meat of the highest quality and flavour,' say the couple. They sell a variety of meat boxes, including a Herdwick box with a leg joint, loin chops, rack of lamb or individual cutlets. Meat is delivered in a fleece lined box with photographs of the farm (pictured below), the animals and Caroline and Jon.

Outlets include: *online from the website and direct from the farm.*

Mutton Renaissance
Website: www.muttonrenaissance.org.uk

When Prince Charles sat down for dinner at the Ritz Hotel in London in February 2006 he was doing so in honour of what had become a hopelessly unfashionable ingredient of the British diet. For half a century mutton had almost disappeared from butchers and restaurants in Britain, as consumers chose lamb as their sheepmeat of preference. But in 2004 the Prince of Wales launched Mutton Renaissance and the event at the Ritz was the inaugural dinner of the Mutton Renaissance Club, a club open to anyone producing, processing, selling or serving mutton.

The hotel's head chef, John Williams, offered three dishes for the assembled gathering of farmers, butchers, chefs and retailers. The breeds he used were a Cumbrian Herdwick from 'Farmer' Sharp (who was one of those present, see p80), a Beulah Speckled Face sheep and a Lleyn from the Prince's farm in Gloucestershire.

What Mutton Renaissance aims to do is not only persuade people of the meat's merits but ensure that farmers get better prices for older sheep. The broad definition of mutton is meat from wethers (castrated males) or ewes which are two years old or over, the meat having to be well matured for quality and flavour. A number of farmers, producers and butchers now sell mutton in Cumbria. One of them, Mansergh Hall, offers organic mutton (see p82).

Several months before the Ritz dinner, mutton was featured at the inaugural event of the Cumbria branch or convivium of Slow Food (see p106) which took place at the First Floor Café at Lakeland in Windermere. Steven Doherty, who runs the café/restaurant (see p180), created a shepherd's pie from Herdwick mutton and Swaledale lamb, to go with all the other food that Cumbrian producers had supplied for the evening. Steven, too, was at the Mutton Renaissance Club dinner with Prince Charles.

Cheese

Slack House Farm

Gilsland, Brampton CA8 7DB
Tel: 016977 47351
Website: www.slackhousefarm.co.uk

In 1688, a certain Barbara Gilmour brought a recipe for sweet milk cheese to Ayrshire in Scotland from Ireland. This is the cheese that Eric (below left) and Dianne Horn produce on their organic farm, close to Hadrian's Wall and the Roman fort of Birdoswald. Warm milk from their small herd of Ayrshire cows is hand worked for something approaching five hours to give a product – Birdoswald organic farmhouse cheese – that is then matured for up to six months.

There's a tea room and small visitors centre at the farm. B&B is also available.

Outlets include: online from the website; own farm shop; farmers' markets in Carlisle, Borderway Mart, Carlisle and Brampton; Alston Wholefoods; Half Moon Wholefoods in Brampton.

Thornby Moor Dairy

Crofton Hall, Thursby, Carlisle CA5 6QB
Tel: 016973 45555
Website: www.thornbymoordairy.co.uk

Bewcastle is famous for its cross and Croglin is famous for its vampire. These two places are also the names of cheeses made by this well known and much liked Cumbrian cheese maker, which celebrated its 30th anniversary in 2009. Thornby Moor Dairy (below right) produces about a dozen different cheeses, ranging from the Crofton to the creamy-textured Cumberland Farmhouse. Crofton is a semi-soft cheese made with cows' and goats' milk while Cumberland Farmhouse uses single herd Dairy Shorthorn milk.

Former photographer Carolyn Fairbairn made her first cheese, Allerdale, at home with milk from her pet goats, then a short time later started production of Cumberland Farmhouse (a gold medal winner at the British Cheese Awards 2008), using unpasteurised milk from a neighbour's herd of cows. In 1994, because of expanding business, she moved to an old piggery in the grounds of Crofton Hall. Eight years later Allerdale won the *Cheese Lovers' Trophy* at the British Cheese Awards.

It's still at Crofton Hall that Carolyn, her daughter Leonie and a small team make the cheeses, all of them with unpasteurised milk. Cumberland Oak Smoked, Cumberland Herb, Tovey, Curthwaite, Eden Valley, Allerdale Herb, Allerdale Smoked and Stumpies are the others not mentioned so far. The Stumpies are small, goats' milk cheeses which are often served grilled. Carolyn and Leonie hold cheesemaking courses by arrangement.

Outlets include: Thornby Moor Dairy shop (open Mon–Fri 9–17.30, Sat 10–16.30); Low Sizergh Barn Farm Shop near Kendal; Westmorland Farm Shops on the M6; Laird's Larder at Houghton Hall near Carlisle; Lucy's Specialist Grocers in Ambleside; Churchmouse Cheeses in Kirkby Lonsdale; the Farm Shop at Rheged near Penrith; Cockermouth Farmers' Market.

Ice Cream

Abbott Lodge Jersey Ice Cream

Clifton, Penrith CA10 2HD
Tel: 01931 712720
Website: www.abbottlodgejerseyicecream.co.uk

Three generations of Claire Bland's family have farmed on the Lowther Estate near Penrith but the Jersey cows have only been here since February 2002 when Claire and her husband Steven (below) re-stocked after the 2001 foot and mouth epidemic. The herd of 250 Jerseys provide the milk which goes into over 30 varieties of ice cream, made at the farm and sold in the tea room (a cabinet usually has 16 on display). This itself is a converted gin case, used by horses in the past to drive farm machinery.

Ice cream varieties include the best selling Just Jersey and flavours such as banana, trifle, rum and raisin, cherry, chocolate, liquorice, raspberry pavlova, green apple, coconut, and honey and ginger. You can see the Jersey cattle in the nearby fields and their milk is available to buy in bottles.

Open: *Easter–end Oct, daily 11–17; Nov–Easter, Sat–Sun, Tue–Thu 11–17.00.*

Taste Of Eden

The Dairy, Winskill, Penrith CA10 1PB
Tel: 01768 881221

For about 75 years ice cream vans from Slee's of Winskill have been plying the Eden Valley between the months of March and November. When David and Deborah Rackham took over the business in 2004 they decided to add another dimension to it and the result was Taste of Eden, a producer and supplier of ice cream (in tubs) and sorbets to shops, cafés, restaurants, hotels, pubs and other places around Cumbria.

The 20 or so flavours of ice cream include strawberry, chocolate, blackcurrant, peach and mango, ginger, cinnamon, mint chocolate chip and raspberry pavlova. The selection is wider than that available on the ice cream vans but the milk used is all from the same farm at Appleby. Sorbets range from lemoncello, mango, and bucks fizz to cranberry and orange, and pineapple.

While most of the ice cream is made with cows' milk, David is also developing ice cream that is produced from ewe's milk.

Outlets include: *Old Smithy Tea Room in Caldbeck; Houghton Hall Garden Centre near Carlisle; Ice Cream Garden and Tea Room at Penrith; Lakeside Tea Gardens in Keswick; and Yew Tree Restaurant at Seatoller.*

Page 87.
Above left: Carolyn and Leonie Fairbairn, Thornby Moor Dairy
Above right: Susan Aglionby with her Longhorn cattle (see p78)
Below left: Andrew 'Farmer' Sharp (see p80)
Below right: Jayne Knowles with her Rough Fell sheep (see p80)

Cakes, Pies and Puddings

Burbush Penrith

The Eden Game Bakery, Gilwilly Road, Penrith CA11 9BL
Tel: 01768 863841
Website: www.burbushs.co.uk

For over 20 years Burbush pies – which celebrated receiving three gold stars at the Great Taste Awards in London in 2008 – have been a familiar sight on the shelves of food shops in Cumbria and beyond. Founded by Tim Burbush, but now owned by Martyn and Melanie Reynolds, the company's range takes in hot crust pies (lidded or topped with fruit), short crust pies, fruit pies, sausage rolls, pasties and hams. The couple source most ingredients from local suppliers.

Amongst the Burbush savoury pies are steak and ale; game; steak and red wine; steak and kidney; chicken and ham; cheese, onion and leek; and sweet potato and Stilton. A duckling, honey and marmalade pie was the one which gained them the three gold stars, only 72 products out of about 4,800, entered for the 2008 Great Taste Awards, managing to achieve this.

Burbush fruit topped pies include pork and caramelised gooseberries; and pork and Stilton with apple and ginger chutney. Fruit pies are a developing area and so are frozen pies which are made for customers to bake themselves.

Outlets include: *Westmorland Farm Shops on the M6; Carleton Farm Shop near Penrith; Greystone House Farm Shop at Stainton; Laird's Larder at Houghton Hall near Carlisle; The Honeypot in Hawkshead; Low Sizergh Barn Farm Shop near Kendal; Artisan in Kendal; Pooley Bridge post office; Langdale and Penrith Co-ops; Carrock Meats in Dalston; Dobies garden centres.*

Cartmel Sticky Toffee Pudding Company

The Bakery, Moor Lane, Flookburgh LA11 7LS
Tel: 015395 58300
Website: www.stickytoffeepudding.co.uk

In the multi-million pound industry that is horse racing, it's reassuring to know that a few quaint traditions still exist. One of them occurs at Cartmel Races where the owner, trainer and jockey of every winning race is given a Cartmel Sticky Toffee Pudding as a prize.

The origins of the sticky toffee pudding may be a matter of debate but one thing is certain: the Cartmel marque is a famous Cumbrian food name, the pudding itself sent all over Britain (over 500 delis and food shops) and overseas.

In 2009 it was 20 years since Howard and Jean Johns started their business in the shop and post office of this small village in south Cumbria. They still own the shop (see p121) but the puddings – sticky toffee along with sticky banana, sticky ginger and sticky chocolate – are now made a short distance away in Flookburgh.

After developing their own recipe in 1984, the couple made the sticky toffee pudding in a restaurant they ran in Grange-over-Sands. When they took over the village shop in Cartmel they continued to do so, along with other dishes. But sticky toffee outsold them all. So they moved production to bigger premises at home and then to the Flookburgh bakery.

Outlets include: *online from the website; Cartmel Village Shop; Booths stores; Waitrose stores; Selfridges (London, Birmingham and Manchester); and Fortnum and Mason in London.*

Country Fare

Dalefoot Farm, Mallerstang, Kirkby Stephen CA17 4JT
Tel: 017683 71173
Website: www.country-fare.co.uk

Wild and peaceful, source of the River Eden and location of Pendragon Castle. This is Mallerstang, home territory of Country Fare, well known Cumbrian cake maker and, since 2002, winner of numerous golds, silvers and bronzes at the Great Taste Awards in London. In 2008, for instance, it won five golds, including two two-star golds for its gingerbread and its iced Christmas cake.

What started with the sale of some cakes at a farmers' market in Appleby in 1999 quickly expanded into a business making cakes, biscuits, desserts, pickles, preserves and such like. Today the focus is entirely on cakes, a range of about 50 being produced every week in a large barn on Dianne and Tony Halliday's farm. Fruit cakes are Dianne's speciality, all of them based on two recipes – one for glacé fruit cake and the other for rich fruit cake. The glacé fruit cake featured in Lakeland's Christmas catalogue for 2006 and 2007. And 2008.

Dianne's husband Tony and their three sons are all involved in the business, alongside a dozen or so local women.

Outlets include: *online from the website; Artisan in Kendal; Lakeland at Windermere; Churchmouse Cheeses in Kirkby Lonsdale; Westmorland Farm Shops on the M6; Holker Food Hall at Holker Hall, Cark-in-Cartmel; the Co-op in Penrith; and the House of Bruar near Blair Atholl in Perthshire. Farmers' markets in Carlisle, Orton, Kendal and Pooley Bridge.*

Country Puddings

Lodge Farm, Dacre, Penrith CA11 0HH
Tel: 017684 80864
Website: www.countrypuddings.co.uk

Although it was Lynne Mallinson's rich, tasty gravy that was praised in a speech on her wedding day, it was her sticky toffee pudding that got this farmer's daughter and former bank manager into business in 2000. Looking for some part-time work while two young children were at home, Lynne started making and selling puddings to the Carleton Farm Shop near Penrith. Within a few months she had approached another four or five outlets. After that shops simply came knocking on the door. Delicatessens, food halls, farm shops and garden centres all over the country now stock her produce.

Originally the intention was to make 900 puddings a week but these days the figure is closer to 1,000 a day. Four sponge-based puddings are the staples of her range – sticky toffee ('a light date sponge with a creamy butterscotch toffee sauce'), chocolate fudge, sticky ginger and tangy lemon pudding. The lemon pudding was voted *Best Hot Pudding or Dessert* at the 2008 North West Fine Food Awards.

Lynne also makes creamy rice pudding, luxury Christmas pudding, summer pudding, sticky toffee sauce and chocolate fudge sauce.

Outlets include: *online from the website; Cranstons Cumbrian Food Hall at Penrith; Carleton Farm Shop near Penrith; Westmorland Farm Shops on the M6; Greystone House Farm Shop at Stainton; Thomason's (butchers) in Keswick; W Lindsay & Sons (butchers) in Cockermouth; Country Cuts at Santon Bridge; and House of Bruar near Blair Atholl in Perthshire.*

The Pie Mill

Blencathra Business Park, Threlkeld, Keswick CA12 4TR
Tel: 017687 79994
Website: www.piemill.co.uk

When their sales of handmade pies reached 14,000 a year Jim and Margaret Hodge and daughter Amanda realised that their pub kitchen was no longer big enough to cope. So they shifted production to a place down the road, called it the Pie Mill, set up a website and never looked back.

They and their team produce about ten savoury pies, all with names that evoke the fells, lakes and dales of Cumbria. Blencathra, for instance, is made with Cumbrian Galloway beef and Jennings Cumberland Ale, and won Amanda the title of *National Steak Pie Champion* in the English Beef and Lamb Executive's countrywide competition of 2005. 'Deliciously succulent,' was one judge's view of the Blencathra.

The same pie also received a silver at the Great Taste Awards in London in 2006 while Lowes Pike (beef, black pudding, caramelised mushrooms and red wine gravy) won a gold at the awards in 2007, having received a silver the year before. In 2008 golds in London went to the Sharp Edge pie (venison, Stilton and pork) and to the Pie Mill's venison pâté and duck pâté.

Other pies include Buttermere, with its roasted vegetables, Old Man (wild venison and cranberry), Grizedale (pork, Cumberland sausage and apple), Swindale (wild venison, pheasant and rabbit) and Souther (lamb and apricot). Fruit pies are produced as well.

The origins of the business go back to 2000 when Jim and Margaret took over the Mill Inn at Mungrisdale. After months of research into shortcrust pastry and fillings, they put pies on the menu. With growing numbers of people taking the pies away to eat, the couple realised the potential of the business. Pie Fest, first held in November 2002 (for charity), whetted people's appetites even more. The move to the Pie Mill came in 2005. In April 2008 the business appeared on the TV shopping channel QVC with considerable success.

Outlets include: *online from the website; Westmorland Farm Shops on the M6; Farm Shop at Rheged near Penrith; Low Sizergh Barn Farm Shop near Kendal; and the Lakeside Inn at Center Parcs, Whinfell Forest, Cumbria.*

Great Taste Awards
www.finefoodworld.co.uk

Every year dozens of Cumbrian producers enter the Great Taste Awards in London and every year dozens of awards head back north to Cumbria. Organised by the Guild of Fine Food, the awards started in 1993 and, says the Guild, are the 'national benchmark for speciality food and drink'. The annual results are announced in August.

John Farrand of the Guild of Fine Food says: 'Interest in regional and local food, made with ingredients from or inspired by a region, is at an all time high. In 1994 the Great Taste Awards had just 240 entries. In 2008 the number was just under 4800 entries, from over 1000 producers.'

'Cumbria is a county with producers who understand its food traditions and heritage. But it also has brave individuals who're producing foods that are inspired by more national and international palates,' he adds. The Guild of Fine Food, which has more than 1,300 members, also organises the World Cheese Awards.

Jams, Chutneys, Pickles, Mustard

Claire's Handmade

Unit 8, Miller Park, Station Road, Wigton CA7 9BA
Tel: 016973 45974
Website: www.claireshandmade.co.uk

What began as a sideline in their AA-rosetted hotel restaurant in Cornwall turned into a business for Claire and Michael Kent when they moved back to Cumbria in 2002. Claire's Handmade produces a range of chutneys, piccalilli, jams, marmalade, curds, ketchups and Cumberland sauce.

Winner of numerous Great Taste Awards, including a gold in 2005 for the beetroot chutney with fresh ginger (this was also *Best Overall Preserve* in the North West Fine Food Awards in the same year), Claire's Handmade products extend to over 30. They include apricot and apple chutney, red onion marmalade, plum ketchup, Cumberland bean piccalilli and fresh lemon curd.

Outlets include: *online from the website; J&J Graham in Penrith; Laird's Larder at Houghton Hall near Carlisle; FondEwe Fine Cheeses in Keswick; Thornby Moor Dairy at Crofton near Carlisle; and Booths stores.*

Cumberland Honey Mustard

16 Hillhouse Lane, Alston CA9 3TN
Tel: 01434 381135
Website: www.cumberlandmustard.com

It's a quarter of a century since Marilyn Avens and Geoffrey Cole set up their business in Alston, and the longevity of the brand and its popularity has made it one of the best known producer names in Cumbria. The first mustard the couple created, the Original is still the best seller and most versatile. These days the range includes Garlic; Horseradish; Vulcan (seriously hot); Green Peppercorn; Whisky (made with 10 year old Isle of Jura single malt); Raspberry; Seville Orange and Organic.

The couple also make a fruit vinegar, using Glen Ample raspberries from the Eden Valley, vinaigrettes and three pickles – cherry, damson and cranberry. The fruit vinegar goes into the pickles as well.

Outlets include: *Booths supermarkets in Cumbria; Cranstons in Penrith, Carlisle and Brampton; J&J Graham in Penrith; Westmorland Farm Shops on the M6; and Low Sizergh Barn Farm Shop near Kendal.*

Demels

Cross Lane, Ulverston LA12 9DQ
Tel: 01229 580580
Website: www.demels.co.uk

Winner of a number of gold, silver and bronze awards at the Great Taste Awards in London, Demels was founded by Manel Trepte in 1996, using recipes handed down through her Sri Lankan family. Today, in the hands of Howard Wilson and John Tiscornia, Demels produce a range of nine Sri Lankan chutneys, including tomato, lime pickle, hot tamarind and mild mango. All four have won gold awards at the Great Taste Awards.

Others in the range are sweet mango chutney, hot and spicy mango chutney, date and lime pickle chutney, apricot and ginger chutney, pineapple chutney and an aubergine pickle. Two curry powders, one for fish and vegetables, the other for chicken and red meats, are produced as well.

Outlets include: *online from the website; Westmorland Farm Shops on the M6; Holker Food Hall; The Honeypot in Hawkshead; Cranstons Cumbrian Food Hall at Penrith; Millstones at Bootle; Low Sizergh Barn Farm Shop near Kendal and FondEwe Fine Cheeses in Keswick.*

Friendly Food and Drink

Unit 1, Staveley Mill Yard, Staveley, Kendal LA8 9LR
Tel: 01539 822326
Website: www.friendlyfoodanddrink.co.uk

In 2007, a year after Geoff Monkman and Lorraine Stobbart set up their business they won gold at the Great Taste Awards in London for their St Clement's marmalade. The marmalade is one of about 30 jams, marmalades, fruit curds, chocolate curds, chutneys, savoury sauces, mustards and coulis which they produce at their Staveley premises, where there's a shop as well.

Those 30 products – packaged in their trademark square jars – include tomato and coriander chutney, beetroot and bell pepper chutney, roasted pepper sauce, strawberry and mint coulis, chocolate and chilli curd, cherry jam, rhubarb and apple jam, damson and gin jam, grapefruit marmalade, hot chilli mustard, and lemon and lime coulis.

'All of these items contain fruit sugar rather than cane sugar. That gives them a lower Glycemic Index value which we feel makes them more suitable for diabetics,' says Lorraine. She and Geoff also make ice cold smoothies at the numerous agricultural and food shows they attend in Cumbria and beyond during the year.

Outlets include: *online from the website; their own shop (open Mon–Sat 10–16); Holker Food Hall at Holker Hall; Westmorland Farm Shops on the M6; the Cumbrian Way in Ulverston; Artisan in Kendal; Churchmouse Cheeses in Kirkby Lonsdale; Love the Lakes in Bowness-on-Windermere; and A Taste of Lakeland (Stewart Cunningham outdoor centre) in Ambleside.*

Below right: the headquarters of Hawkshead Relish

Hawkshead Relish Company

The Square, Hawkshead LA22 0NZ
Tel: 015394 36614
Website: www.hawksheadrelish.com

Speciality Producer of the Year at the Great Taste Awards in 2005 and winner of about 40 awards at the same competition since 2002, Mark and Maria Whitehead's company had its beginnings at their café in Hawkshead where they used to make chutneys and pickles, to serve with customers' meals. When 2001's foot-and-mouth outbreak hit the business the couple decided to go into jam, chutney and sauce-making full time.

The first four products they offered were a Westmorland chutney, Cumberland sauce, sticky toffee sauce and a wholegrain mustard, but things have moved on hugely since then. The range now extends to more than 100 and includes relishes, preserves, mustards, vinegars, flavoured oils, pickles, chutneys and sauces and mayonnaises.

Golds at the Great Taste Awards have come the way of their lemon and lime marmalade, Ballachong prawn chutney, apple and lavender jelly, fig and orange jam, Indian capsicum pickle, five fruit marmalade, Hawkshead relish, chillililli, Cumberland sauce, and pink grapefruit and ginger marmalade. For some time Mark and Maria operated out of their café kitchen but in 2007 moved a short distance to a restored 16th-century barn on the shores of Esthwaite Water. The old café is now a Hawkshead Relish shop (see p127).

Outlets include: *online from the website; the company's Hawkshead shop; Holker Food Hall at Holker Hall; the Cumbrian Way in Ulverston; Booths stores and Lucy's Specialist Grocers in Ambleside.*

Moss Howe Farm Foods

Moss Howe Farm, Witherslack, Kendal LA11 6SA
Tel: 015395 52585
Website: www.mosshowefarm.co.uk

If you've ever been tired of stoning damsons, spare a thought for Annette Cook. She gets through about a ton and a half of the small ruby/purple fruit each year, spreading the September harvest between the four damson products she makes on her farm in the Winster Valley: a jam, a chutney, a jelly and a syrup. They come in two different size jars with distinctive labels.

'They're all produced to traditional recipes which have been handed down locally,' says Annette whose damson jam and syrup also go into Steve Duffin's Windermere Ice Cream.

While damsons are Annette's preserve, her husband John produces lamb and beef from the Swaledale sheep and Dexter cattle on the 600-acre (243ha) farm. The Dexter beef, he says, has proved very popular.

Damson outlets include: *Holker Food Hall at Holker Hall; Low Sizergh Barn Farm Shop near Kendal; The Honeypot in Hawkshead; Ainsworth Specialist Grocers in Grange-over-Sands; and Levens Hall.*
Meat outlets include: *online from the website; contact farm to order.*

Wild and Fruitful

Hillside, Cuddy Lonning, Wigton CA7 0AA
Tel: 016973 44304
Website: www.wildandfruitful.co.uk

Within two years of starting Wild and Fruitful Jane Maggs was named *Joint Overall Champion* at the North West Producer of the Year Awards 2003 for her hedgerow chilli jelly. The jelly is made from crab apples, hawthorn haws, rosehips and chilli peppers. Since then her range of products has increased considerably, to include jams, marmalades, chutneys, pickles, savoury jellies, salts, oils and vinegars, all made in the kitchen of her home with her helper Jill Perry. Jane read forestry and agriculture at Oxford University – where she was also a rowing blue – and later became a landscape architect.

What makes the business unusual is that she either grows the ingredients herself (fruit, vegetables, herbs) or gets them from other people's gardens, from nurseries, orchards, farms or National Trust properties. The origins as well as the ingredients are detailed on the labels.

Other products include chilli, garlic and ginger oil; gooseberry chutney; honey and cinnamon mustard; rhubarb, lime, pineapple and lemongrass chutney; raspberry and rhubarb jam; lemon curd (gold at the Great Taste Awards) and pear and stem ginger conserve.

Outlets include: *online from the website; Artisan in Kendal; Laird's Larder at Houghton Hall near Carlisle; and the Westmorland Farm Shops on the M6.*

Cumbria on a Plate

Ostle House, Mawbray, Maryport CA15 6QS
Tel: 01900 881356
Website: www.cumbriaonaplate.co.uk

Meet the producers, taste the food and savour the country-side. This triple bill of attractions is at the heart of the day-long food safaris, hosted by one of the great champions of Cumbrian produce, Annette Gibbons (pictured below). Presenter of four series of *Home Grown* for ITV Border and author of *Home Grown in Cumbria*, Annette has also run cookery courses at her house on the Solway coast for over 20 years.

Cumbria on a Plate offers visits to some of the best known artisan food producers in the county: butter, cheese, chocolate, jam and preserve makers, a working watermill that produces stone-ground, organic flour, top quality meat producers and farmers who keep rare breed animals. What you get with Annette is an immensely enthusiastic and knowledgable guide, a member of Slow Food Cumbria and a regular cookery demonstrator at events and shows around the county. She was also *Cumbria Woman of the Year* 2006–7.

The itinerary varies from tour to tour but the safari days normally go from 9.30–17.30, with Annette meeting you at a pre-determined location and then driving you around. Some of the places visited are not usually open to the public. Lunch is taken at a private estate, with much of the food coming from that estate. Apart from meeting the producers and seeing how they work, the safaris also offer the opportunity to purchase some great Cumbrian produce.

Price: £120 per person. Numbers: up to six people. Annette can also organise one day food safaris, followed by a cookery demonstration the next day at her home overlooking the Solway. She runs Fine Dining with Annette Gibbons, a club whose members dine at celebrated restaurants in Cumbria, Lancashire, Northumberland and the south of Scotland. Home Grown in Cumbria is published by Zymurgy Publishing and costs £17.

More Producers
The Watermill

Little Salkeld, Penrith CA10 1NN
Tel: 01768 881523
Website: www.organicmill.co.uk

Restored in 1975 by Nick and Ana Jones, this pink-washed, 18th-century watermill produces about two tons of baking and bread making flour a week, specialising in organic and bio-dynamic standard British wheat, rye, barley and oats. 'Bio-dynamic not only means organic but maximising the vital energies of the plant by sowing and harvesting in tune with solar and lunar influences, and enhancing soil fertility through adding natural substances,' says Nick.

He and Ana make a range of stoneground flours that include 100% Wholewheat Flour, 85% Wheatmeal Flour, 100% Wholewheat Self-Raising Flour, Granarius Malted Flour, Rye Flour, Special Blend Flour and Miller's Magic Maslin Flour. A variety of oats and oatmeals, including quick porridge oats

and giant oats, are available, and so too are bran, flakes and muesli, and other products. Flour is supplied to several artisan bakers in Cumbria, Millstones at Bootle and Staff of Life in Kendal amongst them.

Nick believes that the combination of traditional milling using millstones – French burr stones grind the grain – and highest quality grains result in flours of an exceptional standard.

Outlets include: *online from the website; The Watermill's own café/ shop (see p170); Booths in Kendal and Windermere; Appleseeds in Ulverston; Half Moon Wholefoods in Brampton; and Nature's Own in Penrith.*

More Food and Drink Producers

Cowmire Hall Damson Gin

Cowmire Hall, Crosthwaite, Kendal LA8 8JJ
Tel: 015395 68200
Website: www.cowmire.co.uk

Just over 400 years after her ancestor Anne Briggs left Cowmire Hall to marry a man called Edward Stanley, Victoria Stanley returned to the same Crosthwaite property after her marriage to Oliver Barratt. Not long afterwards the couple embarked on their damson gin enterprise, inspired by the Westmorland Damson Association's campaign to revive the damson orchards of the Lyth and Winster valleys.

The business began as a trial run in their kitchen, with their own fruit and supermarket gin producing about 400 bottles. Although production has increased considerably and moved from the kitchen to a converted stable known as the ginnery – it now also uses damsons from nearby farms – the basic process remains the same. The damsons are all frozen at harvest time, put into a large tank with cane sugar and specially blended London Gin and steeped for two or three months. About five batches a year are filtered and then bottled, at ABV 26%, into elegant Italian bottles.

Victoria is the author of *A Taste of Damsons: From Jelly to Gin*. A farmhouse holiday flat – The Bothy – is available.

Outlets for the damson gin include: *J&J Graham in Penrith;, Holker Food Hall at Holker Hall; Artisan in Kendal; Cartmel Village Shop; Low Sizergh Barn Farm Shop near Kendal; the Farm Shop at Rheged; House of Bruar near Blair Atholl in Perthshire; and Fortnum and Mason in London.*

Damsons in the Lyth and Winster Valleys

Until the formation of the Westmorland Damson Association in 1996 brought renewed interest in this little fruit, there was general agreement that the damson's purple patch here was in the first half of the 20th century. Originating in an area around Damascus in present-day Syria, this member of the plum family most likely found its way into England through the Romans. Damson stones have been found in archaeological digs at their ancient camps and settlements across the country.

By the middle of the 17th century damson trees were certainly in evidence in Westmorland where they thrived on the well-drained, shallow, limestone soils in an area to the south west of Kendal, the Lyth and Winster valleys. Around 60 or 70 years ago the blossom on the estimated 30–40,000 damson trees attracted huge numbers of people, many making the journey from Lancashire mill towns to see the spectacle.

By the 1970s the numbers of the trees had declined significantly. Changing farming practices, changing eating habits, less people on the land willing or available to carry out the arduous task of picking the fruit, and jam makers sourcing fruit elsewhere all played a part in the demise of the orchards.

Peter Cartmell, whose family had lived in the area for centuries, witnessed the decline and was determined to do something about it. So in 1996 he and a number of enthusiasts formed the Westmorland Damson Association. Its aim was to restore the orchards to their deserved glory, promote the cultivation and use of Westmorland damsons, extend the market for damson products and look after the interest of local growers.

Website: www.lythdamsons.org.uk

Lizzie's Home Made

The Bank, Dockray, Penrith CA11 0LG
Tel: 017684 82487
Website: www.fruttacotta.co.uk

So great was the impression that the local food left on Lizzie Smith during a holiday in Umbria in 2004 that when she returned to Cumbria she immediately started researching Italian recipes. The former nurse launched the first of her 'puddings in a jar' in 2005. Cumbrian Frutta Cotta was pretty well an instant success, the tasty mix of organic dried apricots, figs and prunes in a spiced rum syrup winning gold at the Great Taste Awards in London in 2006.

A subsequent pudding called Cumbrian Frutta Cotta Mostarda was *New Product of the Year* at the North West Fine Food Awards 2007. Her Damson Fruit Gem won the same title in 2008.

Outlets include: *Artisan in Kendal; Laird's Larder at Houghton Hall Garden Centre near Carlisle; Lucy's Specialist Grocers in Ambleside; Low Sizergh Barn Farm Shop near Kendal; Harvey Nicols in Manchester and Valvona and Crolla in Edinburgh.*

Truffles Chocolates

2 Kingwater Close, Brampton CA8 1PD
Tel: 016977 42539
Website: www.truffleschocolates.co.uk

'Made by a chocoholic for those who enjoy good chocolate,' says Lorna Tampling of her range of 25 different flavoured truffles. It takes three days for her to hand make them, the first part of the process involving the creation of the filling or ganache, using local cream. This ganache is then piped into chocolate shells, the shells then sealed and rolled in tempered chocolate. Some are also rolled in either coconut, sugar or vermicelli.

Flavours include lime Martini (bronze award at the Great Taste Awards in 2006), Champagne (which is made with pink Champagne), passion fruit, cream, vanilla, dark rum, orange and brandy, and Black Russian. The latter is made with plain chocolate, vodka and Tia Maria, rolled in plain chocolate and with white chocolate decoration.

Outlets include: *online from the website; Westmorland Farm Shops on the M6; Cartmel Village Shop; Half Moon Wholefoods in Brampton; and Skrumshus in Corbridge.*

Wooden Spoon Fudge Company

Colton, near Ulverston LA12 8HF
Tel: 01229 861029

Three years after starting her business Claire Waller won a gold for her 'original' fudge at the Great Taste Awards in London. She followed that up a year later with two more golds (maple syrup fudge and ginger fudge) and a silver for the cappuccino.

A trio of bronze medals came in 2006. In all Claire makes eight different varieties of fudge at her home in the Rusland Valley, a rich chocolate, a cranberry, cherry and almond, and a chocolate topped ginger being the other four. 'They're all made in a traditional way, stirred in a big pan with a wooden spoon,' says Claire.

Outlets include: *Low Sizergh Barn Farm Shop near Kendal; Cumbrian Way in Ulverston; shops at Levens Hall, Brantwood (Coniston) and National Trust properties in Cumbria; Farrer's in Kendal; Holker Food Hall at Holker Hall; Westmorland Farm Shops on the M6; Churchmouse Cheeses in Kirkby Lonsdale; and the Farm Shop at Rheged.*

Below: chocolates from Truffles Chocolates

Breweries

Coniston Brewing Company

Coppermines Road, Coniston LA21 8HL
Tel: 015394 41133
Website: www.conistonbrewery.com

It took Ian Bradley only three years in business before his Coniston Brewing Company's Bluebird Bitter was pronounced *Champion Beer* of CAMRA's 21st Great British Beer Festival in London in 1998. Winning the title meant a big demand for this session ale, so he had to ask other breweries to help him out with production.

Bluebird Bitter (ABV 3.6%) and the ruby red Old Man Ale (ABV 4.2%) – one named after speed ace Donald Campbell's boat *Bluebird*, the other after the nearby fell of Coniston Old Man – were Ian's first two beers. The third regular one in the stable is Premium XB Bluebird Bitter (4.2%).

Ian was pretty much born with beer in his blood because his parents, Ron and Sue, have run the Black Bull in Coniston (see p54) for over 30 years and he, himself, worked in the pub for almost five years.

Later Ian and his father went on a two day brewery start-up course at Sunderland University and not long afterwards Coniston Brewing Company, located just behind the Black Bull, produced its first pint. Oliver's Light Ale (3.4%), the dark, seasonal Blacksmith's Ale (5%) and the golden amber ale Quicksilver (4.3%) are three more Coniston beers.

Pubs which serve Coniston Brewing Company's beers include:
the Black Bull Inn and Hotel in Coniston, Britannia Inn at Elterwater, Wateredge Inn and Queen's Hotel in Ambleside, Dog and Gun in Keswick, Angel Inn at Bowness, Sun Inn at Crook, Kings Arms Hotel in Hawkshead, Wilson Arms at Torver, Watermill Inn at Ings and the Stickle Barn Tavern, Great Langdale. Bluebird Bitter, Coniston Old Man, Premium XB Bluebird Bitter, Oliver's Light Ale, Blacksmith's Ale and Quicksilver are all available in bottles.

Middle right: a view across Coniston Water from John Ruskin's home of Brantwood

Cumbrian Legendary Ales

Old Hall Brewery, Hawkshead LA22 0QF
Tel: 015394 36436
Website: www.cumbrianlegendaryales.com

Such was the beauty of innkeeper's daughter Mary Robinson that after Joseph Budworth mentioned her in his 1792 book *A Fortnight's Ramble to the Lakes* people came from far and wide to gaze at her face. William Wordsworth and Samuel Taylor Coleridge both wrote about her, Melvyn Bragg's book *The Maid of Buttermere* told Mary's story and Cumbrian Legendary Ales toasts her in a beer named Buttermere Beauty (ABV 4.8%).

The ale is one of several in the range here – like Wicked Jimmy (ABV 3.6%), the best bitter King Dunmail (4.2%), the golden bitter Dickie Doodle (3.9%), the creamy stout Claife Crier (5%), Langdale Moonshine Ale (4.4%) and Scary Mary (4.2%) – that trawl Cumbria's legends and history.

The brewery is run by David and Liz Newham, and David and Gill Frost, and was launched in June 2006. It is beautifully located in a renovated Victorian barn at Esthwaite Old Hall, which is beside Esthwaite Water near Hawkshead. Naturally Old Hall Mild (3.2%) is named after this little bit of history. The website gives details of each beer.

Pubs which serve Cumbrian Legendary ales include: *the Gate Inn at Yanwath, near Penrith, Strickland Arms at Sizergh, Newfield Inn at Seathwaite, Eagle and Child in Staveley, Wheatsheaf at Brigsteer, The White House in Bowness. A dark beer called Croglin Vampire (ABV 8%) – named after the legend of a vampire in a Cumbrian fellside village in the 17th century – is available in bottles at Holker Food Hall and the Farm Shop at Rheged.*

Geltsdale Brewery

Old Brewery Yard, Craw Hall, Brampton CA8 1TR
Tel: 016977 41541
Website: www.geltsdalebrewery.com

Former archaeologist Fiona Deal has revived a brewing tradition in Brampton that started in the late 18th century. The original brewery closed many years ago but in 2006, having learnt about beer making while living in the Shetland Isles, she began production in a unit housed within Brampton's Old Brewery and now brews two or three times a week.

Her beers are Brampton Bitter (ABV 4.2%), King's Forest Best Bitter (ABV 3.8%), the golden ale Tarnmonath (4%), Bewcastle Brown Ale (4%), the pale ale Cold Fell (3.9%), Hell Beck Ruby Ale (4.2%), and the dark mild Black Dub (3.6%), all names associated with the history and countryside of the area around Brampton. Fiona produces and bottles Geltsdale Lager as well.

Pubs which serve Geltsdale beers include: *the Pheasant Inn at Cumwhitton, Blacksmiths Arms at Talkin, String of Horses at Faugh, Woodrow Wilson in Carlisle, Belted Will at Hallbankgate, Cumberland Hotel in Alston, Centurion at Walton near Brampton, Crossings Inn at Roweltown (north of Carlisle) and Nag's Head at Brampton. All seven beers and the lager are available in bottles.*

Below left: David and Liz Newham, Cumbrian Legendary Ales
Below: Fiona Deal at Geltsdale Brewery

Hawkshead Brewery

Mill Yard, Staveley, near Kendal LA8 9LR
Tel: 01539 822644
Website: www.hawksheadbrewery.co.uk

Although it's based in Staveley, the brewery's origins lie in an 18th-century barn near Hawkshead where former BBC foreign correspondent Alex Brodie started producing beer in 2002. The move to Staveley came four years later, demand, by then, outstripping ability to supply. His purpose-built German Moeschle plant trebled capacity and by October 2007 Hawkshead had brewed over one million pints (571,000 litres) of cask ale at the new site.

In a relatively short time Hawkshead's regulars – Hawkshead Bitter (ABV 3.7%), Lakeland Gold (ABV 4.4%), Red (4.2%), Brodie's Prime (4.9%) and Lakeland Lager (5%) – have become well known and much liked. Bottled Hawkshead Gold, for instance, has won gold three times in five years at the SIBA (Society of Independent Brewers) North Brewing Awards. In 2005 Lakeland Gold (cask) won gold at SIBA's national final.

Other, more seasonal, Hawkshead beers include Ulverston Pale Ale (ABV 4.1%), 5Hop (4.2%), Damson Stout (4.3%) and the Christmas ale Jingle Fells (4.5%). An organic beer is planned. Tours of the 20 barrel brewing plant go from the Beer Hall (see p65) which is open daily.

Pubs and other places which serve Hawkshead beers include:
Watermill at Ings, Brewery Arts Centre in Kendal, Sun Inn at Kirkby Lonsdale, Masons Arms at Strawberry Bank, Eagle and Child in Staveley, Britannia Inn at Elterwater, Church House at Torver and Farmers Arms, Ulverston. Hawkshead Red, Gold, Brodie's Prime, Damson Stout and Lakeland Lager are all available in bottles.

Hesket Newmarket Brewery

Old Crown Barn, Hesket Newmarket CA7 8JG
Tel: 016974 78066
Website: www.hesketbrewery.co.uk

Spring 2008 saw the 20th anniversary of this well known brewery which produces ten beers at its premises behind the Old Crown pub in Hesket Newmarket (see p60). Originally started by Jim and Liz Fearnley, it was taken over by the Hesket Newmarket Brewery Co-operative in 1999 when the couple retired. Ninety shareholders, who put up £1,500 each, take their dividend in beer, money or a combination of both. The most famous and most popular beer in the stable – and the one that Prince Charles drank in the Old Crown on his visit there in 2004 – is the full flavoured, fruity beer called Doris's 90th Birthday Ale (ABV 4.3%), named after Liz Fearnley's mother.

The rest are named after Lakeland Fells: Blencathra Bitter (ABV 3.2%), Great Cockup Porter (3%), Helvellyn Gold (4%), Skiddaw Special Bitter (3.7%), Old Carrock Strong Ale (6%), Sca Fell Blonde (4.4%), High Pike (4.2%), Haystacks (3.7%) and Catbells Pale Ale (5%). The last five in that list, plus Doris's 90th, are also sold as bottle-conditioned beers (the beer still active inside). The bottling is done on site.

There's a small visitor centre and shop at the brewery, with tours available by appointment. The Old Crown pub is run by a co-operative as well.

Pubs which serve Hesket Newmarket beers include: *the Yanwath Gate Inn near Penrith, Travellers Rest at Glenridding, the Scafell Hotel at Rosthwaite, the Fish Hotel at Buttermere and the Kirkstone Pass Inn. Six beers, mentioned above, are bottled. Beer is sold online through the website.*

Below: the Hawkshead Brewery

Keswick Brewing Company

The Old Brewery, Brewery Lane, Keswick CA12 5BY
Tel: 017687 80700
Website: www.keswickbrewery.co.uk

Thirst Green is not a beer that the Keswick Brewing Company has yet produced but considering Sue and Phil Harrison's strong interest in the environment, it may not be long before they do. The couple began brewing in 2006 and currently produce five regular beers – a bitter called Thirst Pitch (ABV 3.8%), the golden pale ale Thirst Run (ABV 4.2%), the rich malty bitter Thirst Fall (4.8%), the golden bitter Thirst Ascent (4%) and Thirst Rescue (3.7%), another golden bitter. 5p per pint from the latter is donated by the brewery to whichever mountain rescue team the pub nominates.

Seasonal ales include the golden bitter Thirst Blossom (ABV 4.1%), the pale ale Thirst Quencher (4.3%) and Thirst Chestnut (4%), a nut brown ale. Thirst Celebration (7%), an India Pale Ale, was made for the brewery's second anniversary. Originally their beers should have been prefaced by the word 'First' but a slight mishearing on the phone by the company designing the logo and pump clips changed that to Thirst etc. to the delight of Sue and Phil.

They use wool insulation in the brewing vessels while 50p from the price of every brewery tour is split between the Climate Contribution Fund and red squirrel conservation (through Cumbria's Tourism and Conservation Partnership). Brewery tours are £5.50 per person and a brewery shop sells packs of bottled beers, mini-casks, T-shirts and other merchandise.

Pubs and other places which serve Keswick Brewing Company's beers include: *the Dog and Gun and The Square Orange café-bar in Keswick; Royal Oak in Ambleside; Fish Hotel at Buttermere; Yanwath Gate Inn near Penrith; Middle Ruddings Country Inn and Restaurant at Braithwaite; Gosforth Hall Hotel; Glen Rothay Hotel at Rydal. Thirst Pitch, Thirst Ascent, Thirst Run and Thirst Fall and the IPA are all available in bottles.*

Below: Sue and Phil Harrison of the Keswick Brewing Company

Whitehaven Brewing Company

The Brewery, Croasdale Farm, Ennerdale CA23 3AT
Tel: 01946 861755
Website: www.twbcl.co.uk

It was in November 2007 that the Whitehaven Brewing Company produced its debut pint of Ennerdale Bitter (ABV 3.9%), the first ale to be made in this particular part of Cumbria for some years, says managing director and brewer Shelagh Ferguson.

The brewery is located in a converted barn at Croasdale, a short hop from Ennerdale Water. Spring water from nearby Kelton Fell feeds the brewery which was set up with the help of former Jennings head brewer, Peter Laws.

This is red squirrel country and because Shelagh and fellow directors Barrie Roberts and Chris Webber are keen to protect them, 1p from every pint of Ennerdale Bitter sold goes to the *Save Our Squirrels* campaign.

Two seasonal beers are also brewed (at present) and a low alcohol beer called Lonsdale. 'It punches above its weight,' says Shelagh in reference to boxing's Lonsdale Belt, named after the 5th Earl of Lonsdale.

Outlets which serve Whitehaven Brewing Company's beers include: the Lutwidge Arms Hotel at Holmrook; the Fish Hotel in Buttermere; the Allerdale Court in Cockermouth; the Vagabond in Whitehaven; and the Fox and Hounds and Shepherds Arms at Ennerdale Bridge. Ennerdale Bitter and Ennerdale Blonde are available in bottles.

Below: Ennerdale Water, close to the Whitehaven Brewing Company.
Above far left: Graeme and Caroline Baxter, Yates Brewery.
Above far right: Yates' bottled beers. Below far left: Watermill Brewing Company at Ings (see p62). Middle far right: Hesket Newmarket Brewery (see p102). Below far right: the village of Hesket Newmarket.

Yates Brewery

Ghyll Farm, Westnewton, Wigton CA7 3NX
Tel: 016973 21081
Website: www.yatesbrewery.co.uk

Producers of Yates Bitter, Best Cellar, Fever Pitch and Sun Goddess amongst others, this is the longest established small brewery in Cumbria. It was set up in 1986 by Peter and Carole Yates and then changed hands ten years ago, its new owners, Graeme and Caroline Baxter, having seen the brewery advertised for sale in a national newspaper.

In 2006 the couple put in a new brewhouse along with a new reedbed system for waste water and a year later Yates celebrated 2,500 brews, which approximated to eight million pints of beer. The original Yates yeast is still used: more than 2,800 generations of yeast have now gone through the brewing process.

A number of Graeme and Caroline's beers have won awards. The pale coloured, hoppy flavoured Fever Pitch (ABV 3.9%) was a finalist in the *Best Bitters* category of the Great British Beer Festival in 2003, their IPA (ABV 4.9%) was the winner of the Cumbrian Micro-Brewery Challenge in 2001, 2006 and 2008, and the golden coloured Yates Bitter (3.7%) was an early winner at the Cambridge Beer Festival.

Other beers include Sun Goddess (ABV 4.2%), Spring Fever (4.5%), the light, hoppy Winter Fever (4.5%), Solway Sunset (4.3%), Mad March Hare (4.2%) and the rich, dark Best Cellar (4.6%). This last beer was originally brewed at Christmas but is now bottled all year round.

Pubs which serve Yates beer include: the Manor Arms at Broughton-in-Furness; the Old Dungeon Ghyll in Langdale; The Screes Inn at Nether Wasdale; King's Head in Carlisle; and the Blacksmiths Arms at Talkin near Brampton. Yates Best Bitter and Best Cellar are both available in bottles. Check out the website for Yates online shop.

Slow Food

Introduction to Slow Food
Websites: *www.slowfood.com* or *www.slowfood.org.uk*

It says much about our food culture that the term 'fast food' needs no introduction at all. Mention the phrase 'slow food' and an explanation is often required, even though the Slow Food movement is over 20 years old. It was founded in Italy in 1986 by Carlo Petrini, a journalist who was concerned that fast food production and standardisation of taste was threatening the existence of distinct, traditional and regional foods. Today Slow Food has some 80,000 members in 130 countries, those members belonging to local groups or convivia.

Slow Food celebrates small-scale agriculture, artisan food production, sustainable approaches to fishing and farming, differences in flavour and a slower pace of life. Good, clean and fair are three key words. Food should taste good and be produced in a way which doesn't hurt the environment, animal welfare or human health. Those who produce it in the first place should receive fair reward for their effort. For obvious reasons the snail is Slow Food's emblem.

Slow Food Cumbria
The Cumbria Convivium was established in 2005 and its inaugural event at the First Floor Café at Lakeland in Windermere gave a pretty good flavour of what Slow Food is all about. Amongst the produce on display – to eat or for sale – was air-dried Herdwick mutton and Herdwick mutton salami from Farmer Sharp, wild boar prosciutto and a roasted leg of wild boar from Peter Gott's Sillfield Farm, about 30 jams and relishes from Wild and Fruitful, and smoked roe deer and smoked salmon from Cartmel Valley Game Supplies. Richard Woodall's Cumbrian pancetta and Cumbria air-dried ham was also on offer, as was a colourful salad from Howbarrow Organic Farm (mizuna, rocket, oak leaf lettuce and nasturtium leaves and flowers were some of the ingredients), Staff of Life bread, Cream of Cumbria butter, Morecambe Bay shrimps from Furness Fish, Game and Poultry Supplies, Birdoswald organic cheese, and Cumbrian Frutta Cotta (Lizzie's Home Made). Damson gin from Strawberry Bank and organic wines from Organico were the drinks.

'A big part of Slow Food is bringing people together to celebrate taste and flavours and to learn about different foods. It's also about encouraging people to seek out and buy artisan products,' says Cumbrian food producer Peter Gott (pictured below). So since that 2005 gathering the Cumbria Convivium has put on numerous other events, to give members and sometimes non-members the chance to find out about the wealth of food and drink here.

The convivium's most significant current objective is to help promote awareness of good local produce by setting up a system which recognises producers, retailers and eating places that adopt the principles of Slow Food. Shops and restaurants which do will receive a Slow Food 'snail' sticker to put in their windows, while producers will be included on a list of Slow Food Cumbria's Guide to Recommended Producers.

In spring 2008 the UK arm of Slow Food chose Cumbria for its second AGM. Slow Food members came from all over the country to the event, and so too did the general secretary of Slow Food International, Paolo di Croce.

For more information about Slow Food Cumbria: email Peter Jackson at pbj@slowfoodcumbria.org.uk.

What's what in Slow Food

Convivium. Based on the Latin word for feast or banquet, convivium means a local group of Slow Food members. There are some 850 Slow Food convivia across the world, 40–50 in the UK. Convivia organise a variety of events, such as tastings, visits to food and drink producers or dinners with a particular theme. Cumbria's convivium is currently setting up a system to recognise producers, retailers and eating places who adopt the principles of Slow Food.

Slow Food Foundation for Biodiversity. Any appreciation of food must include the safeguarding of food resources. That was the reasoning behind the 2003 creation of this foundation whose aim is to organise and fund projects which protect agricultural biodiversity and the traditions of gastronomy, particularly in developing countries.
Website: www.slowfoodfoundation.com

Ark of Taste. Herdwick sheep (three tups or rams pictured below), Lyth Valley damsons, char (found in Windermere) and Morecambe Bay shrimps are four of over 500 products worldwide on the Ark of Taste. Formed in 1996, the Ark's aim is to rediscover and catalogue food and drink products, animal and fish breeds and fruit and vegetable varieties which are in danger of disappearing forever.

Presidia. This working arm of the Ark of Taste began in 2000 with two small-scale projects in Italy. Now it has nearly 300 worldwide. Presidia helps artisan food producers with business advice, marketing, establishing and maintaining the quality of their products and making sure that there is a secure future for them. In the UK Presidia have been formed for artisan Somerset Cheddar, Three Counties Perry, Old Gloucester beef, Gloucester cheese and Fal oysters in Cornwall.

Terra Madre. This biennial event was held for the first time in Italy in 2004 and brings together 'food communities' – farmers, fishermen, processors, cooks and such like – from more than 100 countries, to discuss a wide range of food and food-related issues. *Website: www.terramadre.info*

Salone del Gusto. Another biennial event, Salone del Gusto is held in October in a former Fiat factory in Turin. It's really a huge food and drink market, a showcase for small scale producers from all over the world. There are taste workshops, cookery demonstrations and culinary excursions.
Website: www.salonedelgusto.com

Cheese. The international festival of artisan cheeses and cheese makers is held in Bra, the same place in northern Italy where Slow Food has its main offices.
Website: www.cheese.slowfood.com

Slow Fish. Taste workshops, seminars, conferences and a seafood market are all part of Slow Fish which is held in Genoa every two years. It brings together fishermen, consumers, processors and others in the responsible enjoyment of fish.
Website: www.slowfish.it

Even More Producers

Bennett's Solway Shrimps

Tel: 016973 32571
Website:
www.bennettssolwayshrimps.co.uk
Two Silloth based boats fish for Bennett's Solway brown shrimps, many of which are later cooked in a blend of spices, placed into pots and sealed with butter, for potted shrimps.

Bessy Beck Trout Fishery

Tel: 015396 23303
Website: www.bessybecktrout.co.uk
The fishery at Newbiggin-on-Lune, near Kirkby Stephen produces fresh rainbow trout, smoked trout, smoked trout fishcakes and other smoked foods. There's a tea room, and a small farm shop which sells other local produce as well.

Border County Foods

Tel: 01228 672020
Website: www.cumberland-sausage.net
Based near Carlisle, Austen Davies produces rare breed pork and Cumberland sausage, dry cured and oak smoked bacon, black pudding, pancetta, Cumberland Dux (faggots) and other pork products.

Page 110
Above left: Broughton Village Bakery, Broughton-in-Furness (see p115)
Above right: Westmorland Farm Shop (see p145)
Below left: Organico, Staveley (see p144)
Below right: Artisan, Kendal (see p128)

Carrs Flour Mills

Tel: 01228 554600
Website: www.carrs-flourmills.co.uk
Jonathan Dodgson Carr founded the Carr's biscuit and flour business in Carlisle in 1831. Today Carrs Flour Mills at Silloth produce a range of flours, including three breadmaker varieties: strong white, strong brown and wholemeal

Cartmel Valley Game Supplies and Smokehouse

Tel: 015395 36413
Jonathan and Susan Stott's business near Cark-in-Cartmel supplies game, poultry, fish, venison and wild boar to hotels, restaurants, pubs and food and farm shops. They also produce sausages and smoked foods.

Cream of Cumbria

Tel: 01228 675558
Website: www.creamofcumbria.co.uk
Sue Forrester produces salted and unsalted butter near Carlisle, shaping the butter with butter pats or 'Scotch hands'. She makes buttermilk, rum butter, brandy butter, scones and a variety of cakes as well.

English Lakes Ice Cream

Tel: 01539 721211
Website: www.lakesicecream.com
Peter and Frances Fryer's Kendal based company, established more than 20 years ago, makes a range of luxury dairy ice creams and regular ice creams, diabetic ice creams and sorbets.

Agricultural and Country Shows

If you're looking for an attraction that combines the great outdoors and an insight into the farming life of Cumbria, then the annual agricultural and country shows (most take place between June and September) are hard to beat. Showing and judging livestock are at the heart of almost all the shows - the Cumberland Show and the Westmorland Show are the two biggest - but there are plenty of other things going on as well. Food tents selling Cumbrian produce are an attraction at a number of shows.

Cumberland and Westmorland Foods

The old counties of Cumberland and Westmorland disappeared more than thirty years ago but the names live on in many foods. There's Cumberland sausage and Cumberland sauce, Cumberland or Westmorland courting cake, Cumberland rum butter, Westmorland parkin, Cumberland rum nicky and Westmorland pepper cake. As for some other names, there's Grasmere gingerbread, Borrowdale tea bread, Lamplugh pudding, Hawkshead wigs, Ennerdale cake and Kendal mint cake.

www.artisan-food.com

This popular online food magazine was launched in 2006 by Martin and Cecilia Campbell and is aimed at those who love Cumbrian food. Profiles of food producers, restaurant reviews, job opportunities in Cumbria's catering and hospitality sector, details of farmers' markets and food shops, and information on cuts of lamb and beef are some of the subjects the website covers. Cecilia is the writer and designer, Martin the photographer and website builder.

Jennings Brothers

Tel: 0845 1297185
Website: www.jenningsbrewery.co.uk
Jennings in Cockermouth, part of the Marston's Beer Company, is the biggest of about 25 breweries in Cumbria. It produces Cumberland Ale, Jennings Bitter, Sneck Lifter, Cocker Hoop and numerous other ales.

Jeremy's Soups

Tel: 017683 53311
Website: www.jeremyssoups.co.uk
Jeremy and Helen Kent make a range of about a dozen soups at their production kitchen in Appleby. The soups – they change with the seasons – include leek and potato, tomato and basil, curried parsnip, and chickpea and harissa.

Lakeland Willow Water

Tel: 015395 59452
Website: www.willowwater.com
Over 800 years after the monks of Cartmel Priory discovered the benefits of drinking their local well water, it became available to millions of people when bottling started at Flookburgh, near Grange-over-Sands in 2004. The company produces a still and sparkling water, both of which contain salicin naturally.

Lakes Speciality Foods

Tel: 01539 822713
Website:
www.lakesspecialityfoods.co.uk
The company is based in Staveley, near Kendal and supplies beef, lamb, pork, game and poultry to hotels, restaurants and pubs. It launched the Pinks – Lake District Sausage and Bacon Company in 2008.

Mawsons

Tel: 019467 28278
Website:
www.mawsonsofbaileyground.co.uk
The Mawson family has farmed at Bailey Ground Farm, Seascale for over 60 years. These days they're producers of milk, cream, butter, rum butter, smoothies, cheese and ice cream.

Sue Prickett

Tel: 015242 71435
In the kitchen of her farmhouse near Kirkby Lonsdale, Sue makes a range of chutneys, jams, jellies and marmalades, available from Kitridding Farm Shop (see p133). Her blackcurrant jam won her *North West Producer of the Year* in 2004.

The Pudding Room

Tel: 07769 697868
Website: www.thepuddingroom.net
Helen Boardman makes a range of puddings at Coniston, including rum 'n' raisin sticky date pudding with butterscotch sauce, lemon pond pudding, rich chocolate brownie and traditional bread and butter pudding.

Ray's Shrimps

Tel: 016973 31215
Website: www.raysshrimpsltd.co.uk
Three generations of one family have been involved in this business, founded by the late Alan Ray in the 1960s. Alan's son Joe and daughter Julie, and Julie's son Jason carry on the tradition of selling fresh and potting Solway brown shrimps.

South Lakes Organic Milk

Tel: 01229 586153
Swarthmoor Hall Farm at Ulverston has been producing organic milk and cream since 2001. It supplies Booths supermarkets, a number of food and farm shops in Cumbria and other dairy outlets.

Strawberry Bank Liqueurs

Tel: 015395 68812
Website:
www.strawberrybankliqueurs.co.uk
Mike and Helen Walsh produce damson gin, sloe gin, blackberry liqueur, blackberry gin and strawberry vodka at their production unit just outside Kendal.

Mr Vikki's

Tel: 01768 899023
Website: www.mrvikkis.co.uk
Between them Adam Marks (Mr Vikki's) and Mary Ballantyne (Mary's Homemade) make a range of chutneys, pickles, pastes, sauces, mustards, jams and savoury jellies at their home near Penrith.

Wardhall Dairy

Tel: 016973 21917
Website: www.wardhalldairy.co.uk
At Ewe Close Farm, Arkleby near Wigton, Lynn Ballantine Dykes produces cheeses from cows' and goats' milk, including Wardhall Blue, Bridekirk, Gillands Beck and Parsonby. She makes butter as well.

Food and Drink Shops/ Farm Shops

Alston

Alston Wholefoods

King's Arms Buildings, Front Street, Alston CA9 3HU
Tel: 01434 381588
Website: www.alstonwholefoods.com

Local, organic, Fairtrade and special dietary products are well supported by this shop, just down the cobbled street from the market cross in Alston. You'll find Cream of Cumbria butter and cream, Wild and Fruitful jams, Cumberland Mustard products (made in Alston), Sillfield Farm bacon, Hawkshead organic trout, Mr Vikki's spicy sauces, flour from The Watermill at Little Salkeld and more.

The good range of 40–50 cheeses – a few chalked up on a blackboard outside sometimes – includes those from Thornby Moor Dairy and Slack House Farm in Cumbria, and Cotherstone in County Durham. The shop is happy to take special orders and, like the nearby Moody Baker, with whom it works closely, is run as a workers' co-operative. Alston Wholefoods takes fresh Moody Baker bread every Saturday morning.

Open: *Mon–Sat 9–17, Sun 11–16.*

Below right: Alston, home to the Moody Baker

The Moody Baker

3 West View, Front Street, Alston CA9 3SF
Tel: 01434 382003
Website: www.themoodybaker.co.uk

Towards the upper end of Alston, this popular little bakery produces a range of breads, cakes, stotties, and meat and vegetarian pies and pasties. Like Alston Wholefoods, it's a workers' co-operative, and in the seven years the bakery's been running it's made something of a name for itself. In 2006 the Moody Baker was judged the *Best Local Food Retailer in the North West*, in a competition run by the Countryside Alliance, and in 2007 it won *Best Vegetarian Product* in the North West Fine Food Awards for its carrot and almond nut loaf.

Many of the ingredients for the 50–60 products are organic, Fairtrade or locally sourced, the recipes coming from the ten or so members of the co-operative. Those products include a spicy lentil pasty, walnut bread, roasted vegetable tart, chilli bean wrap, blueberry cheesecake, chocolate brownie and olive bread. A miner's pasty they created specially for the nearby Nenthead Mine has minced pork and root vegetables at one end and apple at the other. It's available from time to time.

Open: *Mon–Sat 8–17.*

Ambleside
Lucy's Specialist Grocers

Compston Road, Ambleside LA22 9DJ
Tel: 015394 32223
Website: www.lucysofambleside.co.uk

Given the variety of food ventures which Lucy Nicholson has created in and around Ambleside over the last 20 years, there's a strong case for nicknaming the town 'Lucyside'. Café and restaurant (see p11 and p160), wine bar, cookery school (see p154), hampers, outside catering and mail order are all part of the Lucy brand, although it's this enticing and well known delicatessen which lies at the heart of an ever expanding business.

Lucy Nicholson's original ambition was to be an actress. Her father urged her to have a back-up job for the times she might be 'resting' and so she enrolled for a year's secretarial course at Lucie Clayton's in London. Marketing work in the music business followed and it was for the promotion of a cassette recording that featured the tales of Beatrix Potter which first brought her to the Lake District in 1978. She moved here four years later and opened Lucy's Specialist Grocers on Church Street in Ambleside in 1989.

The emphasis then was on local produce, and Cumbrian names are still much in evidence in the new and bigger premises on Compston Road. A range of breads are delivered daily. Behind the pay counter there are porridge oats, organic muesli, spelt flour and rye flour from The Watermill at Little Salkeld.

New names and ranges regularly appear. Bread dippers, compotes, tapenades, and warm and cold dips from the Canadian company Wildly were an instant hit when Lucy's started stocking them in summer 2008. French soups, Pain is Good sauces (from the American company Original Juan) and Woodchester sauces are also on the shelves.

There are heaps of jams, jellies, chutneys, mustards, relishes, dressings, a range of rice and beans, plus pasta, Italian biscuits, salts, beers (mostly local), damson gins, fruit wines, tea, coffee and Lizzie's Home Made produce. Enthusiastic notes about the food and drink are dotted around everywhere. Plenty of tasters are available and there are regular in-store tastings.

A lovely old dresser is stacked with olive oils and vinegars while the deli counter has about 40–50 cheeses, together with hams, salamis, bacon, sausages, pies and patés. Cookware is stocked as well and there's even room for a few seats for people to take coffee and cakes.

Open: *Nov–Mar, daily 9–18; Apr–Oct, daily 8–20.*

Below left: Lucy Nicholson

Ambleside

Organico

Fisherbeck Mill, Old Lake Road, Ambleside LA22 0DH
Tel: 015394 31122
Website: www.organi.co.uk

When Sue and Peter Jackson started importing wine from a few estates in Italy in 1997, it was more of a hobby than a business. But in 2005 they opened this outlet in Ambleside and in early 2008 another outlet – considerably bigger – in Staveley near Kendal (see p144).

There's a range in Ambleside of about 200 wines and although Italy and France are the two countries best represented, there are wines from Argentina, Austria, Australia, Chile, Germany, New Zealand, Portugal, South Africa and Spain. All of them, says Peter, are produced without the use of pesticides, fungicides, herbicides or chemical fertilizers. Amongst the Jacksons' favourite red wines are the biodynamic reds – Rosso di Montalcino, Brunello di Montalcino and Morellino di Scansano – from the Corte Pavone and Val di Falco estates in Tuscany.

Open: *Tue–Sat 10–17.30.*

Appleby-in-Westmorland

TM Ewbank

12 Boroughgate, Appleby-in-Westmorland CA16 6XB
Tel: 017683 51462

You can't miss the shop because it's got a window display that's unlike any other butchers in Cumbria. 'Good meat deserves good wrapping,' says Trevor Ewbank and so beef, lamb, pork, bacon and sausages (no poultry except for turkeys at Christmas) are reverently packaged in the greaseproof paper which hangs up behind a long mahogany counter.

Founded over a hundred years ago by Trevor's great grandfather, it's still very much a family business. Trevor's wife Brenda works in the shop, as do his parents Malcolm and Eleanor. Ewbank's has its own farm, for rearing cattle – 'as near to organic as you can get,' says Trevor – and abattoir. Customers come from all over the north of England. Meat, particularly the Cumberland pork sausage, is despatched even further afield. Two mobile shops serve the local area.

Open: *Mon 7.30–12.30, Tue–Wed, Fri–Sat 7.30–17,*
Thu 7.30–16.

Bootle

Millstones Bakery/Food Hall

Bootle, Millom LA19 5TJ
Tel: 01229 718772/718775 (food hall)
Website: www.millstonesbakery.com

After three years of working in hotels and restaurants elsewhere in Cumbria, Toni Sim decided to set up a bakery in the area she grew up in. The business opened in 2006 and produces a range of breads and pies, using stone–ground flour from The Watermill at Little Salkeld and milk, cream and butter from Mawson's of Bailey Ground Farm, Seascale.

Breads might be sun-dried tomato; walnut; mozzarella and rosemary; and green olive. Pies, which are Toni's speciality, include pork, apple and cider; chicken with roasted leek and pancetta; lamb with apricots and orange; and venison and cranberry. Desserts such as pecan pie, zesty apple crumble, and strawberry and vanilla tart are made here too. Toni's mother, Dorothy, helps with the baking.

Next door is Rachel Curry's food hall which stocks a range of jams and chutneys (Claire's Handmade and Hawkshead Relish amongst others), cheeses, mustard, Hartley's ice cream, locally sourced lamb, cured meats, Cartmel Valley sausages and game, and a range of Suma products. The whole complex at Millstones – there's a café here as well (see p160) – is set in old farm buildings that belong to Rachel and her family.

Bakery open: *Tue–Sat 10–16.30. Food hall open: Tue–Sun 10–17 but closed after Christmas until end Jan.*

Brampton
Half Moon Wholefoods

14 Front Street, Brampton CA8 1NG
Tel: 016977 3775

This may not be the biggest of shops but Alison Cheetham and Kathleen Ward certainly know how to make the most of its space. They sell wholefoods, local foods and natural products, with a good showing of Cumbrian producers.

Thornby Moor Dairy and Slack House Farm (organic) cheeses are amongst the 30 or so cheeses, there's honey from Nook Farm and nearby Castlesteads, salami, pancetta, chorizo and Parma-style ham from Shaw Meats, flour and porridge oats, truffles made in Brampton, puddings by Taylors Classics, Cream of Cumbria butter and cream, and jams and chutneys. Soft drinks, natural remedies and toiletries are also sold. The shop provides an Ecover refill service for laundry and cleaning products.

Open: Mon–Sat 9–17.

Below left: Toni Sim of Millstones Bakery
Below: the baker's table at the Broughton
Village Bakery. Picture by Helen Whitaker

Broughton-in-Furness
Broughton Village Bakery

Princes Street, Broughton-in-Furness LA20 6HQ
Tel: 01229 716284
Website: www.broughtonvillagebakery.co.uk

Lara and Darren Napton were on the verge of moving to Australia, Lara's home country, when the chance arose to buy this bakery in the pretty village of Broughton-in-Furness. This was Cumbria's gain because not only do the couple sell good quality bread from their shop but you'll see them at farmers' markets at Orton, Kendal and Pooley Bridge.

For the markets they usually have a range of some 20 breads, made with organic flour from The Watermill at Little Salkeld. These include walnut; hazelnut and cranberry; olive; chilli; sun-dried tomato and herb; spinach and feta twist; cheese and garlic twist; and caramelised onion.

Only some of these breads are sold in the shop and café at Broughton, along with rustic white, wholemeal, seven grain, granary and so on. The bakery produces cakes, custards and quiches, the cakes often inspired by Australian and American recipes (the couple spent five years in the United States).

Two seasonal products are stollen and hot cross buns, while wheat-free chocolate cakes, cinnamon scrolls – like a Chelsea bun – and sweet chilli and cheese scrolls are three more offerings. You'll see some of the range on the huge baker's table just inside the front door.

Open: Tue–Fri 9–17.30, Sat and Sun 9–17 (during school holidays open Mon 9–17). Café closes half an hour before shop.

Farmers' Markets

More than a dozen farmers' markets are held in Cumbria every month, giving people a chance to buy a wide range of locally produced food and drink, to meet the producers and help support the local economy. For many producers the markets are a valuable source of income and a direct way of finding out what consumers think of their products. A number of the farmers' markets are run by Made in Cumbria, some come under the Eden Farmers' Market Network and a few – like Orton Farmers' Market, named *Farmers' Market of the Year* in 2004 – are independent. This is the schedule at time of writing. Most start at 9–9.30 and end about 13–15. It's best to check first. The Made in Cumbria website – *www.madeincumbria.co.uk* – has a calendar of the markets.

Brampton, by Moot Hall: last Saturday of every month.
Brough, Memorial Hall: third Saturday of every month.
Carlisle, city centre: first Friday of every month.

Carlisle, Borderway Mart, Rosehill (Harrison and Hetherington): second Saturday of every month.
Cockermouth, Market Place: first Saturday of every month.
Egremont, Market Hall: first Saturday and third Friday of every month.
Greenhead (Northumberland), village hall: second Sunday of every month.
Kendal, Market Place: last Friday of every month.
Milnthorpe: second Friday of every month.
Orton: second Saturday of every month.
Penrith, Market Square: third Tuesday of every month.
Pooley Bridge: last Sunday of every month (Apr–Sep).
Sedbergh, Joss Lane car park: selected Wednesdays (Apr–Oct).
Ulverston, outside Market Hall: third Saturday of every month.

Below: farmers' market in Carlisle

Cark-in-Cartmel

Holker Food Hall

Holker Hall, Cark-in-Cartmel,
Grange-over-Sands LA11 7PL
Tel: 015395 59084
Website: www.holkerfoodhall.co.uk

The food hall is stylishly fitted out with local oak, and slate from five Holker Estate quarries. The list of producers whose food and drink is sold here reads like a roll call of many of Cumbria's best. Cartmel Valley Game sends sausages, venison and smoked fish and Sillfield Farm delivers bacon, sausages and ham.

McClure (Flookburgh potted shrimps), Low Sizergh Farm (organic milk and cheese), The Toffee Shop in Penrith, Country Fare (cakes), Moss Howe Farm (jams and jellies), Dent and Hawkshead breweries and Cowmire Hall (damson gin) are amongst other local names on the shelves.

From Holker Hall's own estate comes Martin Gott's cheeses, David McClure's honey, venison, Shorthorn/Highland cross beef, Herdwick lamb and Saltmarsh lamb, though the last three are only sold at certain times of the year. The shop also sells soups and ready meals, made on the estate.

It was the promotion of their tenant farmers' Saltmarsh lamb, after the foot-and-mouth outbreak of 2001, that provided the catalyst for Holker's owners Lord and Lady Cavendish to set up the food hall. The shop, right opposite the attractive Courtyard Café, has wine, cheese and olive oil from Italy, amongst other non-Cumbrian foods. Holker Hall has been home to the Cavendish family for 250 years and, with its garden, is open to the public.

Open: *daily 10.30–17.30 Mar–Oct; 10.30–16 Nov–23 Dec, early Jan–Feb.*
Directions: *Holker Hall is on the B5278, about 6 miles (9.6 km) west of Grange-over-Sands.*

Carlisle

Bell's Fishmongers and Cumbrian Game

16 Westmoor Road, Kingstown, Carlisle CA3 0HD
Tel: 01228 542924
Website: www.bellsfishmongers.co.uk

For 19 years Tony Bell had a fish stall in Carlisle's market hall but a few years ago he moved lock, stock and pallet to Kingstown on the city's northern outskirts, where the family's wholesale business was based (Tony's brother Steven works here and parents Jimmy and Alison used to).

Of the 15–20 tons of fish and shellfish which pass through every week much is destined for hotels and restaurants. But there's a retail outlet which sells fresh and frozen fish, fresh and frozen shellfish, fresh and frozen game, smoked produce and other foodstuffs like kangaroo steak and foie gras. Game includes pheasant, partridge, grouse, wood pigeon, mallard, guinea fowl, widgeon, snipe, teal, wild rabbit and hare. Venison generally comes from local estates. Smoked produce takes in salmon, kippers, mackerel, rainbow trout, shellfish, chicken, duck, venison and wild boar.

As for fish and shellfish, that can include tuna, turbot, mussels, squid, Dover sole, skate wings, swordfish, crayfish tails, red snapper, sea bream, monkfish, lobster, wild salmon, anchovies and roll mop herrings. Some of these are also frozen.

Open: *Tue–Thu 8.30–15, Fri 8.30–16.45, Sat 8.30–12.30.*
Directions: *from Junction 44 of the M6, head towards Carlisle on Scotland Road, take second right into Kingstown Broadway and when the road starts to bend round to the right, turn left into Brunthill Road and then left again into Westmoor Road.*

Eva's Organics

Tel: 016977 41906
Website: www.evabotanicals.co.uk

This is not a shop but an organic (Soil Association certified) fruit and vegetable box scheme which delivers to homes in north and west Cumbria, west Northumberland and across the border into Dumfriesshire.

Mike and Debbie Simpson's motivation for setting up the business five years ago was simple. 'We just wanted to be sure that the fruit and vegetables that we ate ourselves had not been treated with pesticides'.

Customers choose from a range of box values (£10, £15 or £20), the most popular combination, says Mike, being the £10 worth of fruit and £10 worth of vegetables. £10 vegetables might include potatoes, carrots, onions, parsnips, French beans, leeks, red peppers, tomatoes and broccoli.

The couple have outdoor raised beds and a number of polytunnels at their own market garden at Low Luckens Farm, north of Carlisle, where they grow seasonal vegetables, salad crops and culinary and medicinal herbs. They supplement this by buying in, as locally as possible, from other producers and suppliers. The contents of boxes vary with the seasons.

Left: Tony Bell of Bell's Fishmongers and Cumbrian Game
Above: Debbie and Mike Simpson of Eva's Organics

The Laird's Larder

Houghton Hall Garden Centre
Houghton, Carlisle CA6 4JB
Tel: 01228 400610
Website: www.thelairdslarder.co.uk

A garden centre may not be the most obvious place to find local food and drink but this spacious shop is stocked with a good amount of Cumbrian produce. You'll see names like Thornby Moor Dairy (cheeses), Richard Woodall (bacon and pancetta), Wild and Fruitful and Claire's Handmade (both jams and chutneys), Cumberland Honey Mustard, Lizzie's Home Made (Cumbrian Frutta Cotta) and the breweries Hawkshead, Hesket Newmarket, Coniston, Geltsdale and Jennings.

Fruit and vegetables are on the left as you go in, followed by bread and cakes, and then an expanding hamper area.

The butchery sells its own sausages, and lamb and Galloway beef from the Dumfriesshire farm of the garden centre's owners. That beef and lamb is also used in a number of the ready meals at Laird's Larder, and in the pies and pasties made in the kitchen here. A range of cakes and biscuits is produced by the in-house bakery.

All the milk, butter and cream that's sold in the shop comes from Cumbria while under the words Select Local are shelves of jam, chutney, mustard, flour, honey, tea and coffee from Cumbrian producers (the tea and coffee comes from Farrer's in Kendal).

There's a delicatessen counter, which has about 40–50 Cumbrian and other British and continental cheeses, olives, antipasti, smoked produce from Saddleback Foods and Smokerie, Burbush pies and paté, and Solway salami from Shaw Meats. You can find Laird's Larder branded wines amongst the beers and wines. Paella, Yorkshire puddings, raspberries, croissants, breaded scampi and such like – all in the frozen foods section – go like hot cakes, says Laird's Larder manager Lorraine Phillips.

Open: *Mon–Wed, Fri–Sat 9–18, Thu 9–20, Sun 10.30–16.30.*
Directions: *Houghton Hall is on the east side of the M6, about 1 mile (1.6km) south of Junction 44, off the A689.*

Bells of Lazonby

Website: www.bellsoflazonby.co.uk

It was in 1946 that John Bell started a small bakery business in the centre of Lazonby near Penrith. He later opened shops in Langwathby and Penrith, and expanded his fleet of mobile shops, selling breads, cakes and groceries to communities throughout the Eden Valley and beyond.

These days Bells of Lazonby is run by John's son Michael, the business incorporating five shops in Cumbria, The Village Bakery in Melmerby (see p133 and p173) and OK Foods (see below). At Bells' Edenholme Bakery in Lazonby there's also an outlet shop, open 9–12 on Saturday morning for coffee and the sale of breads and cakes. In 2006 Bells received the *Queen's Awards for Enterprise: Innovation Award* for its OK Foods and Village Bakery brands.

The company established OK Foods in 2003 with the aim of producing a range of allergy friendly foods, suitable for coeliacs and vegetarians. To this end a dedicated gluten free, wheat free and dairy free bakery was built at its Lazonby premises. The OK Foods range (*www.ok-foods.co.uk*) takes in cakes, fruit fingers, sponge puddings, cake slices and mini bites. The products can be purchased from all major supermarkets.

Bells' shops are at 57 Warwick Road (01228 527268) and 19 Fisher Street (01228 521013), both in Carlisle, 12 Middlegate, Penrith (01768 866870), 1 Market Place, Wigton (016973 42273) and 3 Moor Close, Workington (01900 67435). The Penrith shop has a café.

Pippa Sedgwick Wines

Tel: 01228 573354
Website: www.pippasedgwick.co.uk

Pippa Sedgwick set up this business 15 years ago in the grounds of Crosby Lodge Country House Hotel near Carlisle (see p37). There's no shop as such – visits are by appointment only or you can order online from the website. Some 300 wines from across the world are on her list, 'something for everyone', says Pippa. They include ports, sherries, Madeiras, Champagnes and sparkling wines, a collection that has a leaning towards France, Italy and Portugal.

Portuguese wines include wines from Soalheiro, Luis Pato, Niepoort and Quinta dos Roques (see Pippa's website for the awards they have received). Wine prices range from £5.95 upwards. 'What really drives my passion is the thrill of finding exciting wines, many from small producers, and seeing my customers enjoy them,' she says.

Pippa holds informal wine classes at Crosby Lodge and once or twice a year joins Joan Gate and Margaret Brough of Food & Company at Mirehouse near Keswick, to talk about wine at their cookery workshops (see p152). Pippa also offers a wine and food matching service in private homes. She'll produce a selection of tapas and wines, take them to people's houses and explain the interest of marrying the two.

Cartmel

Cartmel Village Shop

The Square, Cartmel, Grange-over-Sands LA11 6QB
Tel: 015395 36280
Website: www.stickytoffeepudding.co.uk

There's no blue plaque on the wall outside to advertise the fact but this is the birthplace of the famous Cartmel sticky toffee pudding (see p90). Because of demand the Sticky Toffee Pudding Company's range – toffee, banana, ginger and chocolate (all sticky) is now made down the road in Flookburgh. The shop, of course, sells the range, as it does plenty of other good food and drink.

Homemade cakes and tarts and some 30 cheeses are at the lower end of the shop and then elsewhere in this atmospheric little place you'll see jams, chutneys, mustards, beer (Coniston, Tirril and Hawkshead breweries), damson gin, olive oils, vinegars, cooking sauces, bacon, sausages, smoked salmon, chocolates, Italian biscuits, pastas, mint cake, tea, coffee, fudge, toffee and much more. There are plenty of Cumbrian producer names on the shelves. A range of prepared meals, like beef lasagne and Basque chicken, are sold too.

Many years ago the building was used by the farm next door to cure its bacon, which explains the numerous meat hooks in the ceiling. Later the premises became a post office (that's now elsewhere in the village) but the original counter remains in the shop. Race days in Cartmel are always extremely busy for the staff, who keep up a great tradition on such occasions: every winning owner, trainer and jockey is handed a sticky toffee pudding to mark their success.

Open: *Mon–Sat 9–17, Sun 10.30–16.30.*

Howbarrow Organic Farm

Howbarrow Farm, Cartmel, Grange-over-Sands LA11 7SS
Tel: 015395 36330
Website: www.howbarroworganic.co.uk

For ten years Paul Hughes and Julia Sayburn have flown the organic flag high above the village of Cartmel, their home grown and seasonal fruit, herbs and vegetables much in demand. That goes for the fruit and vegetables, meat and other goods which are sourced from organic suppliers elsewhere. All of it is now distributed by The Farmshed, another family organic business in Lancashire.

'All our produce has zero air miles and to offset our own inevitable carbon footprint we support the Sand Martin Wood Project near Faugh in north Cumbria,' says Tom Cropper of The Farmshed.

Take the short trip out of Cartmel and you can buy a range of organic produce at the Howbarrow shop, the Soil Association's *UK Organic Farm Shop* 2002. In one room there are cereals, flour, biscuits, bread, ice cream, soft drinks, rice, pulses, honey, olive oils, jam, butter, pasta, tea, coffee and Howbarrow's tinctures. Some are Fairtrade, some are Suma products.

Fruit and vegetables are in a chilled room, joined in the season by some 60 varieties of herbs and salads (borage, purslane, sage, sweet rocket, chicory, ruby chard, lemongrass and so on) which are grown in Paul and Julia's nine polytunnels. They also own the Grange Bakery (see p124).

Shop open: *Tue–Fri 8–17.*
Directions: *go out of Cartmel past the racecourse and take the first turning on the left where Howbarrow is signposted. The farm offers bed and breakfast.*

Dalston

D Moore of Dalston

*Craft Bakery, 20 The Square, Dalston,
Carlisle CA5 7PY
Tel: 01228 710695*

There will be lots of villages around
Britain that envy Dalston, having both a
baker and a butcher. For over 12 years
David Moore has made breads, cakes,
pies and a range of patisserie at his
busy premises on the village square.
His marmalade and cinnamon tea
bread was voted *Best Marmalade Loaf*
during the second Marmalade Festival
at Dalemain in 2008 and is as popular
as David's treacle bread and Guinness
bread. Originally trained as a chef,
David later went into education before
becoming self-employed.

Open: *Mon–Fri 8.15–17.15, Sat 8.15–14.30.*

Borough Market, London

Every week, in a small corner of Southwark in south east London, three Cumbrian
producers set out their stall at one of Britain's best known food markets. Six
nights a week Borough Market is a wholesale fruit and vegetable market, but on
Thursdays, Fridays and Saturdays it becomes a major draw for food lovers from all
over the capital and beyond, host to some 80–100 producers and farmers selling
everything from meat, game, pies and artisan cheeses to fish, olives, speciality
breads and Spanish hams.

Although a market has existed in this area since Roman times and on the current
site for 250 years, it's only in the last ten years that Borough Market has come into
its own as a retail outlet for fine and specialist foods. One of the early stallholders
was Peter Gott of Sillfield Farm (see opposite page and p85) who was already
working on his mother's market stalls as a young teenager. 'Markets are all about
community spirit, of people meeting up with each other, of shoppers talking to
traders and asking questions about the produce they're selling, of people being
able to touch and smell the food they buy,' he says.

Subsequently his enthusiasm managed to entice both Andrew 'Farmer' Sharp
(see p80) and Les Salisbury of Furness Fish, Poultry and Game Supplies (see
opposite page) to join him. Says Andrew: 'I wasn't that keen at first but I thought
I'd drive down and give it a go. Then I found the customers saying to me "see you
next time then". I didn't really have a choice but to return the following month.'
As for Les Salisbury, it took several months of badgering by Peter before he
succumbed too, but for some years his stall has been one of the biggest at the
Borough Market.

Below: London's Borough Market

Endmoor
Sillfield Farm Shop

Endmoor, Kendal LA8 0HZ
Tel: 015395 67609
Website: www.sillfield.co.uk

Peter and Christine Gott's shop is a splendid showcase for the range of Sillfield Farm products, the shop converted from an old shippon (cow byre). Come through the door and you face a long counter, the centre of which is the meat section. Pork is from Sillfield Farm's rare breed pigs, which a board on the wall explains are Tamworths, Middle Whites and Gloucester Old Spots. Most pigs here, though, are Saddlebacks. There's also meat from the resident herd of wild boar, these being one of the big features of Sillfield Farm.

Just above the counter is a screen relaying pictures of the boar, some distance away. The animals provide meat for pies (there are game, chicken and ham, and pork pies as well), paté, wild boar pancetta, air-dried salami, and wild boar sausage with Chianti and shallots. This is one of over 20 varieties of sausages for sale. You can also buy Cumberland speck, dry-cured back, middle and flitch bacon (some bacon is sliced for you), hams, eggs, waxed cheeses, chutney, mustard and honey. There's more information about Peter Gott on page 85.

Open: *Fri–Sat 10–17, Sunday 10–16. Sillfield Farm also goes to markets in Barrow (Wed, Fri and Sat 9–17); Kirkby Lonsdale (Thu 9–15); Milnthorpe (Fri 9–15); Borough Market, London (Thu–Sat 7.30–18) see p122.*

Directions: *from Junction 36 of the M6, take exit for A65. At first roundabout go left, head for Endmoor and 1/4 mile (400m) after Endmoor, turn right on the Gatebeck Lane. Go over the bridge, over the crossroads, over the motorway bridge and Sillfield Farm is the first farm on left.*

Flookburgh
Furness Fish, Poultry and Game Supplies

Moor Lane, Flookburgh LA11 7LS
Tel: 015395 59544
Website: www.morecambebayshrimps.com

30 years ago Les Salisbury and his wife Carol started selling Morecambe Bay shrimps off a stall at Ulverston market. Today, with an impressive stall at Borough Market in London and this shop at Flookburgh - close to the waters where Les has shrimped and fished for the best part of his life - Furness Fish, Poultry and Game Supplies is a familiar name to foodies in Cumbria, London and elsewhere. At the North West Fine Food Awards 2008 it was *Cumbria Producer of the Year*.

Flookburgh's very much the showroom for all that this family business specialises in. It sells fresh fish, frozen fish (including squid, scallops, prawns, seafood cocktail mixes, fish cakes and fish fingers), Manx kippers, those famous potted shrimps (*Best Fish and Seafood* at the same food awards as above), rabbit, venison, pigeon and, when in season, pheasant, mallard, teal and partridge.

You'll see pies, Sillfield Farm's sausages, bacon and cheeses, oven ready dishes that include stuffed game and poultry (chicken stuffed with a pheasant, for instance), and beef and outdoor reared pork from Bowland Outdoor. Jams and chutneys come from Claire's Handmade and there are Demels' chutneys here too.

Open: *Mon–Thu 9–16, Fri 9–15.*
Directions: *head out of Flookburgh village on Moor Lane and Furness Fish is on the right hand side. The weekly stall at Borough Market in London is Thu–Sat. In Cumbria, Furness Fish also appears at the annual Holker Festival at Holker Hall.*

Below: Furness Fish stall at Borough Market in London

Grange-over-Sands

Ainsworth Specialist Grocers

Kentsbank Road, Grange-over-Sands LA11 7EY
Tel: 015395 32946

John Riley's shop in Grange has the lovely scent and feel of an old fashioned grocers and is packed with good food of all kinds. There's a selection of some 50–60 cheeses, smoked salmon, pancetta, a splendid range of pasta, a big choice of jams and marmalades (Wilkin & Sons on one hand, the Cumbrian producer Wild and Fruitful on the other), chutneys, olives, continental chocolates, biscuits, soups and plenty of other things. At Christmas the shelves are even fuller. A new range of kitchen products — pottery, gifts and olive dishes — has also been introduced. Malt whiskies, damson gin and unusual liqueurs are sold as well.

Open: Mon–Sat 9–17, Sun (summer only) 11–15.

Grange Bakery

Newlyn, Kents Bank Road, Grange-over-Sands LA11 7EY
Tel: 015395 36330
Website: www.grange-bakery.co.uk

In the autumn of 2007 Grange Bakery was taken on by Paul Hughes and Julia Sayburn, owners of Howbarrow Farm (see p121) and pioneering names in Cumbria's organic movement. The bakery produces a traditional range of breads and cakes but from spring 2008 it added organic bread, buns, scones and cakes to its 140–150 item product list. Every item carries the distinctive fragment of rice paper proclaiming its organic status.

You can buy the bread and cakes at the shop in Grange (there are shops in Dalton-in-Furness and Barrow as well) and they're also delivered to a number of hotels, restaurants, shops and post offices in south Cumbria. Paul says the bakery uses free range eggs and organic fruit in its cakes, Fairtrade sugar, and organic cream and dairy products. Nuts and seeds are either organic or Fairtrade as well.

Open: Mon–Wed, Fri 9–16, Thu 9–15, Sat 9–14.

Higginsons & Daughter

Keswick House, Main Street, Grange-over-Sands LA11 6AB
Tel: 015395 34367
Website: www.higginsonsofgrange.co.uk

The queues outside Higginsons may be largest at Christmas when the free range Bronze turkeys are on sale, but at any time of the year this is a very popular shop. Once voted *Best Butchers in Britain* in a competition run by the Meat Trades Journal, it was opened in 1983 — in Stuart's home town — by Stuart and Pauline Higginson, who had met while working in Australia. Over 25 years later it's still very much a family business. Stuart's brothers Nigel and Don are amongst the 20 staff, daughter Sarah is a director and mother Jessie only retired in 2007.

Cheeses, cold meats and pies (over 20 varieties) are to the left when you go into the shop, while to the right is the extraordinary range of meat and meat products. There are about 30 types of sausages, Saltmarsh lamb, garlic chicken, Texas rib-eye steaks, ribs of beef, honey and ginger duck fillets, stuffed racks of lamb, chicken cushions, lamb Henrys, homemade beef burgers and so on. Over 600 items are on the product list.

'Traditional butchers with modern ideas,' is how they describe themselves. The shop also delivers to a number of well known hotels and restaurants in the Lake District. Higginsons & Daughter are members of the Guild of Q Butchers. Their beef, lamb, pork and poultry suppliers are chalked up on a board next to the weekly specials.

Hearty and infectiously enthusiastic, Stuart has a life-long love of his trade. As a youngster he started as a 'Saturday lad' in the butchery department of the local Co-op and now, after a busy day in Grange, he heads for the hills to look after his herd of rare breed Saddleback pigs.

Open: Mon–Sat 8–17.

Above far left: Higginsons & Daughter's shop in Grange
Above far right: Stuart Higginson of Higginsons & Daughter
Far left and right: Cartmel Village Shop (see p121). Pictures by Helen Whitaker

Grasmere

The Grasmere Gingerbread Shop

Church Cottage, Grasmere LA22 9SW
Tel: 015394 35428
Website: www.grasmeregingerbread.co.uk

It's 9.15 in the morning and the first customers are through the front door within minutes, scenting the aroma of baking gingerbread as they step into the small shop. In 1854, four years after the death of poet William Wordsworth, this is where Sarah Nelson began selling the confection that carries her name, and for the next 50 years of her life it went to locals and tourists alike.

Little has changed in that respect except that her ginger-bread has become very well known indeed and is now sent all over the world. That's why this former village school on the edge of St Oswald's churchyard in Grasmere — where both Wordsworth and Sarah Nelson are buried — does a brisk trade all year and can be exceptionally busy in the holidays. This is the only place in the world where you can buy Grasmere gingerbread made to Sarah Nelson's original recipe, claims the current custodian Joanne Wilson.

The gingerbread is pale and crumbly in appearance but chewy on the inside, and although the shop sells a number of other foodstuffs — rum butter (made on the premises), fudge and toffee from The Toffee Shop in Penrith, Farrer's Lakeland tea, Romney's Kendal mint cake and after dinner mints, Cartmel sticky toffee sauce, Lyth Valley damson jam and Coniston honey — the gingerbread is the major draw. You can buy it in individual pieces or in parchment-wrapped packages of six or 12 pieces. Tins are sold as well and so are small wooden boxes of gingerbread and rum butter.

After Sarah Nelson's death in 1904, the business passed to a relative called Agnes German and was then later sold to one Daisy Hotson. She went into partnership with Jack and Mary Wilson and in 1969 Jack's nephew Gerald bought the business with his wife Margaret, the parents of Joanne. As for the recipe, that's been kept in a bank in Ambleside for many, many years. Joanne's husband Andrew Hunter is the 'chief gingerbread man' now, leader of the small team which bakes the product every day and the man who mixes the in-gredients. In 2007 Sarah Nelson's Grasmere Gingerbread was named *Best Regional Product* in the Food Northwest Awards.

Open: *Mon–Sat 9.15–17.30, Sun 12.30–17.30.*

Hawkshead

Hawkshead Relish

The Square, Hawkshead LA22 0NZ
Tel: 015394 36614
Website: www.hawksheadrelish.com

This is the place where the Hawkshead Relish Company started. When Mark and Maria Whitehead's café got hit by the foot-and-mouth outbreak of 2001 they decided to go into jam and chutney making full time. Café customers had often commented favourably about the homemade pickles and chutneys they served with meals, so the couple reckoned they could turn it into a business.

For a while the range was made in the old kitchens here but in 2007 they moved production to Esthwaite Water. The move freed up the property to act as a showcase for the range of Hawkshead Relish produce (see p94) which means a big selection of jam, marmalade, pickles, relishes, sauces, mustards, dressings, oils and vinegars. Hawkshead beers and a range of cookware are sold as well.

Open: *daily 9–17.*

Opposite: Nigel Prickett (above) and Andrew Hunter (below) of the Grasmere Gingerbread Shop

The Honeypot

The Square, Hawkshead, Ambleside LA22 0NZ
Tel: 015394 36267
Website: www.thehoneypotinhawkshead.co.uk

There's any amount of pretty and historic buildings in Hawkshead, the village where William Wordsworth went to school. The Honeypot is no exception and, as it's in the village square, Fiona Wilson's shop is not difficult to miss. She's a great one for stocking the shelves with local produce, even foods made seasonally and by one person.

You'll find damson jam, damson syrup and damson chutney from Moss Howe Farm, Nook Farm honey (jars and combs) and other local honey when available, Coniston Lodge gingerbread, Claire's Handmade jams and chutneys, Thornby Moor Dairy cheeses, Richard Woodall's bacon and sausages, Silver and Green olives (Penrith), English Lakes ice cream, puddings from the Sticky Toffee Pudding Company (Cartmel), Cumberland mustards, Honeypot branded jams and chutneys, and smoked salmon and pastrami from Saddleback Foods and Smokerie.

Breads and cakes, says Fiona, are delivered every day from The Apple Pie in Ambleside, and take-away tea, coffee and filled rolls are also sold by the friendly staff. And as Fiona is married to Andrew Wilson, of Wilson's in Kendal, you'll come across the firm's Kendal mint cake, chocolates and novelty chocolates. The latter includes rabbit droppings and chocolate cow pats.

Open: *daily 9–17.*

Kendal

Artisan

Wainwright's Yard, Stricklandgate, Kendal LA9 4DP
Tel: 01539 742370
Website: www.booths.co.uk

When Booths opened its new store in Kendal in 2004, it also opened Artisan downstairs. They claimed it as a first in the British supermarket industry: a speciality food shop dedicated to showcasing local produce that wasn't necessarily available throughout its entire chain. Added to that was a café and restaurant which would make full use of local food and drink. The latter has nibbled into the shop space a bit, but there's still a good range of jams, chutneys, relishes, mustards, ice cream, dressings, flour, herb salts, bread, bacon, sausages and such like.

Most impressive is the cheese counter, developed in conjunction with Neal's Yard in London, where up to 20 British cheeses are on display, with notes on each. A number are in big rounds. The choice can include Stichelton (organic), Strathdon Blue, St James (made by Martin Gott at Holker Hall), Ragstone, Berkswell, Finn (organic), Tunworth and Beenleigh Blue.

There's a real quality feel to the whole shop, with its polished granite counter, slate floor and oak shelves. The other side of those shelves is the café/restaurant (see p168) while upstairs is the Booths store. Other Booths stores in Cumbria – the firm is a supporter of local produce – are at Keswick, Windermere, Ulverston and Kirkby Lonsdale.

Open: *Mon–Sat 8–19, Sun 10–16.*

Opposite left: Simon Thomas, Staff of Life Bakery
Opposite right: Frank Stainton, Stainton Wines

Farrer's

13 Stricklandgate, Kendal LA9 4LY
Tel: 01539 731707
Website: www.farrers.com

The 17th-century building is listed, the large tea counter inside the entrance is listed and so are the 20 original tea canisters behind it. Some of the floorboards were recycled from ships that were sailing well before Nelson's time. Farrer's, with one of the most attractive shop fronts in Kendal, is certainly a place where the smell of history blends with the aroma of tea and coffee.

Although it sells coffee makers and coffee machines, tea cups, coffee mugs, tea cosies and chocolates, the essence of Gordon and Gillian Grace's business is selling tea and coffee (with a wholesale side as well). The canisters hold teas like Formosa Oolong, Pure Assam, Rose Petal, Large Leaf Ceylon, Green Gunpowder, Keemun and Lakeland Special. Herbal teas are sold too.

The shiny coffee hoppers on the next level up, past the Victorian coffee grinder, are labelled mocha, maragogype, Costa Rica, Java and such like. You can buy the full beans, or the friendly staff will grind them to your requirements. The tea room, for which Gillian does all of the baking, serves teas, coffees, scones, cakes, soups and light lunches. Three of the eight levels in the building – where Liverpool tea merchant John Farrer started his business in 1819 – are tea and coffee lounges.

Open: *Mon–Sat 9–17.30. Café closes at 16.45.*

Staff of Life Bakery

2 Berry's Yard, Kendal LA9 4AB
Tel: 01539 738606
Website: www.artisanbreadmakers.co.uk

To a request for a bread with either cheese or garlic, the enthusiastic Simon Thomas had the perfect answer: a loaf with both. It's called garlic and Parmesan, and it's one of about 15 breads that this well known artisan bakers – run by Simon and his wife Julie – produce for sale at Berry's Yard. The choice includes marinated mixed olives; sun-dried tomato; deli rye; basil pesto; pane rustica; pistachio kernels; and Romano with caramelised red onions. Every loaf, he says, is cut, kneaded and shaped by hand.

Added to the breads are a range of cakes and flapjacks, Julie's award-winning gingerbread (gold in the Great Taste Awards 2007), and 'ultimate chocolate brownies', the latter, says Simon, made with 73 per cent cocoa solids and including pecan nut chocolate brownies and morello cherry chocolate brownies. When you buy them they're individually wrapped in greaseproof paper.

Simon started making bread at an early age, encouraged by his grandmother and mother. He also did the bread when he and Julie ran a café in Kendal, and it was appreciative customer comments that encouraged them to set up a bakery in 1996. The move to Berry's Yard came three years later. In early 2008 he began using a wood-fired oven in a former smokehouse behind Booths supermarket in Kendal. There he makes bread for both Booths and for Staff of Life.

Open: *Mon–Sat 8 until the bread runs out.*

Stainton Wines

1 Station Yard, Kendal LA9 6BT
Tel: 01539 731886
Website: www.stainton-wines.co.uk

What better way to celebrate an upcoming silver jubilee than by moving into shiny new premises which treble your shop space, give customers plenty of car parking and bring you bang next door to your own very large warehouse? Clad in cedar on the outside, the new shop is just past reception, while upstairs are offices, and a tasting room, which can be used for wine launches and the wine training of restaurant staff. Wine is always available to taste in the shop.

Frank Evan Stainton is like a premier grand cru of Cumbrian wine merchants, nearly 50 years of experience in the trade, very well known, and a supplier to many of the top hotels and restaurants in the Lake District. His three sales staff – Chris Leather (a director), Tom Wall and Jane Boothroyd – have over 55 years of experience between them.

The list of Stainton Wines runs to about 1,000, a number shipped directly from as far as Chile and South Africa. Once, the emphasis was very much on French wines but the range is now spread across the board. One thing that hasn't changed since setting up in 1984 is Frank's keenness to source many of his wines from smaller, independent producers.

Open: *Mon–Sat 9.30–17.*
Directions: *from the town centre, take the A6 north. Just before Kendal station, turn left into Station Road and look for Atlantis Kitchens. Turn left there and go to the end of Station Yard where there's free parking.*

Keswick
Bryson's of Keswick

42 Main Street, Keswick CA12 5JD
Tel: 017687 72257
Website: www.brysonsofkeswick.co.uk

For the 60 years since its birth, Bryson's bakery, shop and tea room have stood on the same site in Keswick, making and selling breads, cakes, biscuits, pies and pasties to locals and visitors, as well as supplying many of the same products to shops in and around the Lake District.

The left of the shop is dedicated to the sale of breads, cakes and savouries, those breads including wholemeal, granary and farmhouse loaves. There's also Bryson's speciality and artisan breads, such as muesli, marmalade, tomato, olive and the famous Lakeland plum bread, the plum here referring to currants, raisins and sultanas. There are Florentines, Borrowdale tea bread ('great with Wensleydale cheese'), Cumbrian fruit cake and other gift items. Celebration cakes can be made on request.

JB's coffee bar is to the right, serving coffee, sandwiches, panini and snacks, either to eat at JB's or to take away. Upstairs is Bryson's traditional tea room which has waitress service and offers hot breakfasts, afternoon teas, meals and snacks. There's a children's menu too.

Shop open: *Mon–Sat 8.30–17.30, Sun 9.30–17.*

Cornerwise of Keswick

13 Lake Road, Keswick CA12 5BS
Tel: 017687 73874
Website:
www.whiskyatcornerwisekeswick.com

What started as a sweet shop had, within a year, turned to selling whisky and wine. A quarter of a century later there can be few other places in the north of England that offer the range of whiskies which you'll find here. Some 400 different malts and blends are on the shelves, the vast majority from Scotland. Mary Reeves also stocks Irish whiskeys, Bourbons and Canadian whiskies. Limited editions and a nine year old Speyside malt, called Keswick, prove popular.

Miniatures are another big thing here and so are liqueurs. A range of about 200 includes an Italian artichoke drink called Cynar and a bright green banana liqueur named Pisang Ambon. Rums (including Jefferson's from Whitehaven) and wines almost complete the picture. There are hip flasks, water jugs and glass and ceramic decanters too.

Open: *daily 10–19.*

FondEwe Fine Cheeses

9 Packhorse Court, Keswick CA12 5JB
Tel: 017687 73377
Website: www.fondewe-cheeses.co.uk

A few steps from Keswick's Moot Hall, this specialist cheese shop is run by Faith and Brian Watterson and offers some 55 or so British and continental cheeses. Cumbrian names include Thornby Moor Dairy and Low Sizergh Barn. The shop - finalist in the *Best New Deli* award at the British Cheese Awards 2008 - stocks a variety of biscuits to accompany cheese, a range of olives, and stuffed pumpkins and red peppers.

There are also locally made cheese boards (sycamore, beech or cherry), cheese knives, fondue sets and raclettes. The raclettes, which people can hire first to find out what they're like, cook vegetables, meat and fish on a stone while melting cheese underneath. There's a choice of chutneys, teas, coffees and sticky toffee puddings. Olive oil and vinegars are on tap: buy your first bottle, fill it up and then bring it back to get it refilled.

Open: *daily 9.15–17.15*
(closed Sun Jan–Feb).

Open All Hours

5 St John Street, Keswick CA12 5AP
Tel: 017687 75414
Website: www.personaldrinks.co.uk

For over 25 years Alan and Heather Dunn have run this convenience store, dispensing groceries and household products to locals and tourists alike. What sets the place apart is the great selection of bottled beers which the shop offers – 200 at any one time, including 40 or so Cumbrian ones.

They include Yates, Hesket Newmarket, Geltsdale, Keswick, Watermill, Hawkshead, Dent, Jennings and Tirril. The overall selection made Open All Hours the *Best Independent Beer Retailer* for both 2006 and 2007 in the *Off Licence News*. Alan also runs the Personal Drinks Company, a way that beer and wine can be specially labelled to celebrate special occasions.

Open: *daily 8–22.*

Below far left: Derwentwater, beside Keswick
Below left: Cornerwise of Keswick
Below: FondEwe Fine Cheeses

Kirkby Lonsdale

Churchmouse Cheeses

4 Market Street, Kirkby Lonsdale LA6 2AU
Tel: 015242 73005
Website: www.churchmousecheeses.com

Almost five years to the day since its opening, John and Jules Natlacen travelled to London to receive the award for *Best Independent Cheese Shop* in Britain. The prize, at the 2007 Retail Cheese Awards, sponsored by Dairy Crest and The Grocer magazine, was thoroughly deserved. Churchmouse Cheeses is a very inviting shop, not massive in size but big on enthusiasm.

It offers more than 100 cheeses from Cumbria, Northumberland, Yorkshire, Lancashire, Devon, Cornwall, elsewhere in Britain and the continent. There are organic and vegetarian cheeses and those made with cows', ewes', buffalo and goats' milk. Names include Lancashire Black Bombs, Lord of the Hundreds, Yorkshire Fine Fettle, Rooks Nest, Croglin, Trotter Hill Tasty Lancashire and Goosnargh Gold. Their website gives descriptions of them all. John and Jules's wedding cake cheeses are also very popular.

How the couple got to open the shop in the first place was a mixture of accident and good fortune. Jules broke her leg two weeks before their wedding in 2001 and walked down the aisle with plaster on her right leg. The honeymoon in Devon had to be cancelled and instead the newly-weds spent a few days in Cumbria. It was then that they spotted vacant premises in Kirkby Lonsdale and within minutes had decided to quit their jobs – John a financial advisor, Jules a venue-finding agent – and open a cheese shop.

There are jams, chutneys, pickles, tea, coffee, biscuits, butter, sauces and puddings for sale as well. Bowls of olives stand on a mahogany table just inside the front door, the table a present to Jules's grandmother on her wedding day. A chest of drawers, a bureau and a piano – which is played on Fridays, Saturdays and Sundays – all add atmosphere to a place that has already got more than its fair share: oak beams, a woodburning stove behind the counter, a part-timber, part-flagstoned floor and the remains of 18th-century panelling on the walls.

Open: *Mon–Sat 9.30–17.30, Sun 12–16.*

Below: John Natlacen of Churchmouse Cheeses

Melmerby
The Bakeshop

The Village Bakery, Melmerby, Penrith CA10 1HE
Tel: 01768 881811
Website: www.village-bakery.com

Bread, cakes and biscuits are only part of the organic offering in this flagstoned shop, next to the café/restaurant (see p173) at the famous Village Bakery. You'll also find its range of jam, marmalade and chutney, bacon and sausage from Mansergh Hall, flour from The Watermill, cheese, chocolate, tea, coffee and soft drinks. The granola on the shelves is made here, as are the biscuits, shortcake and scones.

Wooden bread trays are for sale along with bread boards, books on bread, storage containers and such like. The organic bread – produced down the road at Bells of Lazonby (see p120), owners of The Village Bakery – includes Russian inspired rye (Rossisky), spelt, mixed seed, sunflower, and brazil nut and linseed. The luxury organic chocolate almond cake was *Best Speciality from the North West* at the Great Taste Awards 2007. If you go upstairs to the small art gallery you'll pass more Village Bakery awards on the way.

Open: *Mon–Sat 8.30–17, Sun 9.30–17*
(slightly shorter hours in winter).

Old Town
Kitridding Farm Shop

Old Town, near Kirkby Lonsdale LA6 2QA
Tel: 015395 67484
Website: www.kitridding.co.uk

An expanded shop and a new tea room was the result of much building work in 2007 at Stewart and Christine Lambert's farm. The shop sells beef and lamb from animals born and reared at Kitridding, pork from pigs which are also reared here, homemade pies and burgers, and its own 20 varieties of sausage, like pork and blue Stilton, and pork, apple and sage.

Free range chickens from Levens, locally sourced vegetables, cheese, homemade cakes, Jeremy's soups, Forest of Bowland butter, puddings from Country Puddings, damson products from Moss Howe Farm, Lizzie's Home Made Primi Prunes and Posh Prunes, and Sue Prickett's jams and jellies are amongst other products available. Those jams and jellies come with toast and crumpets in the oak-floored tea room next door (see p175), as does some of Kitridding's meat, bacon, burgers and sausages.

Open: *Fri–Sun 10–17.*
Directions: *the farm is on the B6254 on the Kendal side of Old Town.*

Orton (Eden)

Kennedys Fine Chocolates

The Old School, Orton, near Penrith CA10 3RU
Tel: 015396 24781
Website:
www.kennedyschocolates.co.uk

The signpost says Orton but it could just as easily say 'chocolate heaven'. For 12 years Kennedys' shop and production unit has been based at the old village school, a display cabinet just inside the front door giving a pretty good idea of its range. The firm, run by David Kennedy and his sister Alison (a former head of patisserie at Sharrow Bay) makes 80–90 different varieties of chocolate, including sticky toffee pudding, sloe gin, passion fruit and galliano, chocolate fudge cake, Calvados truffle and apple crumble. Along with the changing range of chocolates, there are seasonal specialities, chocolate novelty items, chocolate bars and gift boxes. There's also a café serving light refreshments.

Open: *Mon–Sat 9–17, Sun and public holidays 11–17.*
Directions: *from the M6, exit at Junction 38 and turn left at the first roundabout for Orton.*

Penrith

Brunswick Deli

9 Brunswick Road, Penrith CA11 7LU
Tel: 01768 210500

Set up by Archie and Susan Bell in 2000, this small delicatessen won *Best Paté and Terrine* at the 2008 North West Fine Food Awards, for its chicken liver paté with brandy. In 2007 at the same awards, the deli won *Best Cake* for its chocolate brownie, and *Best Biscuit* for its caramel shortcake. The shop specialises in homemade ready food, offering meals, sandwiches, quiches and salads to customers who come into the shop, or office workers who want the food delivered. Brunswick Deli also sells cheese, cooked meats, chutneys, olives, olive oils, pasta and so on. Archie and Susan also have a bed and breakfast establishment in Penrith called Albany House (*www.albany-house.org.uk*).

Open: *Mon–Tue, Thu–Sat 9.30–16, Wed 9.30–14.30.*

Opposite, clockwise from top left: Artisan in Kendal (see p128), the Farm Shop at Rheged (see p136), Churchmouse Cheeses (see p132), Ullswater, close to the food shops in and around Penrith, shrimping in Morecambe Bay (see p123), Farrer's in Kendal (see p128).

Penrith

Carleton Farm Shop

Carleton, near Penrith CA11 8RQ
Tel: 01768 210027
Website: www.carletonfarmshop.co.uk

'A taste of the country on the edge of town' is this farm shop's slogan, situated as it is on the outskirts of Penrith, on the A686 towards Alston. Neil and Jean Hodgson's big sellers are the fresh vegetables, many grown on the farm here: leeks, potatoes, carrots, cabbage, turnips, broccoli, sprouts and more. Meat and sausages from Mansergh Hall, Slack's bacon, flour from both The Watermill at Little Salkeld and Heatherslaw Corn Mill in Northumberland, free range eggs, cakes, honey, jam and preserves are stocked as well.

Open: *Mon–Sat 9–17.30, Sun 10–16.*
Directions: *on the edge of Penrith on the A686 Penrith to Alston road, just opposite Penrith Rugby Club.*

Below left: chocolates at Kennedys Fine Chocolates
Below: David and Alison Kennedy of Kennedys Fine Chocolates

Penrith

Cranstons Cumbrian Food Hall

Ullswater Road, Penrith CA11 7EH
Tel: 01768 868680
Website: www.cranstons.net

A very well known food name in Cumbria, Cranstons began business in 1914 with a small butcher's shop in the village of Kirkoswald. It's still a family firm – brothers Roger and Philip Cranston, great nephews of the founder Stan, are both in the business – but now it's got butcher's shops in Penrith, Brampton, Hexham and Allendale and food halls in Carlisle and Penrith.

The latter is its biggest premises, selling bread from Bells and The Village Bakery, fruit and vegetables, fish, eggs, desserts, beer, cheese, jam, chutney, tea and coffee, olives and a lot more.

There's also a very large meat counter here, offering beef, lamb (including Saltmarsh and Herdwick lamb), pork, chicken, sausages, bacon, black pudding, burgers, pies and such like. A notice indicates where farm-assured beef and lamb has been sourced that month (usually from about 20 local farms). Take-away food is available at lunchtime while a wide range of fresh produce, including Cumberland sausage and bacon, can be ordered from Cranstons' website.

A major extension of the food hall was planned for 2009, with a café upstairs.

In 2007 Cranstons won gold for its own-recipe dry-cured back bacon at the Great Taste Awards in London, and then later picked up six golds, and a Diamond Award 'for outstanding product performance', at the Smithfield Awards (for members of the Guild of Q Butchers). Picking up the prizes were the traditional Cumberland sausage, dry-cured streaky bacon, and honey and mustard roast ham. Cranstons was also the North West's *Best Rural Retailer* (2005) in a competition run by the Countryside Alliance.

Open: *Mon–Sat, 8–18.*
Directions: *On Ullswater Road (A592) on the outskirts of Penrith, close to Junction 40 of the M6.*

Farm Shop at Rheged

Redhills, Penrith CA11 0DQ
Tel: 01768 868000
Website: www.rheged.com

The Farm Shop at Rheged – to the right as you come in to the main building – is a combination of food hall and café, inside what's described as Europe's largest grass covered building. The two-tiered shop sells some 30–40 cheeses, plus pies, breads, cakes, biscuits, chocolates, honey, jam, chutney, cooking sauces, pastas, fruit juices, bacon, sausages, paté, air-dried wild boar prosciutto, smoked salmon, mustard and cider.

Lamb and beef comes from the farm of the Dunning family (a few miles away) who own both Westmorland Services (see p145) and Rheged. Increasing space in the shop is devoted to English wines, Scotch whiskies and local beers, and there is a growing selection of kitchenware.

The food bar serves breakfast, lunch and afternoon tea, using ingredients from Cumbria and elsewhere in the north of England that can be bought in the shop. Light lunches might feature salmon quiche and salad leaves (£6), potted shrimps and salad leaves (£4), soup and soda bread (£3.50) and cheese platter (£6) amongst other dishes.

There are two more cafés within Rheged: Café Pod for Fairtrade tea and coffee, soups and hot roast sandwiches (meat from the Dunning family farm), and the Rheged Café (with table service) in the Mountain Hall. Special menus are available here for the under 12s.

Rheged also has a 156 seat cinema, with a large format film screen, a number of shops and an indoor play area. There are exhibitions, other events and pottery and painting workshops too.

Open: *10–17.*
Directions: *Rheged is just outside Penrith, a short distance from junction 40 of the M6, as you head west along the A66 towards Keswick.*

Right: part of the meat counter at Cranstons Cumbrian Food Hall
Far right: J&J Graham

J&J Graham

6–7 Market Place, Penrith CA11 7BS
Tel: 01768 862281
Website: www.jjgraham.co.uk

Housed in one of Penrith's most recognizable and attractive buildings, James and John Graham first started business in 1793, selling seeds, fertilizers and household goods to farmers and their families. For the last 20 years or so the emphasis has been very much on specialist food and drink, Graham's being one of Cumbria's early delicatessens.

Straight ahead as you walk in is the cheese counter, with some 60–70 cheeses. Many of them are from Cumbria, Northumberland, Lancashire and Yorkshire. Cold meats, pies, quiches, Slack's sausages and Richard Woodall's bacon and hams are also sold in this central part of the shop. On the shelves all around you'll see more Cumbrian producer names amongst the jams, chutney, flour, pasta, chocolate, sticky toffee pudding, olives, olive oils, savoury biscuits, tea, coffee, wine, beer and more. Just before the check-out counter is a range of bread and cakes, delivered from Bryson's and The Village Bakery.

Graham's also offer 15 different hampers which make good presents throughout the year, not just at Christmas. The Windermere (£30) includes cake, fudge, chutney, jam, marmalade, coffee and tea while The Cumberland (£57.50) has some of the above, plus sticky toffee pudding, Woodall's air-dried ham, smoked Cumberland sausage and local cheese. Most expensive is The Greystoke (£300 in a card box, £350 in a wicker basket) which includes Champagne, port, wines, smoked salmon, smoked chicken and cheeses.

Open: *Mon–Sat 9–17.*

Penrith

Saunders Chocolates

Rheged, Redhills, Penrith CA11 0DQ
Tel: 01768 860098
Website: www.saunderschocolates.co.uk

Saunders Chocolates has been producing handmade truffles and chocolates at Rheged since 2003. Its shop is right beside the production area where over 40 different centres – including dandelion and burdock, orange and cardamom, blackcurrant and chilli, and apricot and ginger – are created.

Champagne truffles are very popular, and so too is the 'pudding collection' which has flavours such as chocolate fudge, pecan pie, black forest, and strawberries and cream. Plain chocolates have a 60 per cent cocoa content, explains Bob Cullen, who runs the business with his wife Jane. As far as they're concerned the proof of the pudding is in both the appearance and the taste of their truffles and chocolates. 'That's why we hand polish every mould with cotton wool before it is used. It helps give our chocolates a real sheen,' says Bob. The polishing, blending, piping, sealing and other parts of the process can be seen by the public through a large window into their kitchen.

In the shop itself you can buy loose chocolates, boxed chocolates and other gifts. Chocolates in boxes (with the boxes themselves being made of chocolate) are increasingly bought as wedding favours. Other food shops, like Cranstons Cumbrian Food Hall in Penrith, Artisan in Kendal, Orton Grange and Laird's Larder at Houghton Hall (both near Carlisle), sell their chocolates too.

Open: *daily 10–17.*
Directions: *Rheged is located just outside Penrith, a short distance from junction 40 of the M6, as you head west along the A66 towards Keswick.*

The Toffee Shop

7 Brunswick Road, Penrith CA11 7LU
Tel: 01768 862008
Website: www.thetoffeeshop.co.uk

It's not long now until The Toffee Shop celebrates its centenary. In that time royalty, musicians, film stars, television personalities and politicians have all beaten a path to the shop in Penrith, or had the trademark boxes – white, with gold edging and black lettering – delivered to their homes. The Toffee Shop, producers of fudge and toffee, has become one of the most famous of all Cumbrian brands.

Walk through the front door and to the right of the rather plain counter you'll see a photograph of the Queen and the Duke of Edinburgh receiving a box of fudge. Another picture shows Prince Charles stirring one of eight brass fudge pans with a wooden spoon when he visited the shop in 2003. Then there's a cutting on the wall from a national newspaper which lists Neil and Pat Boustead's business as one of the 50 best food shops in Britain.

The fudge is hand made in small batches from butter, sugar and milk and comes in three flavours: butter, chocolate or mint. After cooking, the mixture is cooled and then cut by hand into slabs. A little more force is used for the toffee which is made with sugar, butter and syrup or black treacle. Having cooled in trays, it's broken up with a hammer and the pieces individually wrapped. That's how you'll find them when you open a box of either butter or treacle toffee. Perhaps those boxes should come with a warning. 'Once you start eating you may it find it difficult to stop'.

Open: *Mon–Sat 9–17.*

Below left: Saunders Chocolates shop
Below right: chocolates from Saunders Chocolates

Brougham Hall Foods

Tel: 01768 890270
Website: www.the-old-smokehouse.co.uk

This is an online shop, the 'home of Cumbrian artisan foods', says Richard Muirhead who runs the business. You can buy fresh meat and fish, smoked salmon and other smoked foods like poultry, cheese, meat, fish, sausages and vegetables. The website also sells game, pies, patés, cheese, puddings and cakes, cider, apple juice and beer, jams, chutneys and mustards.

Richard says there's a choice of hundreds of products from about 20 different Cumbrian producers. The smoked foods are from the Old Smokehouse at Brougham Hall which Richard used to own but is now part of Brookside Products (see p84). Richard, though, still works there. Hampers, and gourmet dinners for two or more people can also be ordered online from Brougham Hall Foods.

Sedbergh
Steadmans

2 Finkle Street, Sedbergh LA10 5BZ
Tel: 015396 20431
Website: www.steadmans-butchers.co.uk

Sedbergh is England's Book Town but looking at the list of Garth Steadman's sausages it could easily pass for 'banger town'. Over 100 varieties, including beef and horseradish; and venison, pork and cranberry, are offered at this well known Guild of Q Butchers shop. Free range local pork is a speciality, bacon and hams are dry-cured and the shop produces a pancetta and a Parma-style ham.

Beef generally comes from two local farmers, as does lamb (usually Rough Fell cross). Steadmans is also licensed to sell game, and it stocks organic free range chicken. Voted the *North of England's Best Butchers* by the Meat Trades Journal in 2006, it was the *North West's Best Rural Retailer* (local food category) in 2007 in a competition run by the Countryside Alliance. In the same year Steadmans won seven gold awards for its products at the Guild's Smithfield Awards in London.

Open: *Mon–Sat 7–17.*

Below left: fudge from The Toffee Shop, Penrith
Below right: toffee from The Toffee Shop, Penrith

Sizergh

Low Sizergh Barn Farm Shop

Low Sizergh Farm, Sizergh, Kendal LA8 8AE
Tel: 015395 60426
Website: www.low-sizergh-barn.co.uk

'Scrummilicious biscuits from Highland Croft in Perth. Get the kettle on', said the board at Low Sizergh Barn, one of Cumbria's best known farm shops. The enthusiasm here for good, tasty food is catching and that's why the place is so popular. Every little corner of an atmospheric 18th-century Westmorland barn (below and top three pictures opposite) seems to be filled with jams, chutneys, breads, butter, cakes, pies, puddings, biscuits, mustards, flours, beers and cider. Then there's lamb, pork, beef, bacon, chicken, venison, mallard, partridge, sausages, pancetta and hams. And household goods. Plenty of Cumbrian producers are represented.

Right in front of you, as you come in, are organic vegetables from Growing Well, a social enterprise based at the farm. To the left is the cheese counter with 60–70 varieties (mainly British), including sheep's and goats' cheeses, and three – Kendal Creamy, Kendal Crumbly and Kendal Crumbly with red onion – made by Chris Sandham in Lancashire, with organic milk from the farm's 120 dairy cows. A cheese of the week is chalked up every Friday. Eggs from the resident hens are sold, as is Windermere ice cream, also produced with the farm's organic milk.

The Park family moved to Low Sizergh in 1980 and opened the farm shop in 1991. Since then they've won numerous awards, including *Best Independent Specialist* in the 2005 Retail Cheese Awards, sponsored by Dairy Crest and The Grocer magazine, and a silver (*Best Organic Dairy Farm*) in the 2006 Soil Association Organic Food Awards.

Downstairs from the food shop is the Shippon Gallery (mind the low beams and uneven floor) where you'll find rugs, baskets, pottery and other craftwork. Upstairs, on the way to the tea room (see p177), is an area selling clothes, cards and children's toys. A 2-mile (3.2 km) farm trail starts near the large car parking area.

Open: *daily 9–17.30 (closes slightly earlier Jan–Easter).*
Directions: *4 miles (6.4 km) south of Kendal on the A591.*

Below left: Burbush Penrith pies sold by Brougham Hall Foods (see p139).
Pictures above by Helen Whitaker

Stainton (Penrith)

Greystone House Farm Shop

Stainton, Penrith CA11 0EF
Tel: 01768 866952
Website: www.greystonehousefarm.co.uk

John and Marjorie Dawson's farm shop and tea room – son Tom is in the business as well – was the overall winner of the *Cumberland News* Countryside Awards in 2004 and, looking at the popularity of the place, visitors heartily agree with the judges' decision. A butcher's counter in the shop sells beef and lamb from the farm of which 286 acres (116 hectares) are organic. There's locally sourced pork, homemade sausages and burgers. Wicker baskets stock fruit and vegetables, while bread, jam, preserves, tea, flour, mustard, butter and cheese are on offer too.

Upstairs is the Lofthouse Tea Room where 'great homemade, wholesome food,' is served, says one regular. A small number of tables and chairs are in the shop (pictured above right), for those unable to get up to the tea room.

Open: *daily 10–17.30.*
Directions: *from M6 junction 40 take A66 westbound until first roundabout. Take A592 towards Ullswater and then first right into Stainton. The farm shop is on the first crossroads you come to.*

Butchers

Look at any photograph of any high street of any town in Britain 50 or 60 years ago and chances are you'll spot a local butcher's shop. Visit many of those same places today and you'll be hard pressed to find any butchers at all. Almost 2,000 of them, it seems, were lost between 2000 and 2007, bringing the numbers down to little more than 7,000.

Cumbria is probably better off than most places, the butcher's shop still being a familiar sight in plenty of towns. 'It's probably a lot due to the support and loyalty of rural customers in what is a big farming county. We're still seen as an important part of the community but we're also lucky to have so much excellent produce,' says Stuart Higginson at Higginsons & Daughter in Grange-over-Sands (see p124). The small town supports three butchers.

Just outside Carlisle at Corby Hill, Steven Wilson goes to Carlisle auction mart every Monday, to buy cattle and sheep, mainly from farmers he knows. The beef and lamb, butched and boned by Steven and staff, is later sold in his shop, along with his own sausages, pies, potted meats and black puddings, his own-cured bacon and cooked meats. 'Many of our customers like the idea of knowing where the meat comes from, and most of it has travelled less than 20 miles,' he says.

As for local butchers themselves, says Stuart Higginson 'they've got to be friendly, chatty and ready to offer advice on how to cook meat, if people want help. Above all they've got to make customers confident in what they're buying. That's very important these days,' he adds.

A handful of butchers are featured in this chapter, and below are a few more around Cumbria. Opening times vary, so it's best to check first if travelling far.

Ambleside: *Clayton's*
Compston Road.
Tel: 015394 32143

Bootle: *W Bewley*
Main Street.
Tel: 01229 718792

Bowness: *Richardson's Butchers*
Windermere
Queen's Square.
Tel: 015394 43135

Broughton-in-Furness:
Melville Tyson
Princes Street.
Tel: 01229 716247
Website: www.melvilletyson.co.uk

Cockermouth: *W Lindsay & Sons*
Station Street.
Tel: 01900 823143

Corby Hill: *Steven Wilson's Family Butchers*
near Carlisle.
Tel: 01228 560896

Egremont: *Wilson's Butchers*
Main Street.
Tel: 01946 820036

Great Orton: *R&J Mulholland*
The Shop.
Tel: 01228 710298

Kendal: *Marsden Bros*
New Shambles.
Tel: 01539 720033

Kendal: *Watson and Woollard*
Market Place.
Tel: 01539 720198

Keswick: *Thomason's*
Station Street.
Tel: 017687 80169

Kirkby Lonsdale: *Dales Traditional Butchers*
Market Street.
Tel: 015242 71278
Website: www.dalesbutchers.co.uk

Shap: *JN Bellas*
Main Street.
Tel: 01931 716624

Ulverston: *Irvings Butchers*
Market Street.
Tel: 01229 583181

Whitehaven: *Haighs*
King Street.
Tel: 01946 692715
Website: www.haighs.com

Wigton: *RJ Harrison & Sons*
King Street.
Tel: 016973 42192

Windermere: *Huddlestons*
Crescent Road.
Tel: 015394 43080
Website:
www.cumberlandsausage.co.uk

Windermere: *Claytons of Windermere*
Crescent Road.
Tel: 015394 43071

Opposite clockwise from top left: Trevor Ewbank at TM Ewbank (see p114), Trevor Ewbank and his father Malcolm, staff at Steven Wilson's Family Butchers (Terry Studholme, Michael Jupp, Steven Wilson, Sheila Wilson, Ray Parkin, see above), meat and then pies at Higginsons & Daughter (see p124), meat at Greystone House Farm Shop (see p141).

Staveley

Organico

Mill Yard, Staveley, Kendal LA8 9LR
Tel: 01539 822200
Website: www.organi.co.uk

A chance remark from the owners of an organic winery in Tuscany – 'why don't you sell our wine in England?' – prompted Sue and Peter Jackson to do just that. What began as a small-scale business in 1997 turned, eight years later, into the 'UK's first dedicated organic wine shop', based in Ambleside (see p114). In early 2008 Organico opened a second outlet at spanking new premises in Staveley, near Kendal. Here, on the oak-floored ground level, you'll find about 200 different wines, most of them certified as made from organically grown grapes. Others come from estates where, Peter says, 'we know the wine is made naturally and without chemicals, even if the product isn't actually certified as organic'.

The ground floor houses three large wine tanks, from which private or trade customers can fill their bottles or other containers to take away. There's also a display of every wine that Organico sells and an area offering wine books, wine accessories and other products from vineyards which supply the Jacksons with wine. At the back of the building, beyond the large warehousing area, is a room with decking that overlooks the River Kent. This is used for wine tastings and wine courses. Up the oak staircase to the next floor is a bar/bistro, opening 2009.

Although Italy and France are the countries best represented at Organico, wines also come from Argentina, Austria, Chile, Australia, France, Germany, New Zealand, Portugal, South Africa and Spain. 'We try to impart the passion of our wine growers to the customers we serve,' says Peter. Among the favourites is the 2006 Riesling Johannisberg (Austria).

The Jacksons themselves (their son Chris is also in the business) run the self-catering holiday firms Tuscan Holidays and Heart of the Lakes and are leading lights in Cumbria's Slow Food convivium (see p106). Apart from the outlet at Staveley, Organico supplies wine to a growing number of hotels and restaurants in the Lake District and elsewhere.

Open: *daily 10–18 and later when bar/bistro opens.*

Tebay
Westmorland Farm Shops

Tebay Services, Westmorland Place, Orton, Penrith CA10 3SB
Tel: 01539 711341 (northbound) and 01539 711342 (southbound)
Website: www.westmorland.com

The farmyard's nowhere to be seen and the cattle and sheep are somewhere out on the fells. No matter. These two farm shops are a real bonus for drivers pulling into Westmorland Services on the M6. They had barely been open a year when they were named *Best Local Food Retailer* in the BBC Radio 4 Food and Farming Awards in 2003.

The shop on the southward side is bigger than the one opposite and it has a butcher's counter as well – which must be a first for a motorway services in Britain. The butcher's sells lamb and beef from the nearby farm of the Dunning family, who own Westmorland Services, plus locally reared pork, game and chicken.

Both shops are very well stocked and, given their location, they're ideally placed for drivers who want to take home a taste of Cumbria. One couple from London say they regularly buy supplies here on their way up and on their way back. Cool bags and ice bricks can be provided and orders phoned ahead, for collection.

Apart from the meat mentioned above you can buy bacon, hams, Herdwick mutton, pies, patés and sausages. Richard Woodall, Sillfield Farm, Deer 'n Dexter and Kitridding Farm are four Cumbrian producers who supply sausages. A cheese counter includes local makers, and bread, milk and fruit and vegetables are sold too. Shelves are groaning with jams, chutneys, olive oils, vinaigrettes, tea, coffee, cakes, biscuits, sauces, coulis, chocolates, mustards, honey and more. The southbound café/restaurant was completely redesigned in 2008. It sells local sausages and homemade burgers, sandwiches, cakes, salads etc. See also Farm Shop at Rheged (p136).

Open: daily 7–23.
Directions: the farm shops are at the Westmorland service areas, northbound and southbound on the M6 between Junctions 38 and 39 near Tebay.

Below: Butcher Jim Taylor at the Westmorland Farm Shops

Waberthwaite
Richard Woodall

Lane End, Waberthwaite, near Millom LA19 5YJ
Tel: 01229 717237
Website: www.richardwoodall.co.uk

'There's an old saying that you should never cure a pig unless there's an R in the month,' says June Woodall, as we gaze at the empty hooks above us. So if you come here between October and April (September might still be a bit warm) you'll see up to 80 hams hanging from the ceiling. June and her husband Richard are the seventh generation of the family in this business which produces hams, bacon, sausages and pancetta (see p85). Their nephew Colin is the eighth generation.

Just inside the front door is the grocery and post office side of the shop, beyond that the room selling Woodall's products. The ceiling hooks, flagstoned floor, old tea cannisters and a certificate from the Royal Agricultural Society's International Show at Kilburn (north London) in 1879, awarding Woodall's second prize for their British hams, give the place a certain character. Outside on the wall, the Royal Warrant – to supply the Queen with Cumberland sausage, bacon and hams – stands out a treat on an otherwise unassuming looking building.

Open: *Mon–Fri 8.30–12.15, 13.15–17.30. Sat: 8.30–12.*

Windermere
Oak Street Bakery

1 Oak Street, Windermere LA23 1BH
Tel: 015394 48284

Six mornings a week Phil Eastwood rises before the lark to start work at this busy, open-plan bakery in Windermere town. For over eight years he and his wife Ruth have run the business, offering a range of some 30 different breads (17 or 18 on any given day), cakes, scones, croissants, Danish pastries, filled rolls, sandwiches, baguettes, traybakes, celebration cakes (when requested) and more.

The range of breads include white farmhouse, crusty bloomer and wholemeal, as well as Italian, French, Spanish, Polish and German breads: ciabatta, focaccia, Pugliese and the very tasty Bayerisch Donker, for example. A big seller is their Mediterranean bread, packed with pesto, basil, cheese, sun-dried tomatoes, olives and roasted peppers.

The Oak Street Bakery also supplies Lucy's of Ambleside and a number of cafés, hotels and restaurants in the Lake District. Next door to the bakery is Ruth and Phil's Coffee Bar 7, serving tea, coffee, cakes, croissants and sandwiches. The café is the venue for occasional 'stitch and bitch' evenings, an opportunity for people to knit and sew, and have a good gossip at the same time.

Open: *Mon–Fri 8.30–17, Sat 8–16. Open: Sun during summer holiday 8–16. In winter bakery closes a bit earlier. Café open: daily 10–17 but in summer holiday 8–20. Shorter hours in winter. Check first if coming a distance.*

More Food and Farm Shops

Airey's Farm Shop

Ayside, near Low Newton LA11 6JE
015395 31237.
www.aireysfarmshop.co.uk
This family shop, just off the A590, stocks local, rare and traditional breed beef, pork and lamb, including Herdwick lamb and mutton. Airey's has an abattoir as well which serves a wide area.

Baycliffe Farm Shop

Baycliffe, near Ulverston LA12 9RW
01229 869257.
www.farmshopbaycliffe.co.uk
Five miles (8km) along the coast from Ulverston, the Barlow family shop stocks beef, lamb and cooked meats, plus bread, cakes and pies, baked on the premises. The shop also has an outside catering business.

Brown Horse Farm Shop

Winster, near Bowness-on-Windermere LA23 3NR
015394 43443 (pub).
www.thebrownhorseinn.co.uk
Located at the Brown Horse pub, the shop sells beef, lamb, pork, and game (when in season) from the local Brown Horse Estate. Other Cumbrian produce is stocked as well.

Page 148
Above left: two images from Bread Matters, Melmerby (see p151)
Above right: Ivan Day's preparation for kippered salmon and ducks à la braise (see p153)
Below left: a pyramid of fruit created by Ivan Day (see p153)
Below right: homemade jams and jellies at Acorn Bank, Wetheral (see p150)

The Cumbrian Way

Brogden Street, Ulverston LA12 7AH
01229 588906.
www.cumbrianway.co.uk
Plenty of Cumbrian names are amongst the jams, jellies, pickles, chutneys, cheeses, smoked foods, fudge and toffee, sold at The Cumbrian Way. It does hampers and outside catering too.

HDM Spice Shop

Brook Street, Carlisle CA1 2HU
01228 522579.
www.hdmspiceshop.co.uk
A range of Asian foods are stocked here: spices, sauces, pastes, oils, pickles, chutneys, flour, rice and such like. The shop sells Halal chicken, beef, lamb and mutton, and there's a selection of Indian cooking ingredients and free recipes.

Love the Lakes

Ash Street, Bowness-on-Windermere LA23 3EB
015394 46298.
www.lovethelakes.net
Food and drink from Cumbrian producers takes up part of the shelf space in this attractive shop. The range includes jams, marmalades, beers, damson gin, chutneys, pickles and spicy sauces.

More? The Artisan Bakery

Mill Yard, Staveley, Kendal LA8 9LR
Tel: 01539 822297
Website: www.moreartisan.co.uk
Patrick Moore sells a range of breads, cakes, puddings, sandwiches, cheeses and charcuterie. His More muddee won three gold stars at the 2008 Great Taste Awards where the brownie was *Best Speciality from the North West* and a *Reserve Supreme Champion*.

Plumgarths Farm Shop

Crook Road, near Kendal LA8 8LX
01539 736300.
www.plumgarths.co.uk
Plumgarths sells beef, lamb, pork, bacon and sausages, as well as jam, honey, mustard, pickles, chutneys, Cumbrian beers and sticky toffee pudding.

Relish Deli

36-38 Market Place, Kendal LA9 4TN
01539 727279
Cheeses, chutneys, pickles, olive oils, truffle oils and balsamic vinegars (6 and 12 years old) are some of the many foods - from Cumbria, Italy, China, Japan and elsewhere - stocked by this deli. The shop sells sandwiches and hampers and does outside catering as well.

Shill's of Station Street

11 Station Street, Cockermouth CA13 9QW
Tel: 01900 826427
Website:
www.shillsofstationstreet.co.uk
Nick and Wendy Shill's deli sells French cheeses, pâté, charcuterie and wines (Nick spent two years buying from the Rungis food market in Paris) and other wines and cheeses, including those from Cumbria. You'll also see olives, flours from The Watermill at Little Salkeld, Saunders chocolates, Cuban cigars and much more. Monthly wine tastings take place. Check website for dates.

Opening days and times vary between the food and farm shops on this page, so it's best to check first if travelling far.

Cookery and Baking Courses

Acorn Bank

Wetheral, Carlisle CA4 8JG
Tel: 01228 561434
Website: www.acornbank.co.uk

Fortunately, for all those who enjoyed the food and hospitality at Isabel and Geoff Ferguson's Carlisle restaurant, Number 10, the couple didn't go far when they decided to sell up in 2006 after 15 years. No new restaurant but their cookery days, held in a smart orangerie overlooking the garden of their Georgian home, are almost the next best thing.

The demonstrations – 'informative, entertaining, relaxing and most enjoyable', says one regular – take place on three days in most months of the year. Themes range from *Vegetarian Cookery*, *Cooking with Cheese*, and *Summer Puddings and Desserts* to *Cooking with Shellfish*, *Winter Warmers* (pies and tarts) and *Summer Garden Party*.

Coffee is at 10.30 (18.30 aperitif if it's an evening course) and then the real business starts at 11. 'The more questions the better,' says Isabel who cooks with Geoff for up to an hour and a half. Food is occasionally passed round to taste, but everything which has been prepared in the morning is served at lunch. That takes place in the orangerie as well. Local produce is extensively used and recipes are given out for people to take away.

Price: *from £25 per person includes lunch and wine.*
Numbers: 10–12 on each course. Geoff and Isabel also lay on cookery demonstrations – apart from those advertised – for groups of 8–12. Gift vouchers available. Craft days are run as well. Acorn Bank has two rooms for bed and breakfast and if guests want others to join them for dinner, a limited number are very welcome.
Directions: *Wetheral is on the B6263 about 3 miles (4.8km) east of Carlisle city centre.*

Bay Horse Inn

Canal Foot, Ulverston LA12 9EL
Tel: 01229 583972
Website: www.thebayhorsehotel.co.uk

Robert Lyons has been running his courses at the Bay Horse (see p69) for 15 years, combining his flair for cookery with a liberal sprinkling of humour. It's only on Thursdays and Fridays in November that this former head chef at Miller Howe holds the courses so they tend to get booked up early.

Coffee and homemade biscuits are served at 10.30, the actual demonstration starts at 11. Robert usually goes through the dishes that will be served at lunch, plus others. In the past he's demonstrated food like mustard and leek bread; asparagus and crème fraîche tart; fresh pheasant roasted with pomegranate and crab apple jelly; smoked pork cutlet with sour cream paprika and wild mushrooms; baked dark chocolate pistachio custard on a white chocolate and milk chocolate; and baked peach in a sweet dessert wine.

The three course lunch is at 12.30 in the conservatory, then there's more cookery – questions are encouraged – until 15.30/16. Tea and cakes are served before people leave with a full complement of recipes.

Price: *£70–£75 per person includes lunch and wine.*
Numbers: 12 on each course.
Directions: *as you come into Ulverston on the A590 from Newby Bridge, turn left at the cattle market into North Lonsdale Road and the Bay Horse is just over 1 mile (1.6km) down there.*

Below left: Isabel and Geoff Ferguson of Acorn Bank
Below middle: Isabel Ferguson in the kitchen at Acorn Bank
Below right: the Bay Horse Inn
Far right: Andrew Whitley of Bread Matters

Bread Matters

The Tower House, Melmerby, Penrith CA10 1HE
Tel: 01768 881899
Website: www.breadmatters.com

Long before the word organic passed into common parlance, Andrew Whitley turned his back on London, headed for Cumbria, bought 5 acres of land on which to grow organic fruit and vegetables and converted a stone barn next to his house into a small bakery (with wood-fired oven) and tea room. Such were the modest beginnings in 1976 of The Village Bakery which went on to become one of Britain's great organic bread names.

In 1998 Andrew was the first recipient of the Organic Trophy (for lifetime achievement) at the Organic Food Awards. Four years later he stepped down from The Village Bakery, to spend more time on teaching, campaigning and writing. *Bread Matters*, a book about the 'state of modern bread and a definitive guide to baking your own', was published in 2006 to considerable acclaim. It was *Best Food Book* in the prestigious André Simon Book Awards of that year. Early in 2008 Andrew began work on the Real Bread Campaign.

Bread Matters is also the name of the courses that he runs throughout the year in Melmerby. 'They're for people who love bread, and for those who cook for a living and want to put bread centre-table,' says Andrew. 'All you need is a desire to make proper bread'.

Most courses last two days (from 10.00 on the first day to 16.00 on the second) and include *Bread Matters Fundamental*, *Gluten-Free Baking*, *Sourdough for All*, *French Breads*, *Italian Baking* and *North European Baking*. *Baking for a Living* is three days and *Bread Matters Advanced* lasts five. Whatever the course, everyone is introduced to the fundamentals of fermentation on which, Andrew says, all good bread depends. Coffee, lunch (organic food) and tea punctuate the sessions and as the course progresses you get to sample some of the breads you've made and baked in the wood-fired oven.

The courses, says Andrew, give people a greater under-standing of the processes at the heart of breadmaking, more confidence, a lot of fun and several loaves of their own bread. One participant described their two days as 'a life-enhancing experience'. Andrew also runs *Together We Rise*, team development courses through breadmaking.

Price: *£395 for the two day course, £560 for three days, £850 for five days.*
Numbers: maximum of 8 people. Andrew's book Bread Matters *is published by Fourth Estate and costs £20.*
Directions: *Melmerby is 9 miles (14.4km) north east of Penrith on the A686 road to Alston.*

Augill Little Cooks

Augill Castle, South Stainmore, Kirkby Stephen CA17 4DE
Tel: 017683 41937
Website: www.augillcastle.co.uk

'We don't aim to create little Masterchefs but we do want to inspire children,' say Wendy and Simon Bennett of the cookery courses for 7–14 year olds, held at their Victorian castle in the Eden Valley. The castle, built as a folly by eccentric John Bagot Pearson, is only part of the attraction because there are pigs, chickens and a kitchen garden here as well.

Courses are usually run during school holidays, a typical day starting at 11 with a drink, snack and safety talk. Then the fun starts, the children closely supervised throughout the day, say Wendy and Simon, as they have a go at making breads, meatballs, macaroni cheese, pizzas, pasta, quiches, tarts, cakes, biscuits and such like. Parents, meanwhile, can relax at the castle or go sightseeing in the local area. The day ends at about 16.00 and the children leave with a goody bag, an apron, recipe book and the things they've cooked.

Price: *£45 per child for one day, £80 for two consecutive days. Check the website for dates of courses. Also see p40.*
Directions: *take the A685 from Brough to Kirkby Stephen and you'll see a sign for Augill Castle just outside Brough.*

Cook in Cumbria

High Chapel House, Ravenstonedale,
Kirkby Stephen CA17 4NQ
Tel: 015396 23411
Website: www.cookincumbria.com

Mussaman beef curry, babi pangang, beef rendang and Dutch apple pie. Cook in Cumbria and travel the food world is what Yelly de Jong offers with her cookery courses in this quiet part of Cumbria, within striking distance of the Howgill Fells. She started her courses in autumn 2008 and holds them three times a week, on Wednesday, Friday and Saturday.

Most are day long sessions (until about 16.00) but there are a few evening courses (18.30–21.30) as well. Coffee and homemade cakes and biscuits start the day sessions at 10 and before lunch Yelly, who has a City and Guilds diploma in professional cookery, runs through four to five dishes in her open plan kitchen/dining room. Whatever she's demonstrated that morning you get for lunch. She offers advice on sourcing ingredients too.

After lunch there's another demonstration before you have a go yourself, preparing dishes around the large dining table until about 16.00. Each class has a different theme, including Thai, Chinese, Malaysian, Indonesian, Greek, Dutch (Yelly herself was born in Holland), French and 'Best of Cumbria'. This means that one day she might be demonstrating Chinese hot and sour soup and Chinese red cooked lamb while another time it might be Cumbrian venison and cherry Cumberland sauce, and Westmorland pepper cake.

Price: *£79 per person for day long sessions, £34 for evenings. Numbers: up to 10 on each course. Yelly is happy to organise cookery days with special themes on request. Discounts are offered on group bookings of five or more. Gift vouchers are available. Yelly's High Chapel House also offers B&B accommodation (www.highchapelhouse.com)*
Directions: *From M6 Junction 38 follow the A685 towards Brough, turning right into Ravenstonedale after about 8 miles (12.8km). Follow signs to the village and pass the Black Swan. High Chapel House is on your right, on the brow of the hill.*

Far left: ices made by Ivan Day (Historic Food) from original Victorian moulds
Far right: Ivan Day of Historic Food

Food & Company

Tel: 016974 78634
Website: www.foodandcompany.co.uk

There's poetry on the wall of the sheltered verandah as you head into the Garden Hall at Mirehouse, by Bassenthwaite Lake, and there are more winning words in Food & Company's guest book inside. 'Good food, good fun, good fellowship,' writes one person. 'Lovely, relaxing and informative day,' says another.

Joan Gate and Margaret Brough's *food workshops and lunch with friends* take place in a timbered 16th-century building at this historic home beside Bassenthwaite Lake. 'Our aims are to build confidence for beginners and widen the knowledge for the more experienced food lover,' they say. The courses run from spring until late autumn, but judging by the response they could be holding them all year round. In the Cumbria Tourism Awards 2007, Food & Company received the *Taste of Cumbria Award of the Year*.

Sisters, farmer's daughters and 18 years running an outside catering business, Joan and Margaret make an engaging double act. Their workshops are sometimes held on two or three days of the week, with themes such as *Flavour, Sizzle and Smoke, The Spice Trail, Easy Recipes for the Terrified Cook, Easy Entertaining* and *The Italian Evening for Men. Easy Entertaining*, for example, might take you through salmon en croûte, hot roasted smoked salmon, baked chicken Gruyère, asparagus with Hollandaise sauce, prawn galette, lemon pots, and rhubarb and orange compote.

The day starts with coffee and biscuits at 10.30 (evening courses at 18.30) and then comes the cookery demonstration which moves seamlessly between the two sisters, one demonstrating and offering advice, the other chipping in and getting ready for the next course. Questions are encouraged, local suppliers get a good mention and samples of the featured dishes are handed round for people to taste. Napkins, pencils and recipe cards have already been given out at the beginning.

Lunch comes at 13.00 with everyone tucking into a tasty two course buffet. Afterwards, Joan and Margaret throw open the 'Tardis', a cupboard which holds pots, pans and other kitchen utensils for people to buy. Finally there's the chance to wander through the Mirehouse gardens before you set off home.

Price: *about £38 per person (unless otherwise stated). Numbers: up to 30 people on each course. Food & Company also offer corporate and special occasion days. Gift vouchers available.*
Directions: *Mirehouse is about 4 miles (6.4km) north of Keswick on the A591.*

Historic Food

Tel: 01931 716266
Website: www.historicfood.com

It was a chance purchase in a Colchester bookshop that prefaced Ivan Day's lifelong interest in historic food. So amused was the teenager by the references in John Nott's 1723 edition of *The Cook's and Confectioner's Dictionary* to roast lumps, fried maids and stewed ox palettes that he immediately tried one of the recipes himself.

Forty years later Ivan is one of Britain's leading food historians: writer, broadcaster and lecturer (in Britain and the United States), re-creator of spectacular period table settings in museums and stately homes, and an actual cook of historic food, all prepared with the aid of antiquarian cookery books and wonderful old kitchen equipment.

The 16–18 weekend food courses Ivan runs every year at his part-17th century home make full use of these ancient culinary artefacts, which he has collected over many years. That's what makes the courses so unusual.

'I was really bowled over by everything – the amazing sophistication of the recipes and the equipment, and in particular by the incredible depth of Ivan's knowledge. I don't think I've ever been so impressed, to be honest, and I've met most of the world's great chefs,' says one participant.

Taken as a whole the weekend events cover 500 years of history and include *Georgian Cookery, Pie Making and Pastry, Sugarwork and Confectionery, Italian Renaissance Cookery, Victorian Cookery, Dairy and Ices, Period Ham Making, Roasting and Broiling* and *A Taste of Christmas Past.*

The courses are a mix of demonstrations and hands-on experience, introducing you to a world of raised pies, marrow chewitts, powdered geese, mutton dressed like venison, pigeon crostata, pippin knots, flummeries, cullises, hackins and Yorkshire Christmas pies. You will become familiar with clockwork spitjacks, sorbetières and pastry jaggers, and try recipes from Antonin Carême, Charles Francatelli, Agnes Marshall, Edward Kidder and others. Ivan's website gives a detailed run-down of the courses.

Each of the two days starts at 10.00, with an introduction on the Saturday to the specific subject. Lunch is cooked by participants but on the Saturday evening Ivan does the food himself. Expect a showcase of Britain's rich culinary heritage. You'll be amazed at the flavours and saddened that much of this food is almost forgotten.

As one participant says: 'The food we made on the Georgian course was some of the most delicious I have ever eaten, and I learnt so much about the history and forgotten techniques of English cookery. The spit-roasted mutton with anchovies and oysters was exceptional'.

Ivan's book *Cooking in Europe 1650–1850*, published by Greenwood Press in 2008, explores the changes that took place in food and dining between the Baroque and Victorian eras. The book includes almost 200 recipes, many translated into English for the first time.'

Price: *£280 per person (weekend). Numbers: maximum of 6 people. Ivan can suggest a range of places to stay. He will hold courses for private groups, on request.*

LucyCooks

Mill Yard, Staveley, Kendal LA8 9LR
Tel: 015394 32288
Website: www.lucycooks.co.uk

Demo and Dine can be a pretty busy night at LucyCooks but Demo and Do is a better description of the myriad courses which take place at this well known cookery school, a few minutes from Windermere. With 24 work stations in one big, bright room, everyone gets the chance to hone their skills in creating the dish that a chef has only just demonstrated.

Lucy Nicholson opened LucyCooks in 2006, adding another slice to her culinary empire (see p11, p113 and p160). The school runs practical courses and demonstrations every day of the year, apart from a few days around Christmas. Themes embrace *Fabulous Fish, Super Speedy Suppers, Soups, Stocks and Sauces, A Taste of the Orient, Fat Free Cookery, A Taste of France, A Taste of Mexico, A Taste of Italy, A Taste of Spain, Aga Sagas, Brilliant Baking, Cool 4Kids* and such like.

The majority are daytime courses, starting at 9.30 with coffee and scones and a chat from the chef of the day in the Aga Room downstairs. Half an hour later it's upstairs for the first demonstration and after that you're off to your work station, with recipes and pre-weighed ingredients. 'We want to inform and enthuse people and give them plenty of tips,' says Nick Martin who is one of LucyCooks' main chefs, along with Dale Blacow, executive chef of Lucy's of Ambleside.

You get 30–45 minutes to re-create the featured dish and then the chef is ready for the next demonstration. Two of these take place before lunch – which itself draws heavily on Cumbrian produce – and two afterwards. The food you've cooked is packed up and put in a fridge to take home at the end of the day with your information. That's a good time to pop into the LucyCooksShop and check out the kitchen equipment and cookery books that are for sale.

Demo and Dine is usually a three to four hour evening affair (starting 18.30), a 'culinary book club without the homework,' says Lucy Nicholson. The only work you're expected to do is to eat a three course meal with wine, each dish demonstrated by the chef before you try it. A guest chef is invited for Big Friday, a Demo and Dine which takes place regularly throughout the year.

Price: *from £110 per person (day long session), from £70 (morning courses), £40 (Demo and Dine).*
Numbers: up to 24 for cookery demonstrations. LucyCooks offer corporate packages and days for different groups and organisations. Gift vouchers available.
Directions: *Staveley is about 4 miles (6.4km) east of Windermere, just off the A591.*

Smoky Jo's

Castle Court, Shap, Penrith CA10 3LG
Tel: 01931 716638
Website: www.smokyjos.co.uk

For more than three years Jo Hampson and Georgina Perkins ran The Old Smokehouse at Brougham Hall near Penrith, despatching smoked foods all over the country (Harvey Nichols and Fortnum and Mason included) and winning numerous Great Taste Awards for their produce. Since 2007 they've been passing on their expertise to people who come to their one and two day home smoking courses which, says Jo, are great fun as well as being informative.

Two day courses (weekends) take participants through hot and cold smoking, smoking of a dozen different foods including trout, salmon, chicken, sausages, mussels and peppers, and smoking on different types of equipment – from biscuit tins to commercial smokers to converted filing cabinets. Their cabinet is called 'Freddy'.

In between you will make your own recipe sausages and smoke them, and do some fishing at nearby Bessy Beck Trout Fishery. The trout is later smoked as well. Unfortunately there's no time for fishing on the one day course.

Jo and Georgina – 'your hosts, tutors and entertainers' – start the day for people at 9.45 with coffee and chocolate biscuits, then the first lesson of each course is how to brine your food in preparation for smoking. Lunch is about 13.00 and on the Sunday of the weekend course (as on the one day session) that means a meal of hot smoked salmon, salad and homemade bread. Notes about smoking food are given out before you leave along with goodie bags of smoked food.

'The tuition and organisation were excellent, the environment perfect and the company brilliant,' enthuses one participant. 'You have a winning formula. It's been a really special day,' says another.

Price: *£99 for one day course, £199 for two days (includes the fishing). Numbers: maximum 8 people. Jo and Georgina also offer B&B accommodation at their house.*
Directions: *Castle Court is near Shap, about 3 miles (4.8km) from junction 39 of the M6.*

Below: Jo Hampson and Georgina Perkins of Smoky Jo's.

The Watermill

Little Salkeld, Penrith CA10 1NN
Tel: 01768 881523
Website: www.organicmill.co.uk

Slow Food supporters Nick and Ana Jones have been producing organic and bio-dynamic flour at their 300 year old watermill (see p97) for many years so it's no surprise that the one day breadmaking and cookery courses entirely reflect their work and their passion for good food. Almost half of the 25–30 courses run during the year are devoted to breadmaking but there are also a number of cookery courses, linked to the seasons: *Saladmaking*, *Hedgerow Cooking* (what to do with the harvest of fruit and berries), *Soupmaking*, *Apple Cooking*, *Christmas Baking* and *Winter Vegetarian Cooking*.

For those who've never made bread or feel that their skills could do with improving, *Breadmaking* is the ideal course, says Ana. 'It's a day spent learning about grain, milling and how to make wonderful tasty bread that takes very little time and effort.' *More Breadmaking* is a step up, looking at using sourdough and experimenting with rye and barley. All courses start at 10 with coffee and go on till about 15.30. Lunch is taken in the Watermill's tea room (see p170). *Breadmaking* and *cake making* are also two of the children's courses run here, the creative courses for children running from 10–12.45.

Price: *check the website or ring for details.*
Numbers: maximum 10 people.
Directions: *The Watermill is 11/2 miles (2.4km) from Langwathby, off the A686 Penrith to Alston road.*

Woodend Cookery

Woodend House, Woodend, Egremont CA22 2TA
Tel: 01946 813017
Website: www.woodendcookery.co.uk

'Good food, good shopping, good cooking' was the ethos that Grainne Jakobson grew up with at her home in Yorkshire. Her mother, Grace Mulligan, presented ITV's *Farmhouse Kitchen* for 15 years in the 1970s and 1980s, so cooking was an important ingredient of family life. Nowadays Grainne passes on her own knowledge and enthusiasm during the courses she holds at her Georgian home, close to glorious countryside in the Western Lake District.

The sessions are held three times a month during most of the year, with a different theme each time. Days might include *A Taste of Spain*, *Summer Alfresco Eating*, *Men Only*, *60 Minute Entertaining*, *Magic of Chocolate* or *Get Ahead for Christmas*. The day and evening demonstrations are held in Grainne's own kitchen which looks out through a large conservatory into the garden. 'There's great emphasis on local and seasonal foods and on presentation. The sessions are informal and very sociable, with plenty of time for chat and exchange of tips. It's really a lovely day out for people,' says Grainne.

Coffee or tea and homemade biscuits start the daytime demonstrations (at 10.30) and then Grainne takes guests through four or five dishes before a two course lunch with wine. Some of the dishes seen during the demonstration are on the menu and when you leave at about 14.30 you'll have recipe sheets to take away with you. Evening sessions (19–23) start with non-alcoholic cocktails and homemade nibbles, and include dinner with wine.

Price: *£34.50 per person. Numbers: 8–12 on each course. Group bookings available at times to suit, with discount. Hands on practical sessions can be tailor-made to requirements. Gift vouchers available.*
Directions: *from the north take the A595 from Whitehaven and after passing through Bigrigg take the first turning on the left signed Cleator and Cockermouth. At the bottom of the hill the road bears round to the left and Woodend House is at the bottom on the right.*

Opposite clockwise from top left: Joan Gate and Margaret Brough of Food & Company (see p152), Mirehouse historic home where Food & Company hold their food workshops, the Cook in Cumbria kitchen (see p152), Ennerdale Water, a few miles from Woodend Cookery, The Watermill at Little Salkeld, High Chapel House where Cook in Cumbria holds its courses

Page 158: Above left: view across Coniston Water from Jumping Jenny at Brantwood, Coniston (see p166)
Above right: Courtyard Café, Holker Hall (see p163)
Below left: Chesters Café by the River, Skelwith Bridge (see p178)
Below right: tea at the Bay Horse Inn, Ulverston (see p69)

Cafés, Tea Rooms, Café/Restaurants

Ambleside

Lucy's on a Plate

Church Street, Ambleside LA22 0BU
Tel: 015394 31191
Website: www.lucysofambleside.co.uk

'A balanced diet is a cake in each hand,' says the menu at Lucy Nicholson's informal and popular café/restaurant. There's certainly plenty of choice (from £1.95): lemon cake, banana cake, carrot and cranberry cake, chocolate and Guinness cake, and more. Gluten free cakes are available as well. Breakfasts include hot fruit compote (£4.50) and Lucy's all day breakfast (£8.95).

Omelettes and savoury croissants are available, and, for lunch, there are soups, salads, pasta, pancakes, dips, hummus, Westmorland rarebit, baguettes and ciabatta. Dishes for youngsters come with names like tiddly breakfast and diddly omelette. Cumberland spiced bread pudding, served with rum butter (£3.95) is one of over 30 homemade puddings.

Open: *daily 10–21. Evening menu is available after 18.00 (see p11).*

Bootle

The Byre

Millstones, Bootle LA19 5TH
Tel: 01229 718757

This is a really welcome stop in south west Cumbria – one way lies the sea and the other Corney Fell. Converted from an old farm building, The Byre (pictured right) is light and spacious inside, with exposed roof timbers, chunky tables and chairs, and a wood burning stove in one corner with sofas beside it. Linda Leece, who runs the café/restaurant, puts great emphasis on Cumbrian produce.

Tea, coffee, Fentiman's drinks, wine and beer (Jennings, Coniston) are served, and, to eat, there are homemade cakes and scones, soups, sandwiches, light meals and specials. Some dishes – like Bewley's Cumberland sausage bun (£3.75), soup (£3.65), bacon roll (£3.50) and ploughman's lunch (£6.75) – are served all day. The children's menu, which might take in poached egg on buttered toast, or peanut butter on two slices of hot toast, includes a free glass of milk. Occasionally there is jazz in the evenings.

Open: *Tue–Sun 10–18 (earlier closing in winter). Also open Bank Holiday Mon.*

Zeffirellis

Compston Road, Ambleside LA22 9AD
Tel: 015394 33845
Website: www.zeffirellis.co.uk

Next to Zeffirellis restaurant in this cinema complex – and applying the same high standards as the restaurant – is this relaxed, vegetarian café, serving tea, coffees, cakes, baguettes, salads and soups. You can also get pizzas (average £7.50–£8.50), pasta (£7–£7.50), jacket potatoes, potato wedges (£3.25) and dishes like bruschetta, toasted with pesto, cherry tomatoes and melted mozzarella, and served with a mixed leaf salad (£3.85).

Desserts include sticky pear and ginger pudding, and Italian chocolate torte (both £3.20). Italianate friezes adorn the walls and classical music plays lightly in the background. You'll find newspapers in a rack and on warmer days you can sit outside on the terrace. The restaurant is open in the evenings (see p13) and there's a jazz café bar here too (see p44).

Café open: *daily 10–16.30.*

Bowness-on-Windermere

Blackwell Tea Room

Blackwell, Bowness-on-Windermere LA23 3JR
Tel: 015394 46139
Website: www.blackwell.org.uk

Even the location above Windermere is put in the shade by the glories of this 100 year old property. Blackwell was built for a Manchester brewer and is one of the most important Arts and Craft houses in England. It's Grade I listed, with almost all of its original decorative features – wood carving, stained glass, the wonderfully vibrant fireside tiling, the plasterwork, wrought iron work and stone carving – still surviving.

What makes the tea room special is that the menu aims to reflect the philosophy of the Arts and Crafts movement with an 'emphasis on quality and the handmade'. Sandwiches, with Blackwell's own baked bread, include slices of Parma ham, with rocket, sun blushed tomatoes and Parmesan shavings (£4.75), and chicken breast with crispy bacon, red pesto and crème fraîche (£4.75). Soup of the day, like red lentil and bacon, or spicy parsnip and apple, with focaccia and butter is £4.25. Specials might include Morecambe Bay shrimps, home potted and served with lemon, toast and a mixed leaf salad, with pine nuts and honey vinaigrette dressing (£7.50).

There's tea, coffees, soft drinks (including homemade lemonade which is steeped overnight), beers and wine. Tea bread, with a slice of Wensleydale cheese, fruit scones, Blackwell's popular chocolate hazelnut brownies and the speciality panforte are on the menu as well. The panforte comes in three flavours – chocolate and black pepper; citrus and almond; and mixed nuts and cherry – and is delicious. Eaten in the tea room it's £1.85, taken away in packs it's £5.95 (because there's more of it). Artwork hangs on the wall – Henry Moore's sheep sketches when I called – and on sunny days you can sit on the garden terraces and gaze at the wonderful view.

Open: *daily except Christmas Day, Boxing Day, and two weeks in early Jan 10.30–17 (10.30–16 Nov–Easter). Check when opening again in Jan 2010.*
Directions: *Blackwell is just south of Bowness-on-Windermere on the B5360, off the A5074.*

Below: the main hall at Blackwell

Brougham

Fusion Café

Brougham Hall, Brougham, Penrith CA10 2DE
Tel: 01768 867888
Website: www.allfusedglass.co.uk

For some years Anne Clayton was front of house at Sharrow Bay Country House Hotel under Francis Coulson and Brian Sack, so she knows a thing or two about the hospitality business. She enthusiastically runs this 24-seat café with her husband Ian in the grounds of what was once the home of the first Baron Brougham and Vaux, Lord Chancellor of England 1830–34. An outside terrace has more seats, and in summer Anne and Ian put tables and chairs on the nearby lawn.

Food is 'lovingly cooked to order' in the small kitchen behind the counter and includes baguettes, with dry-cured bacon and chutney, honey roast ham or roast beef (£3.95), soup of the day (£3.95), salads and panini. Panini could have roast ham and chutney, or bacon, brie and red onion. There are homemade cakes, croissants and chocolate brownies as well. Coffee comes with organic, Fairtrade and Rainforest Alliance certification, while the leaf tea is supplied by Jing, suppliers to Heston Blumenthal and Gordon Ramsay. Mary's jams and chutneys, which Fusion uses, are sold in the café.

The couple hold occasional 'special dinner evenings' where food might be Italian or Indian. Anne teaches jazz piano and singing, so music on those evenings ties in with the meal. She also runs a choir here on Thursday evenings. Ian doubles as a glass artist, his studio being a few steps away from the café.

Open: *daily 9–17 (slightly earlier closing in winter).*
Directions: *Brougham Hall is about 1 mile (1.6km) south of Penrith, on the B6262, just off the A6.*

Caldbeck

Watermill Café

Priest's Mill, Caldbeck CA7 8DR
Tel: 016974 78267
Website: www.watermillcafe.co.uk

Just over 300 years ago the rector of Caldbeck built a watermill close to St Kentigern's Church. The mill is no longer in use but the building, restored in 1986, is home to this busy café, run with very obvious care by Helen and Colin Daglish. In 2006 The Independent newspaper named it as one of the top 50 cafés in the UK. The L-shaped room has exposed roof timbers, stone walls and a wood burning stove, while an outside terrace overlooks the River Caldbeck and the village cricket pitch.

The café serves Fairtrade leaf tea and coffee, soft drinks, homemade cakes, scones and gingerbread as well as soups, sandwiches, ciabatta, baked potatoes and more substantial dishes. These may include the Greek platter, Cumberland ham platter or Watermill cheese platter (all £6.95) and dishes like broccoli and smoked cheese bake, and mushroom, tomato and almond layer. Desserts such as fruit crumble and sticky toffee pudding are £3.75. There's a children's board too.

On the shelves, for sale, are Cumberland mustard, Farrer's tea, flour from The Watermill at Little Salkeld, fudge from the Wooden Spoon Fudge Company and Watermill Café jams and chutneys. There are baby chairs and books for children. St Kentigern's churchyard has the graves of huntsman John Peel and Mary Robinson, the 'Maid of Buttermere'.

Open: *daily 9–17, mid-Feb–Oct, 9–16.30, Nov–Jan.*

Below left: Fusion Café
Below right: Watermill Café

Above: all views from Courtyard Café and Holker Hall apart from the sign at Fusion Café

Cark-in-Cartmel
Courtyard Café

Holker Hall, Cark-in-Cartmel, Grange-over-Sands LA11 7PL
Tel: 015395 58328
Website: www.holker-hall.co.uk

Like the Holker Food Hall (see p117) just across the way, the Courtyard Café has a rather elegant feel to it. Originally part of the stable block, the room is painted in Holker estate colours, with three or four partitions to break the space up, a wooden floor, photographs of Holker Hall's garden on the wall and little trees in plant pots here and there. The café offers tea, coffee, beer and wine, cakes, flapjacks, sandwiches (like beef, ham, tuna mayonnaise, cheese savoury), soups, salads, jacket potatoes and other snacks.

As for prices, a tomato and roasted red pepper soup with roll and butter is £3.95, a cajun chicken baguette, with chips and salad is £5.25, and a chicken and bacon salad is £4.95. In warmer weather the courtyard makes for a lovely place to sit and have your tea. Cream tea is presented on a piece of Burlington slate. The café can be hired for private functions in the evenings. Holker Hall and its garden are open to the public but check for opening times. The Holker Festival is held annually at the end of May.

Open: *daily 10.30–17.30 in high season, 10.30–16 in winter. Closed Christmas–early Jan.*

Carlisle

Hoopers, The Restaurant

Castle Street, Carlisle CA3 8SR
Tel: 01228 524202
Website: www.hoopers.ltd.uk

Hoopers department store stands in a part of Carlisle which encompasses the small but beautiful cathedral, the 11th-century castle and Tullie House Museum and Art Gallery. The light, bright café/restaurant is on the first floor, with large windows on two sides – the cathedral is just across the road – and artwork from Cumbria University students on the other two walls. A softer area in the middle has four leather sofas, tub chairs and low tables.

You can get tea, coffee, soft drinks, wine and bottled lager, scones, homemade cakes, toasted teacakes, gingerbread and such like. 'Lite bites' include either dry-cured bacon or Cumberland sausage in a bap (both £3.95) and there are sandwiches (£5.25–£6.50), salads and panini.

Monthly specials might be Hoopers' ground beef burger, with caramelised red onions and Cajun wedges (£5.95) or poached salmon on herby crushed potatoes, with lemon and Parmesan cheese (£7.50).

Local produce is sourced as much as possible and some is for sale: jams, chutneys, curds, marmalade, jellies and so on from the likes of Hawkshead Relish, Wild and Fruitful, Lizzie's Home Made, Mr Vikki's, and Hoopers' own make. The store itself sells ladies' and men's fashion, shoes, accessories, perfume and cosmetics, gifts and cookware.

Open: *Mon–Sat 9–17, also Sun Nov–Dec 11–17.*

Prior's Kitchen

7 The Abbey, Carlisle CA3 8TZ
Tel: 01228 543251
Website: www.carlislecathedral.org.uk

In that the setting for this café is the stone-vaulted cellar of Carlisle Cathedral's fratry, Victoria Holt and her team are maintaining a centuries old tradition of hospitality. The basis for their soups, salads, snacks and main dishes is pretty well the same as when the monks used to dine here: as much local and organic produce as possible.

'It's food for body and soul,' says Victoria. Organic Longhorn beef comes from Croft Farm Meats near Carlisle and organic Birdoswald cheese is from Slack House Farm at Gilsland. Victoria also uses Thornby Moor Dairy cheese (near Carlisle), vegetables from Eva's Organics and beer from Geltsdale Brewery at Brampton.

The menu is sprinkled with Biblical quotations about food, and starts, unusually, with choices 'for little people'. There's cheese on toast and sliced fruit, or ham, cheese or jam sandwich and sliced fruit (both £2). Grown-ups can tuck into things like fruit scones, carrot cake or gluten-free lemon cake, soup with organic roll (£3), sandwiches (£3.95), quiche of the day and salad (£4.95) and local potted shrimp salad (£6.50).

Specials might include organic beef and ale casserole (£6.50), sweet potato and bean hotpot (£5.95) and pepper and goat's cheese roulade (£5.50). 'It's very good indeed here,' says one visitor. Fairly traded leaf tea, coffee and hot chocolate are served, along with soft drinks and wine. Sugar, honey, jam, fruit, juices and rice are all Fairtrade as well. Prior's Kitchen also caters for special functions.

Open: *Mon–Sat 9.30–16.*

Coniston

Jumping Jenny

Brantwood, Coniston LA21 8AD
Tel: 015394 41715
Website: www.jumpingjenny.com

The spirit leaps even before you step inside Jumping Jenny because few café/restaurants have views like this. Coniston Water lies below, and across the lake are the Coniston fells, a sight to savour when you sit on the terrace outside. Jumping Jenny – located in former stables where four horse stalls are still in evidence, and a wood burning stove is lit on chillier days – is named after a boat of John Ruskin's. The artist, writer, art critic and conservationist lived at Brantwood for the last 28 years of his life.

Tea, coffee, hot chocolate, soft drinks and local beers like Hawkshead, Barngates and Coniston are offered and there are cakes, scones, flapjacks, soups and 'Brantwiches' (sandwiches on wholemeal roll/bread with salad, all about £5). Lunch choice might include casserole of beef in Morocco Ale with a new potato mash (£9.80), pasta with spinach, garlic and mascarpone, with roasted cherry tomatoes and shavings of fresh Parmesan (£7.80), savoury flan of caramelised red onion and Lancashire cheese (£6.80), and sticky toffee pudding with hot fudge sauce, cream/ice cream (£4.50).

The café, run by Gillie and Chris Addison (they also have Belmount Hall at Outgate), is licensed and available for evening party bookings of over ten people.

Open: *daily (summer) 11–18, Wed–Sun (winter) 11–17.*
Directions: *Brantwood is just over 2 miles (about 4km) from Coniston village, on the east side of Coniston Water. Georgian Belmount Hall, completely refurbished in 2006, is available for house parties, weddings and conferences.*
Website: www.belmount.net.

Yew Tree Farm

Coniston LA21 8DP
Tel: 015394 41433
Website: www.yewtree-farm.com

A 17th-century farmhouse in a perfect Lakeland setting. That's a pretty good start but there's more to come. Yew Tree Farm, with its attractive spinning gallery, was once owned by Beatrix Potter and in the 1930s she started a tea room here. Much of the furniture in the cosy flagstoned parlour was provided by the author.

The farm's National Trust tenants, Jon and Caroline Watson, keep Herdwick sheep and Belted Galloway cattle (see p86) so the lamb and beef is as local as the home-grown vegetables. Tea, coffee, hot chocolate and soft drinks are offered, as well as scones, seasonal cakes (£1.60–£2.20), sandwiches, soups, jacket potatoes (£5.95) and dishes like hot Herdwick baguettes (£5.95). The farming year is detailed on the reverse of the menu card and it's Jon and Caroline's keenness in connecting visitors with the land around and the food it produces which I really admire.

Open: *Easter–end Oct, daily 11–16, rest of year and local school holidays, weekends 11–16.*
Directions: *Yew Tree Farm is on the A593 between Ambleside and Coniston, about 2 miles (3.2km) north of Coniston. No parking at the farm but parking very close by. Bed and breakfast available.*

Page 165
Clockwise from top left: Chesters (see p178), Linthwaite House Hotel (see p16), Rothay Manor (see p12), Brysons (see p130), Lucy's on a Plate (see p160)
Below left and right: Jumping Jenny

Hawkshead
Poppi Red

Main Street, Hawkshead LA22 0NT
Tel: 015394 36434
Website: www.poppi-red.co.uk

'Stylish clothes, chic handbags, fabulous jewellery, unique home accessories,' it says on the outside of Poppi Red. No mention of a café but there's one here: six tables, and chairs with brightly coloured cushions, surrounded by the pinks, yellows, reds, blues and lime greens of all those gifts: glassware, jewellery, bowls, plates, mugs, lamps, cards, clothes, paper napkins and more. It's certainly a jolly place inside and owner Kim Merrick wants people to feel a bit spoilt when they come here.

Tea, coffee, soft drinks, soups (£3.95), sandwiches (£3.85), and snacks like smoked salmon with cream cheese, and ham with damson chutney are served, and there are flapjacks, shortbread and cupcakes with pretty, edible flowers on top. Homemade cakes (£2.30) are served on colourful heart-shaped plates and might include lemon sponge, Victoria sponge, carrot cake, and coffee and walnut sponge.

Mulled wine is offered in winter and Pimms, and Champagne and strawberries in summer. You can sip the Pimms and Champagne on the terrace outside and watch Hawkshead go by. Another Poppi Red shop is a few steps away.

Open: *daily 9–18.*

Above left: Yew Tree Farm
Below left: Poppi Red

Kendal

Abbot Hall Coffee Shop

Abbot Hall Art Gallery, Kendal LA9 5AL
Tel: 01539 722464
Website: www.lakelandartstrust.org.uk

It took more than 50 years to realise a vision for Abbot Hall but far less time for this Georgian mansion to turn into one of the finest small art galleries in the country. Not only is there a collection of furniture, paintings and objets d'art here but the changing exhibitions of art – works by Lucian Freud, Paula Rego, Stanley Spencer, Euan Uglow, Sean Scully, Bridget Riley, Walter Richard Sickert, Ben Nicholson, Prunella Clough and Maggi Hambling – have earned Abbot Hall a well deserved national reputation.

As with Blackwell, the Arts and Craft House at Windermere (see p161) also run by the Lakeland Arts Trust, the café aims to complement the gallery experience in what it offers. There are cakes, soups, sandwiches, light meals, tea, coffee, hot chocolate, soft drinks and beer.

Soups might be cauliflower and stilton (£3.20), sandwiches include prawn and mayonnaise (£3.75) and avocado with stilton dressing (£3.25). Morecambe Bay potted shrimps, smoked salmon and scrambled eggs (£5.75 and £5.95) and cheese ploughman's might also be on the menu. Everything is served in a room where there's usually a show of paintings, prints or photographs. A smaller café room adjoins.

Open: *daily Easter–Oct 10.30–17, Nov–Easter 10.30–16. Closed mid-Dec–mid-Jan.*

Artisan

Wainwright's Yard, Kendal LA9 4DP
Tel: 01539 742370
Website: www.booths.co.uk

Good food and good use of Cumbrian producers, attentive service and attractive surroundings – no wonder Artisan had to expand a bit to cope with demand. The café and restaurant is one part of an area below Booths store and is linked to it by staircase. It has a slate wall and windows down one side and its shelves of jams, chutneys, mustards and oils down another.

You can have tea, coffee, cakes, scones and lunches here, the cakes and pastries (£2–£2.50) coming from local producers like Ginger Bakers, Staff of Life and Country Fare, all named on the menu card. Some cakes are also made on the premises. Artisan breakfast (about £6) includes Richard Woodall's bacon, Booths breakfast sausage, beef tomato, black pudding, mushrooms and local free range eggs.

The café/restaurant offers salads, jacket potatoes, savouries like the ploughman's board (£8.75), and sandwiches. Sandwiches might have roast rib eye of beef (£5.95), or salt water prawns (£6.25). Main dishes include the very popular fish and chips, and the Cumberland sausage, with a choice of four different kinds of mash.

Desserts (all £3.75) include fruit crumble and sweet lemon curd posset. 'Excellent,' says a visitor about the food served at Artisan. And if you agree, don't forget the Cumbrian produce sold in the adjacent shop (see p128).

Open: *Mon–Sat 8–19, Sun 10–16.*

Tapestry Tearooms

Friends Meeting House, Stramongate, Kendal LA9 4BH
Tel: 01539 722975
Website: www.quaker-tapestry.co.uk

Considering Cumberland and Westmorland's long association with the Quakers it seemed entirely fitting that the Quaker Tapestry should find a permanent home in Kendal in 1994. The exhibition of 77 embroidered panels 'expressing Quaker insights and experiences over 350 years' was created by over 4,000 men, women and children in 15 different countries.

Right beside it is this 36-seat tea room which won a Vegetarian Society award in 2007 for the *best provision for vegetarians at a visitor attraction*. As you sit down you'll notice that most, if not all, of the seats have little brass plaques on them in memory of a person or some event.

You can have tea, coffee and soft drinks, homemade soups, sandwiches, baked potatoes (£4.75), light bites and daily specials (£5.95). Light bites might include scrambled eggs on toast for £2.95, specials could be creamy vegetable Laksa (a kind of stew/soup) with basmati rice or Tuscan style salad with artichoke hearts, olives and pasta.

Pudding of the week is £2.95–£3.50. Most meals can be made into children's portions. Other specials, such as afternoon tea for two – a cake and a scone with jam and cream, shared between two people, with a pot of tea for £5.95 – are something of a bargain.

Café open: *Mon–Fri (occasionally Mon–Sat) 10–16.30. Closed Bank Holidays.*

Waterside Wholefood

Kent View, Kendal LA9 4DZ
Tel: 01539 729743
Website: www.watersidewholefood.co.uk

'Great vegetarian café,' says one visitor. Overlooking the River Kent, with tables outside and a view to the hills, Toni Yates's café/restaurant/shop has been serving vegetarian and vegan wholefoods for more than a quarter of a century.

Tea, coffee, herbal fruit teas, organic hot chocolate, organic wines and beers are offered and so are homemade scones and cakes, the latter including sticky apricot cake, Yorkshire curd tart, carrot cake and chocolate cake. Soup of the day with a granary roll, a cheese bap or a cheese scone is £3.25, quiche of the day with side salad is £5.95. A salad counter offers three salads for £3.95 and a large salad plate for £5.95.

Main dishes, made daily on the premises, might include hot and spicy chilli on a bed of organic brown rice at £6.50. The café, which uses largely organic and Fairtrade ingredients, has a shop within that sells wholefoods, and an outside catering business. A noticeboard, just to the right as you enter, advertises all sorts of local groups and interests.

Open: *Mon–Sat 8.30–16.30.*

Don't forget that plenty of country house hotels (also some pubs) offer morning coffee and afternoon tea as well.

Kirkby Stephen

Church Gallery Coffee Lounge

3–7 Market Street, Kirkby Stephen CA17 4QS
Tel: 017683 72395

You may not think it's there but amidst the cards and candles, the jewellery, textiles and glassware are two rooms on the first floor where you can sit down and have a cup of tea or coffee. No matter that it's self-service because that's part of the charm. Cakes are on offer too, most of them locally made and organic: lemon cake (£1.50), chocolate cake (£1.50) and apple spice slice (£1), for instance.

There are sofas in one room, a wood burner in the other room and beamed ceilings in both. You'll find The Times, The Guardian, Private Eye, Hello and Good Housekeeping in the newspaper/magazine rack, and in warmer weather you can sit on an outside terrace and gaze across to the fine old church. Pay as you leave – owners Steve and Fiona Simkiss are trusting people – and check out other gifts for sale: pottery, handbags, prints, mirrors, rugs, scarves, garden torches and more.

Open: Mon–Sat 9–17, Sun 10.45–16.

Little Salkeld

The Watermill

Little Salkeld, near Penrith CA10 1NN
Tel: 01768 881523
Website: www.organicmill.co.uk

'There's a sense of discovery about coming here which people really like,' says Nick Jones who with his wife Ana has owned the tea room and 18th-century watermill for over 30 years. Once discovered, never forgotten. Housed in a former milking parlour, with old beams and a wood burning stove, it's cosy and comforting, the perfect match for the tasty and wholesome fare that is prepared just behind the counter. The mill itself produces a range of organic and bio-dynamic flours (see p97).

The café is organic and vegetarian, local suppliers like Howbarrow Organic Farm, South Lakes Organic Milk and Kate Gascoyne being listed on the menu. So too are eggs from the mill's smallholding. The bread is baked every day, using flour produced next door. What bread remains is sold off.

Tea, fruit tea, coffees, hot chocolate, cakes, flapjacks, chocolate brownies and scones are served, along with lunches. The latter might include Watermill rarebit (£6.50), homemade soup (£4.25), vegetarian chilli or Miller's lunch (£6.50) – homemade bread with bio-dynamic cheese from Loch Arthur near Dumfries (Camphill Village Trust), chutney and salad cream.

Open: daily Mar–Nov 10.30–17, Nov–Mar 10.30–dusk. Closed Christmas–mid-Jan.
Directions: The Watermill is 1.5 miles (2.4km) from Langwathby, off the A686 Penrith to Alston road.

Low Newton
Hat Trick Café

Yew Tree Barn, Low Newton,
Grange-over-Sands LA11 6JP
Tel: 015395 30577
Website: www.hattrickcafe.co.uk

Low Newton's been by-passed by the A590 but that's no excuse to miss out on the singular experience that is Hat Trick Café. Hats and helmets, hat boxes and clocks, and photographs of film stars, of early 20th-century street scenes and of old Citroen cars provide a theatrical backdrop to the tea, coffee, hot chocolate, cold drinks, cakes, breakfast and lunches that are served here.

The café, part flag-stoned, part carpeted, is run by Sam and Jane Clee (pictured right) and is located at Yew Tree Barn 'where art meets architectural salvage' (*www.yewtreebarn.co.uk*). The couple sell their own bottled lemonade, salad dressings, pickled garlic and flavoured oils and vinegars.

'Always cheerful chat,' says one visitor in the guest book. 'Really good homemade food', says another. That food includes Hat Trick Café's morning start which is served until 11.30: English breakfast, American breakfast, vegetarian breakfast, breakfast fishcakes (all £5.95) and such like. Lunch offers sandwiches, hot filled jacket potatoes, vegetarian soup of the day, fresh fish soup of the day (you don't see that in many cafés in Cumbria), potato skins with filling (£5.95) and Hat Trick's rarebit. Cakes, such as warm chocolate fudge cake and cream, moist walnut cake with maple syrup and cream, and creamy hazelnut cheesecake (all £3.25), are chalked up on a board.

Open: Mon–Fri 8–16.45, Sat 9–16.45, Sun 10.30–16.30 (slightly earlier closing in winter months).

Maryport

Her Citi

107 Crosby Street, Maryport CA15 6JX
Tel: 01900 810400
Website: www.herciti.co.uk

Annette Gibbons, author of Home Grown in Cumbria (see p96), recommended this place in Maryport and what a good find it is. Former London Centre for Fashion student Debbie Wright opened her 'eatery and interiors' in July 2006 at the time of the Maryport Blues Festival. This explains the first item on the menu, the Big Blues Bap: a generous filling of Lakeland dry-cured bacon, free range egg and Cumberland sausage, served in a homemade bap (£4.50).

The café's located in what was once Bobby Ritchie's, the grocers. A shuffling of his surname's letters came up with Her Citi. Eye-catching chandeliers hang from the high ceiling, there's artwork on the walls and a dresser holds the homemade cakes, scones and biscuits. The bread is made here too. Free range eggs are used in the cooking.

The café serves tea, coffee, hot chocolate, milkshakes and soft drinks, including Fentiman's lemonade, ginger beer, and dandelion and burdock. Light lunch bites have homemade soup (£2.95), sandwiches such as ham and Dijon mustard, and tuna and balsamic mayonnaise, toasted panini and salads – salade Niçoise and chicken Caesar salad are two.

Specials on the board could offer homemade Thai fish cakes, with noodles and salad (£4.95), and homemade sticky toffee pudding (£2.75). Theme nights – Italian, Thai, Indian, Taste of the Mediterranean, Hawaiian and others – are held once a month, some with live music.

__Open:__ Mon–Sat 9–17. Her Citi will open in the evenings for groups of 12 or more.

Mawbray Hayrigg

The Gincase

Mawbray Hayrigg, Silloth CA7 4LL
Tel: 016973 32020
Website: www.gincase.co.uk

A delightful oasis, close to the Solway coast, the Gincase is a popular licensed tea room, craft barn and gallery, owned by Val and John Nattrass. They serve teas, coffees and hot chocolate (often using Val's collection of old tea sets), cold drinks and scones and cakes. Egremont chocolate cake, lemon drizzle cake and coffee cake are all £1.90. The main menu – all the food is homemade – includes soup, savoury flans, ploughman's lunch, with either cheese or ham (£6.50), sandwiches and things for 'little people'.

There's a daily specials menu which could include chicken and ham pie with new potatoes and vegetables (£6.95) or Solway shrimp salad (£6.95). Once a week John adds his rare breed Cumberland sausage. Desserts like apple crumble, sherry trifle and baked cheesecake are all £3.25. In warmer weather you can sit in the garden, and there's a farm park here too.

__Open:__ Tue–Sun 10.30–16.30. Closed Mon except Bank Holidays.
__Directions:__ from Silloth take coast road B5300 south towards Maryport. Go through Beckfoot and at the end of the village you'll see brown signs pointing to Newtown and Mawbray Hayrigg.

Melmerby

The Village Bakery

Melmerby, Penrith CA10 1HE
Tel: 01768 881811
Website: www.village-bakery.com

One of the best known of all Cumbrian food names and winner of Cumbria Tourism's *Taste of Cumbria Award* 2008, The Village Bakery overlooks the large green in this fellside village. The popular café/restaurant, 'committed to organic food since 1976', the year the bakery was founded, is just past the bakeshop (see p133).

Two bright, cheerful rooms have views to the green, with a wood burner in the biggest of them. I like coming here when the place opens for the day, so my latest visit was just after 8.30 in the morning. The sun was streaming in through the window and freshly made scones were being arranged on wooden trays in the shop.

The clearly laid-out menu lists a choice of full breakfast (£9.75), sausage bap, raspberry porridge, vegetarian breakfast (£7.15), smoked salmon and scrambled egg (£6.75) and more. The café/restaurant also offers soups, sandwiches, main meals (steak and kidney pie £8.95; mozzarella, olive and pepper pizza £7.95), puddings, cakes, tea bread, leaf tea, coffee, soft drinks, wine and beer.

Puddings might be fruit pie of the day at £4.15 or bread and butter pudding at £4.25. A children's tea plate (£4.95), served from 15.00, includes a baby gingerbread man, a baby lemon muffin and a choice of small milkshakes. Many meals, says manager Chris Curry, are suitable for people with special dietary needs. A small art gallery is upstairs.

Open: Mon–Sat 8.30–17, Sun 9.30–17 (slightly shorter hours in winter).

Morland

Mill Yard Café

The Square, Morland, Penrith CA10 3AZ
Tel: 01931 714155
Website: www.millyardcafe.co.uk

The café was officially opened in 2007 by the then 97-year old Canon Gervase Markham, former vicar of Morland. Those present will never forget his 40-minute potted history of the village, delivered with humour and without a note. It's his son Freddy, chairman of the first ever Cumbria and Lake District Food and Drink Festival in 2004, who decided to convert a 200 year old building beside Morland Beck into this bright, cheerful café.

Downstairs, two oak-beamed rooms have tables, three sofas and some easy chairs between them, while upstairs – with its lovely Morland oak floor – are more tables, and original paintings and prints on the wall by artist Alan Stones. The café serves leaf tea, Fairtrade coffee, soft drinks, local beers, wines and spirits. On weekdays, you get soups of the day with homemade bread (£3.95), quiches, fish cakes, jacket potatoes, sandwiches, Morland burgers (£5.95) and changing specials till 15.00. From 15–17 afternoon tea is available, with cakes, scones or toasted teacakes. On Sundays, brunches (including full English breakfast, unlimited tea and coffee, croissants and toast etc, £9.95) go from 9.30–15, with tea till 17.00.

Local foods plus frozen soups and frozen meals are sold for taking away. On warmer days there are tables and chairs in the pretty mill yard, with shady awning. Visitors can also explore the 4-acre garden (1.6 hectares) of Morland House next door. Café rooms can be booked for meetings and functions.

Open: Mon–Sat 10–17, Sun (with newspapers for sale) 9–17.
Directions: Morland is 7 miles (11.2km) south east of Penrith.

Old Town

Kitridding Tea Room

Old Town, near Kirkby Lonsdale LA6 2QA
Tel: 015395 67484
Website: www.kitridding.co.uk

The menu can't make it clearer. 'The ethos at Kitridding is to use as much of our own farm produce, along with other carefully selected, locally produced food and drink as possible'. This means plenty of home cured bacon, homemade sausages and burgers, and lamb and beef from Stewart and Christine Lambert's farm.

The oak-floored tea room, next to the farm shop (see p133), serves teas, coffees, cold drinks and scones with butter and Sue Prickett's raspberry jam (£1.40). There's the Kitridding breakfast (£5.95) and a vegetarian option (£5.50), soups, savoury snacks, toasted sandwiches, omelettes, jacket potatoes, quiches, salads, Kitridding's ploughman's (£5.95) and dishes like Cumberland sausage (£6.50), cottage pie, Whitby scampi and more.

Open: *Fri–Sun 10–17 (last orders 16.30).*
Directions: *the farm is on the B6254 on the Kendal side of Old Town.*

Orton (Carlisle)

Orton Grange

Orton, Dalston, Carlisle CA5 6LA
Tel: 01228 711410
Website: www.ortongrange.co.uk

They were blessed with wonderful stone barns, and once the buildings were redundant, Claire Scott and her brother Richard Martin made perfect use of them. Where animals and machinery used to stand, there's now a gift and farm shop, a shop for quilting and patchwork enthusiasts (Quiltessentials), a swimming pool, a meeting room, a hair salon and a café on two floors. Downstairs in the light-filled café are tables and chairs, upstairs on the two mezzanine levels – one at each end of the barn, linked by a glass-sided walkway – there are sofas and a grand piano.

You can get tea, coffee, hot chocolate, soft drinks, beer, cakes (£1.50), scones, soup, sandwiches (£3.75), bagels (£4), panini, baked potatoes and daily specials. Fillings for the sandwiches include Cumbrian ham, cheese, tomato, salad, and smoked salmon.

Orton Grange has about 180 cows, producing over 2.5 million pints of milk a year. Some of the milk goes into its own ice cream, also sold here. There's a farm trail as well.

Open: *Mon–Sat 10–17, Sun and Bank Holidays 11–16.*
Closed for two weeks from Christmas Eve.
Directions: *Orton Grange is on the A595, south west of Carlisle.*

Rydal

Old School Room Tea Shop

Rydal Hall, Ambleside LA22 9LX
Tel: 015394 32050
Website: www.rydalhall.org

Once a place of study for young le Flemings, the family who owned Rydal Hall for four centuries, the old school room was attractively rebuilt in 2007. It's right beside Rydal Falls and a few steps from Rydal Hall's famous gardens, which were restored to their original Thomas Mawson design in the last couple of years. The tea room itself, which has oak beams, a slate floor, big windows and textile art on the stone walls, offers tea, coffee, cold drinks, soups, sandwiches, scones, cakes and cream teas.

Sandwiches (like organic crumbly cheese with Westmorland chutney or tuna mayonnaise) are about £3.50, cakes, flapjacks and shortbread are £1.90–£2.20 and cream teas £3.50. Tea shop policy is to serve fairly traded and local produce wherever possible. There are two sofas at one end near a wood burning stove which throws out a fair heat.

Rydal Hall has belonged to the Diocese of Carlisle since the 1960s and is used for retreats, conferences and holidays, with private guests welcome. The gardens are open to the public and certainly worth a visit. Rydal Mount, William Wordsworth's home for the last 37 years of his life, is just across the road.

Open: *daily 10–17.00 (shorter hours during winter).*

Sedbergh

Weavers Café

Farfield Mill Arts and Heritage Centre, Sedbergh LA10 5LW
Tel: 015396 21958
Website: www.farfieldmill.org

Close to the Book Town of Sedbergh, right beside the River Clough and within sight of the Howgill Fells stands delightful Farfield Mill. For over 100 years it was a thriving spinning and weaving mill, now it's home to some 20 artists and craft makers whose work is displayed on three of the building's four floors, alongside that of many other makers. Two Dobcross looms, which work on most days of the week, can be seen through an internal window in the café.

Tea, coffee and soft drinks are served, as well as homemade scones, cakes (from £1.20), soups, sandwiches, jacket potatoes (all less than £5) and main dishes. Sandwiches might have smoked salmon and cream cheese or Cumberland ham with wholegrain mustard. Weavers' brunches include a slice of crusty bread, lightly grilled and topped with two field mushrooms, crispy bacon and poached egg or two Cumbrian potato cakes, topped with oak smoked salmon and poached egg. A vegetarian option is offered each day, as well as a daily special.

Open: *daily 10–17.*
Directions: *Farfield Mill is 1 mile (1.6km) east of Sedbergh on the A684 to Hawes.*

Sizergh

Low Sizergh Farm Tea Room

Low Sizergh Farm, Sizergh, Kendal LA8 8AE
Tel: 015395 60426
Website: www.low-sizergh-barn.co.uk

Don't be fooled. The tea room TV is not there for Champions League football or day time chat shows. For those not close enough to overlook the parlour below, the screen relays the milking of Low Sizergh's 150 dairy cows. And if you want to know more, there are helpful notes about the cattle and the farm (why each cow is numbered, how much milk they give, how the milking machine works etc) on a nearby dresser. I love these thoughtful touches about Low Sizergh and the evident care for the food here.

'The day starts early on the farm but the kitchen is bursting with activity too, as the day's baking gets underway,' says the menu. That menu offers tea, Fairtrade coffees, milk shakes, soft drinks, sandwiches, toasted sandwiches, soup, jacket potatoes, quiches with salad (£6.25) and the Low Sizergh breakfast.

Sandwiches (£4.95), served with a salad garnish, might be honey roast Cumberland ham, Low Sizergh Farm organic egg with cress, or Kendal Creamy cheese which is made with the farm's organic milk. Soups, like cream of mushroom; potato and watercress; or vegetable barley broth, are about £3.70; jacket potatoes with salad £4.50–£6. An excellent bacon bap (the bacon from Mansergh Hall), plus a pot of leaf tea, should give you change from £5. Children's sandwiches with crunchy potato chips are available too for £1.95.

Specials of the day are chalked up on blackboards, two of the boards in the shape of a cow. The friendly 60–70 seat tea room is located, like the farm shop (see p140), in an 18th-century Westmorland barn. A note on the paper napkin encourages you to 'walk the farm trail, taste our organic dairy products, cook with Growing Well's farm-grown organic vegetables'. The trail starts just outside by the car park.

Open: *daily 9–17.30 (closes slightly earlier Jan–Easter).*
Directions: *4 miles (6.4 km) south of Kendal on the A591.*

Skelwith Bridge

Chesters Café by the River

Skelwith Bridge, Ambleside LA22 9NJ
Tel: 015394 32553
Website: www.chesters-cafebytheriver.co.uk

For over 21 years Chesters has been a familiar name at
Skelwith Bridge, originating as a small café in what was then
Kirkstone Galleries. The galleries later became Touchstone
Interiors and then in late 2007, Chesters Shop by the River.
The café sits alongside the shop, the two of them creating a
very tempting attraction in this part of the Lake District.

There's a great look and feel to the café which was
partly inspired by a restaurant in the French Alps. It's got big
exposed beams, lots of windows (which overlook the wooden-
decked terrace, right beside the River Brathay), and a
part-timbered, part-Kirkstone slate floor. There's a wood
burning stove and two sofas beside it, separated by a low
table on which lie newspapers and magazines. Two big
mirrors are on the wall, four ironwork chandeliers hang from
the ceiling, and jugs, lanterns and old bellows are placed here
and there.

You order your food at the long and deep bar/counter and
give staff your table number. Drinks served include tea, coffee,
hot chocolate, wines, spirits and beers. Tag Lag from nearby
Barngates Brewery is one of the beers. Right from the start,
cakes – toffee apple cake; sticky stem ginger sponge; apricot
and almond puff pastry tart; and Bakewell tart, for example
– have been a big thing at Chesters, made from 'good, old
fashioned, traditional recipes, granny knew best,' as it says on
the menu.

The menu also tells people where the meat for main
dishes (served 12–16) comes from: game and sausages from
Cartmel Valley Game Supplies, all other meat from Higginsons
butchers in Grange. The dishes themselves include ham hock
and pea pie with roasted Chantenay carrots; wild mushroom
and spinach pizza with toasted pine nuts (both £8.50),
Jerusalem artichoke and blue cheese risotto with char grilled
courgette; or smoked haddock and caramelised leek chowder
(both £7.95).

Because this place is so popular a few café tables are in
the shop, which itself sells a small amount of food stuff. Both
are owned by Karen Lawrence and Steph Barton. Steph also
has the nearby Drunken Duck Inn (see p45).

Café open: *daily 9.30–17.30.*
Directions: *Skelwith Bridge is on the A593 Ambleside to
Coniston road.*

Staveley

Wilf's Café

Mill Yard, Back Lane, Staveley LA8 9LR
Tel: 01539 822329
Website: www.wilfs-cafe.co.uk

Well known and well patronised, Wilf's Café was one of the original food businesses on this Mill Yard estate, located in a part of the old bobbin mill, which operated here for over 100 years. A big glass entrance area has the ordering counter to the left and a small number of tables and chairs, while there are sofas in a back room and two more rooms upstairs. An outside terrace overlooks the River Kent. There's artwork on the walls and, for the walkers and cyclists who frequent the café, one or two large-scale maps as well.

A big blackboard behind the counter lists many of the hot drinks, salads and dishes – such as soup of the day (£3.25), Wilf's famous veggie chilli, hot Cumbrian chicken salad (£6.25) and Wilf's rarebits (£4.30–£5.75) – which are available. Another blackboard names the day's specials which could be vegetable crumble or beef moussaka (both £6.25). The menu card lists the breakfast offerings, the snacks, salads, hot drinks, children's menu and more. You can take food through an internal door to the Staveley Beer Hall or bring beer back to have with your meal.

The café, owned by Iain Williamson and Charlotte Webb, puts on slide and supper evenings early in the year, and speciality food evenings (Cuban, Turkish, Mexican, Italian, French). The business can provide buffets for all occasions away from the café and you can also order 'Wilf's Away' meals to take away. The venue is available for evening hire.

Open: *daily 9.30–17 but some seasonal variations.*

Ulverston

Gillam's Tea Room

64 Market Street, Ulverston LA12 7LT
Tel: 01229 587564
Website: www.gillams-tearoom.co.uk

For over 100 years JJ Gillam sold groceries to the people of Ulverston and around. The shop closed in 1994 but 12 years later, when JJ's great nephew, Doug, and his wife Shirley opened this tea room, the surname appeared on the property directly opposite.

Enthusiastic and welcoming, the couple are committed to organic and fairly traded produce. The menu includes soups (£3.20), sandwiches, toasted sandwiches, jacket potatoes, salads (about £5.95), cakes and scones. Fruit scones come with a choice of strawberry, raspberry, damson, blackcurrant, gooseberry or plum jam.

Specials might include roasted courgette and red onion quiche with jacket potato and side salad (£5.95). This being a member of the UK Tea Council's Tea Guild, Gillams serves a variety of teas and coffees. There are also soft drinks, beers, cider and wines.

Doug and Shirley are described as 'lovely people' by one visitor and nothing better illustrates their care for customers than the Little Gillams Tea Party (£3.95) which is on offer for children: cucumber or tomato sandwiches, small scone with strawberry preserve and fresh cream, a gingerbread biscuit, a pot of raisins and a dainty cake, served on a silver tray with a teapot of water and a jug of apple, blackcurrant or orange juice concentrate.

Open: *Mon–Sat 9–17, Sun 10–16.*

Windermere

First Floor Café

Lakeland Limited, Alexander Buildings
Station Precinct, Windermere LA23 1BQ
Tel: 015394 88200
Website: www.lakeland.co.uk

Upstairs from Lakeland's flagship store is this very busy café, its long, curving glass front almost giving it the appearance of an ocean-going liner. A small area at one end of the place has leather tub chairs, the rest is given over to tables and chairs. First Floor is run by Steven Doherty, former head chef of Le Gavroche in London, the restaurant where he retained three Michelin stars in the five years he was in charge.

You can get teas, coffees, hot chocolate, soft drinks, beer, wine and cider. Morning food includes smoked salmon and cream cheese croissant (£3.95), mushrooms on granary or white toast (£3.25) and locally smoked kipper (£5.95). There are soups, sandwiches, filled baguettes, baked potatoes, scones and cakes. Lunchtime specials have such dishes as char-grilled chicken Caesar salad with bacon and soft boiled egg (£5.75), or pan fried fillet of salmon with a creamy Thai curry sauce (£7.95).

Pasta, jacket potatoes, sausage and beans, and fillet of salmon are some of the items on the children's menu. Local suppliers like Claire's Handmade, Farmer Sharp, English Lakes Ice Cream and Cartmel Valley Game Supplies are listed on the back of the menu. No reservations can be made and a pager system operates when the café is really busy. A display at the bottom of the stairs indicates how long you might have to wait for a table.

Open: *Mon–Fri 9–18, Sat 9–17, Sun 10.30–16.*

Although the examples from menus – and the prices – were correct at the time of going to print, they can change over the months. Owners of places may also change.

Francine's Coffee House and Restaurant

27 Main Road, Windermere LA23 1DX
Tel: 015394 44088
Website: www.francinesrestaurantwindermere.co.uk

Francine's is a very well liked café/restaurant, an eatery that would not feel out of place in France or Italy. 'Delicious red lentil, coriander and sweet chilli soup, interesting choice on the menu, very welcoming atmosphere,' reports one visitor. The day starts with the big breakfast (£6), vegetarian breakfast (£6) and breakfast ciabattas, and works its way through morning coffee, cakes, scones, lunch, afternoon tea and, on five nights a week, dinner. Classical and ambient music plays lightly in the background.

Sandwiches include Parma ham with Dolcelatte and plum tomatoes, or pastrami and Wensleydale; lunch offers fresh mussels, confit duck leg, chicken Caesar salad, and crab cake and smoked salmon salad (all £7.95) and more. Lobster thermidor or grilled lobster (whole £32, half £16) is available at both lunchtime and dinner. Ballotine of salmon (£14.95) is another possibility for dinner.

'Seafood is our passion,' say Francine Donaldson and Graeme Wells, who have run the coffee house for four years. They also have plenty of game when in season. Most meals are gluten-free (gluten-free bread is served as well) and vegetarian options are available. Complementary canapés come with dinner, for which you might go for clementine and ginger pudding or pineapple Tarte Tatin to finish.

Coffee house open: *Tue–Sun 10–16.30; restaurant open Wed–Sun 18.30–23.30 but in low season Francine's may close Sun evening. Booking advisable for evening meals.*

Above right: Steven Doherty from First Floor Café. Picture by Helen Whitaker
Right: Francine's Coffee House and Restaurant

More Cafés, Tea Rooms and Café/Restaurants

Alston

Gossipgate Gallery

The Butts, Alston CA9 3JU
Tel: 01434 381806
Website www.gossipgate-gallery.co.uk
Set within this well established gallery, the Gaslight Café offers sandwiches and light bites (using as much organic produce as possible) and cakes made by Alston's Moody Baker. The gallery sells a range of artwork, with changing exhibitions.

Ambleside

Brambles Café

Chapel Stile, Great Langdale LA22 9JE
Tel: 015394 37500
The Langdale Co-op at Chapel Stile – a few miles from Ambleside – was established in 1884 and it's through the shop and up the stairs that you'll find Brambles Café. Gaze at the great views as you savour breakfast, cakes, scones, soups, sandwiches and snacks.

Rattle Gill Café

2 Bridge Street, Ambleside LA22 9DU
Tel: 015394 34403
Within months of honeymooning in Cumbria in 2007, Gareth and Carly Harding packed up their jobs in the south and took over this small café. They offer cakes, scones, soups, sandwiches, snacks, salads, main dishes, a children's menu and the 'Hungry Hiker' packed lunch. Organic milk is used and soya milk is available too.

Appleby

Bojangles

10 Bridge Street, Appleby CA16 4QH
Tel: 017683 52662
Website: www.bojangles-appleby.co.uk
The conversion of this former sports shop won a design award in 2007. There are leather sofas and tub chairs in the oak-floored front room and artwork on the walls. Breakfast, snacks, sandwiches, salads, cakes and lunches are all served.

Barrow-in-Furness

The Custom House

1 Abbey Road, Barrow LA14 5UF
Tel: 01229 823823
Website: www.1abbeyroad.co.uk
The bar/restaurant on the ground floor serves breakfast, snacks, lunch and dinner. Newspapers are available to read and there's internet access in the building. 'Food is good, staff are brilliant and it's very child friendly,' says one visitor.

Brampton

Boathouse Tearoom

Talkin Tarn, near Brampton CA8 1HN
Tel: 016977 41050
Talkin Tarn country park is a popular walking and rowing spot within sight of the Pennines. The tea room, owned by Carlisle City Council, overlooks the glacier-formed tarn and offers cakes, sandwiches, soups, salads and hot snacks.

Lanercost Tearooms

Lanercost Priory, near Brampton CA8 2HQ
Tel: 07821 867496
The enchanting setting of Lanercost Priory near Brampton belies its troubled history. Founded in the 1160s, the canons' peaceful life was often violently interrupted by raiding Scots. Edward I spent his last winter alive here in 1306–7. The tea rooms beside the Priory, open from spring 2009, serve cakes, snacks, sandwiches and lunch.

Carlisle

Eden Coffee Lounge

Wetheral, near Carlisle CA4 8ES
Tel: 07851 313700
Elaine Armstrong's small café, in a village just to the south east of Carlisle by the River Eden, offers soup, sandwiches, snacks, cakes and light lunches. The café does outside catering too. Next door is an equally friendly village shop/post office selling fruit, vegetables and Cumbrian produce.

High Head Sculpture Valley

High Head Farm, Ivegill, Carlisle CA4 0PJ
Tel: 016974 73552
Website: www.highheadsculpturevalley.co.uk
This working dairy farm, about 9 miles (14.4km) south of Carlisle, has a gallery, a 'sculpture valley' and a tea room where you can get scones, cakes, soup, sandwiches, snacks and hot meals.

Linton Tweeds

Shaddon Mills, Carlisle CA2 5TZ
Tel: 01228 527569
Website: www.lintontweeds.co.uk
Homemade cakes are the big thing at the Bobbin Coffee Shop (other food served too), while designer fabrics and women's clothes are sold in the room next door. Over the years Chanel has been Linton Tweeds' most famous client.

John Watt & Son

11 Bank Street, Carlisle CA3 8HG
Tel: 01228 521545
Website:
www.victoriancoffeeshop.co.uk
Watt's has been a name in Carlisle since 1865, starting as a grocers and then becoming a tea and coffee merchants. You can buy a range of teas and coffees in the shop area; the café serves cakes, soups, snacks and sandwiches.

Cockermouth

Merienda

7a Station Street, Cockermouth CA13 9QW
Tel: 01900 822790
Website: www.merienda.co.uk
There's artwork on the walls to buy, newspapers to read and a sofa to relax on. Live music is held on Friday nights. Breakfast and lunch are served, along with cakes, sandwiches and snacks.

Coniston

Bluebird Café

Lake Road, Coniston LA21 8AN
Tel: 015394 41649
Website: www.thebluebirdcafe.co.uk
The café (and outside seating) is right beside Coniston Water with views across to John Ruskin's home of Brantwood. It serves cakes, soup, sandwiches, salads and snacks

Grange-over-Sands

Hazelmere Café and Bakery

1-2 Yewbarrow Terrace, Grange-over-Sands LA11 6ED
Tel: 015395 32972
Website: www.hazelmerecafe.co.uk
The café has several awards for excellence from the UK Tea Council's Tea Guild, including the award for *Top Afternoon Tea* in 2006. Almost 40 varieties of tea are offered, each one described on the menu. You can get breakfast, soup, sandwiches, lunch and cream teas as well. Next door is the Hazelmere Bakery.

Grasmere

Green's Café and Bistro

College Street, Grasmere LA22 9SZ
Tel: 015394 35790
A map on the wall outside shows where Green's local suppliers are based. The café itself serves cakes, salads, sandwiches, snacks and hot meals. A lot of food is gluten free.

Kendal

Brewery Arts Centre

Highgate, Kendal LA9 4HE
Tel: 01539 725133
Website: www.breweryarts.co.uk
A new addition to this arts complex in late 2008, the Warehouse Café is a café bar with a small cinema screen. There are plenty of leather chairs and sofas on which to sit and enjoy coffee, crêpes and snacks. The Brewery also has the Intro Café Bar, the Vats Bar and the Grain Store Restaurant (see p21).

Hideaway Coffee House

Cow Brow, Lupton, near Kendal LA6 1PF
Tel: 015395 67434
Website:
www.hideawaycoffeehouse.co.uk
The coffee house and large garden area are close to junction 36 of the M6, with views towards the Lancaster Canal. You'll find sandwiches, light snacks, cakes and 'kids bites' on offer.

Keswick

Café-Bar 26

26 Lake Road, Keswick CA12 5DQ
Tel: 017687 80863
Website: www.cafebar26.co.uk
This is a café/restaurant by day – serving lunch – and a wine and cocktail bar in the evening. There's live music on Thursday nights.

The cafés, tea rooms and café/restaurants on these pages are grouped around the nearest biggest place. Opening days and times vary, so it's best to check first if travelling far.

The Flock-In

*Yew Tree Farm, Rosthwaite,
Keswick CA12 5XB
Tel: 017687 77675
Website:
www.borrowdaleyewtreefarm.co.uk*
The tea room is on a working farm and
there are great views of Borrowdale
from its garden. You can get soups,
snacks, sandwiches, Herdi-burgers
(Herdwick meat) and cakes. Herdwick
meat, chutneys and jellies are sold to
take away.

Good Taste

*19 Lake Road, Keswick CA12 5BS
Tel: 017687 75973
Website: www.simplygoodtaste.co.uk*
Downstairs is a deli while upstairs is
the coffee shop where you can have
croissants, sandwiches, salads and
snacks. The Good Taste range of jams
and chutneys is sold in the deli.

Lakeland Pedlar Wholefood Café

*Bell Close, Keswick CA12 5JD
Tel: 017687 74492
Website: www.lakelandpedlar.co.uk*
This well known vegetarian café
(and bike centre) offers cakes, soups,
sandwiches, snacks and more. There
are beers from the Keswick Brewing
Company, and organic beers and
wines too.

Old Sawmill Tearoom

*Mirehouse, Underskiddaw,
Keswick CA12 4QE
Tel: 017687 74317
Website: www.theoldsawmill.co.uk*
The tea room is at Dodd Wood, close
to Mirehouse. This historic home, just
north of Keswick, has connections to
William Wordsworth, Alfred Tennyson,
Robert Southey and Thomas Carlyle.
The tea room serves homemade snacks,
lunches, cakes and scones.

Siskins Café

*Whinlatter Forest Park, Braithwaite,
Keswick CA12 5TW
Tel: 017687 78410*
A siskin (finch) appears on each price
tag for the homemade cakes at this
delightfully located café. You can
get 'early birds' breakfast, soup,
sandwiches (design your own with
different fillings), salads and a lot more.
If you have half portions of items from
the main menu and sandwich board
you'll pay half price.

Kirkby Lonsdale

Avanti

*57 Main Street, Kirkby Lonsdale
LA6 2AH
Tel: 015242 73500
Website: www.baravanti.com*
Attractive and popular, this café/
restaurant serves snacks, lunches and
evening meals. There's artwork on
the walls, leather chairs, decorative
ironwork and a floor to ceiling window
at the rear, overlooking a garden where
you can sit. Avanti has a crêperie here
as well.

Penrith

Bewick Coffee House and Bistro

*Princes Street, Penrith CA11 7BJ
Tel: 01768 864764*
Named after the famous
Northumberland wood engraver,
Thomas Bewick, this café/restaurant is
located in a former chapel. Breakfast,
cakes, sandwiches, soups and light
lunches are offered and the Bewick
is also open for dinner on Saturday
evenings.

Dalemain

*near Penrith CA11 0HB
Tel: 017684 86450
Website: www.dalemain.com*
The tea room is in the medieval hall
of this historic home near Ullswater.
You can have snacks, sandwiches,
filled Yorkshire puddings, and what
Dalemain describes as its 'wonderful'
chocolate cake.

Larch Cottage Nurseries

*Melkinthorpe, Penrith CA10 2DR
Tel: 01931 712404
Website:
www.larchcottagenurseries.com*
Set up over 25 years ago, Larch Cottage
Nurseries (south of Penrith) has a huge
selection of plants, a range of statuary,
an art gallery and the Greenhouse
Restaurant and Wine Bar, serving
morning coffee, lunch and afternoon
tea. It's open for dinner on Saturday
evenings.

Mosedale Meeting House

Mosedale, Penrith CA11 0XQ
Tel: 017687 79397 (caretakers)
Homemade soup, cakes, biscuits and shepherd's lunch are served in this delightful 300-year old Quaker building, a few miles west of Penrith. There's very limited opening, from July to mid-September, and then only at certain times Thu–Sun.

Narrowbar Café

13 Devonshire Street, Penrith CA11 7SR
Tel: 01768 891417
Website: www.narrowbarcafe.co.uk
Called the Narrowbar for obvious reasons, the café serves breakfast, cakes, soup, sandwiches, salads and snacks. Wi-Fi is available, and there's artwork on the walls which you can buy.

Number 15

15 Victoria Road, Penrith CA11 8HN
Tel: 01768 867453
Right opposite the well known John Norris fishing shop, this café, with its good mix of customers, has one room at the front and a bigger room at the back. Soups, sandwiches, toasted ciabatta, salads, snacks and more are available, as is Wi-Fi. The artwork on the walls is for sale.

The cafés, tea rooms and café/restaurants on these pages are grouped around the nearest biggest place. Opening days and times vary, so it's best to check first if travelling far.

Ullswater Steamers

The Pier House, Glenridding, Penrith CA11 0US.
Tel: 017684 82229
Website: www.ullswater-steamers.co.uk
You get lovely views of Ullswater from the small pier house tea rooms at Glenridding and Pooley Bridge. Food cruises on the steamers are run on certain dates over the summer months.

Ulverston

Gleaston Watermill

Gleaston, near Ulverston LA12 0QH
Tel: 01229 869244
Website: www.watermill.co.uk
Dusty Miller's is in the old shippon at this 18th-century watermill, with farming implements, old violins and other objects dotted about the place. Breakfast, soups, sandwiches, snacks, cakes and 'comfort puddings' are offered. A wide range of food is gluten free. Children get farm animal crockery to use.

Hot Mango Café

27 King Street, Ulverston LA12 7DZ
Tel: 01229 584866
'Best café in the Lakes', says one visitor and even if the geography's not strictly accurate there's plenty of praise for Hot Mango. Emma and Graham Carrick's ethos of using fresh, local, quality produce as the basis of their food most certainly appeals. Homemade cakes (chalked up), croissants, breakfast, soups, salads, sandwiches, snacks and lunches are all available. The menu changes regularly.

World Peace Café

5 Cavendish Street, Ulverston LA12 7AD
Tel: 01229 587793
Website: www.worldpeacecafe.org
Set up by the Manjushri Buddhist Centre at Conishead Priory in 2002, this organic, vegetarian café offers cakes, soup, sandwiches, snacks and main meals. There's a toy box for children, and books (library and shop) on meditation and Buddhism for adults. Upstairs is a meditation centre, outside a garden.

Windermere

Rambla

Ellerthwaite Square, Windermere LA23 1DP
Tel: 015394 48443
Website: www.ramblabistro.co.uk
Opened by Nathan and Hannah Davies and chef James Byrne in 2008, this welcoming café/bistro serves soups (including fish soup), salads, sandwiches and snacks by day and main meals by night. There are changing exhibitions of artwork (for sale) and newspapers to read.

Above: sheep gathered near Blencathra

Map 187

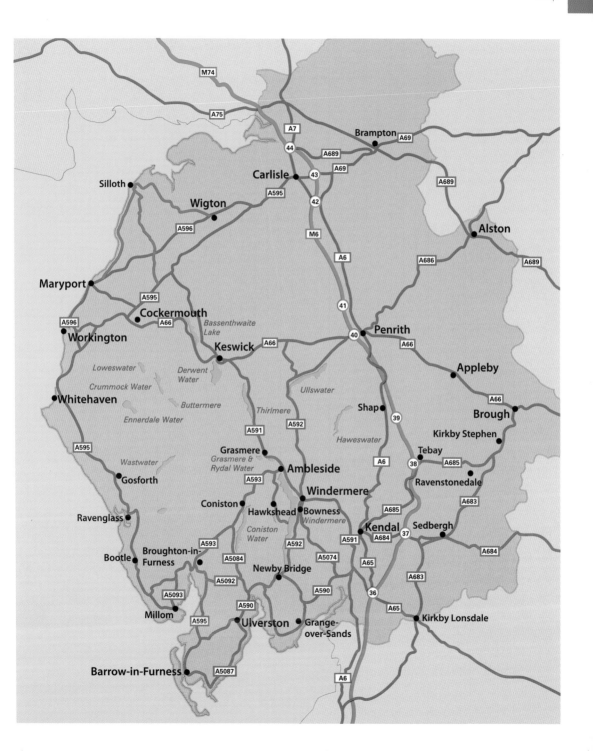

AA Rosette 10, 14, 22, 23, 24,35, 36, 39, 40, 41, 45, 59, 74, 93
Abbot Hall Coffee Shop, Kendal **168**
Abbott Lodge Jersey Ice Cream, Clifton, near Penrith 89
Acorn Bank, Wetheral **150**
Ainsworth Specialist Grocers, Grange-over-Sands 95, **124**
Airey's Farm Shop, near Low Newton 84, **147**
Alston 10, 93, 112, 182
Alston Wholefoods 88, **112**
Ambleside 11, 12, 13, 37, 44, 45, 72, 113, 114, 160, 182
Angel Inn, Bowness-on-Windermere **73**, 100
Appleby 72, 109, 114, 182
Artisan, Kendal 90, 91, 94, 95, 98, 99, **128**, 138, 168
www.artisan-food.com 108
Askerton Castle Estate, near Brampton 78, 83
Augill Castle, near Kirkby Stephen 40, **151**
Augill Little Cooks 151
Avanti, Kirkby Lonsdale **184**
The Bakeshop, Melmerby **133**
Barbon Inn, Barbon 74
Barngates Brewery/beers **45**, 47, 55, 64, 166, 178
Barrow-in-Furness 72, 182
Bassenthwaite Lake 46, 152
Baycliffe Farm Shop **147**
Bay Horse Inn, Ulverston **69**, **150**
Bay Restaurant, Ambleside **11**, 29
beer festivals 71
The Beer Hall, Staveley **65**, 179
Bell's Fishmongers and Cumbrian Game, Carlisle **118**
Bells of Lazonby **120**, 133, 136
Bennett's Solway Shrimps **108**
Bessy Beck Trout Fishery **108**, 155
Bewick Coffee House and Bistro, Penrith **184**
Bistro Déjà Vu, Kendal **39**
Bitter End, Cockermouth **52**, 56
Black Bull Inn and Hotel, Coniston **54**, 100
Blacksmiths Arms, Broughton Mills **47**, 58,
Blacksmiths Arms, Talkin **68**, 101, 104
Black Swan Hotel, Ravenstonedale **60**, 64
Black Swan Inn, Culgaith **75**
Blackwell, Bowness-on-Windermere 14, **161**, 168
Bluebird Café, Coniston **183**
Boathouse Tearoom, Talkin Tarn **182**
Bojangles, Appleby **182**
Booths stores 85, 90, 93, 94, 97, **128**, 129, 168
Bootle 58, 114, 160
Border County Foods 81, **108**
Borough Market, London 80, 85, **122**, 123
Bowness-on-Windermere 14, 16, 73, 147, 161
Bower House Inn, Eskdale **74**
Brambles Café, Chapel Stile **182**
Brampton 17, 56, 68, 78, 88, 99, 101, 115, 182
Bread Matters **151**
Brewery Arts Centre, Kendal 21, 102, **183**
Bridge Street Restaurant, Kendal **21**
Britannia Inn, Elterwater **57**, 100, 102
Brookside Taste of the Lakes 84, **139**
Brougham Hall Foods **139**
Broughton-in-Furness 47, 58, 73, 115
Broughton Village Bakery **115**
Brown Horse Farm Shop, Winster **147**
Brown Horse Inn, Winster **73**, 147
Brunswick Deli, Penrith **135**
Bryson's of Keswick **130**
Burbush Penrith **90**, 119
Burgundy's Wine Bar, Kendal **62**
Butchers **142**
Buttermere 22, 63
The Byre, Bootle **160**

Café-Bar 26, Keswick **183**
Caldbeck 162
Campaign for Real Ale (CAMRA) 47, 52, 56, **58**, 60, 62, 63, 66, 71, 73, 100
Cark-in-Cartmel 117, 163
Carleton Farm Shop, near Penrith 78, 82, 90, 91, **135**
Carlisle 37, 58, 73, 78, 88, 108, 118, 119, 120,147, 164, 182, 183
Carlisle and District State Management Scheme 48
Carrs Flour Mills 108
Cartmel 18, 49, 90, 121
Cartmel Fell 50
Cartmel Sticky Toffee Pudding Company 90, 121, 127
Cartmel Valley Game Supplies and Smokehouse 11, 14, 41, 49, 106, **108**, 117, 178, 180
Cartmel Village Shop 85, 90, 98, 99, **121**
Cask Marque/Cask Marque Trust 71
Castle Green Hotel, Kendal **22**
Cavendish Arms, Cartmel 49
Chesters Café by the River, Skelwith Bridge **178**
Church Gallery Coffee Lounge, Kirkby Stephen 170
Church House Inn, Torver **68**, 102
Churchmouse Cheeses, Kirkby Lonsdale 82, 88, 91, 94, 99, **132**
Claire's Handmade **93**, 114, 119, 123, 127, 180
Clifton, near Penrith 52
Cockermouth 18, 22, 52, 73, 147, 183
Coniston 54, 68, 73, 86, 100,
Coniston Brewing Company/beers 46, 52, **54**, 56, 57, 58, 62, 63, 72, 73, 74, **100**, 119, 121, 160, 166
Coniston Water 68, 166, 183
Cook in Cumbria **152**
Cornerwise of Keswick **131**
Country Fare **91**, 117, 168
Country Puddings **91**, 133
Courtyard Café, Holker Hall 117, **163**
Cowmire Hall Damson Gin **98**, 117
Cranstons Cumbrian Food Hall, Penrith 81, 82, 84, 85, 91, 93, **136**, 138
Cream of Cumbria 106, **108**, 112, 115
Croft Farm Meats, near Carlisle 78, 83, 164
Crosby Lodge Country House Hotel, near Carlisle 37, 120
Cross Keys Temperance Inn, Cautley 51
Crosthwaite, Lyth Valley 55, 98
Cumberland Honey Mustard **93**, 112, 119, 127, 162
Cumberland sausage 81
Cumbrian Legendary Ales 56, 64, **101**
The Cumbrian Way, Ulverston 94, 99, **147**
Cumbria on a Plate (Annette Gibbons) 96
Cumbria Organics 83
The Custom House, Barrow **182**
Dalemain, near Ullswater 29, **184**
Damson Day 29
Damsons in the Lyth and Winster valleys **98**
Dean, near Workington 56
Deer 'n Dexter, near Penrith 78, 83, 145
Demels **93**, 123
Dent Brewery/beers 47, 57, 64, 73, 117, 131
Derby Arms, Witherslack 74
Doi Intanon, Ambleside 37
Drunken Duck Inn, near Ambleside **45**, 178
Duke of Edinburgh Hotel, Barrow 72
Eagle and Child, Staveley **66**, 101, 102
L'enclume, Cartmel 18
Eden Coffee Lounge, Wetheral **182**
English Lakes Hotels 11, 29
English Lakes Ice Cream **108**, 127, 180
Estuary Restaurant, Ravenglass **24**, 38
Eva's Organics 83, **118**, 164

Ewbank, TM, Appleby **114**
Famous Wild Boar Hotel, Crook 54
Farlam Hall Hotel, near Brampton **17**, 27
Farmer Sharp, Lindal-in-Furness 35, **80**, 86, 106, 122, 180
farmers' markets 78, 80, 88, 91, 115, **116**
Farm Shop at Rheged 78, 82, 88, 92, 98, **136**, 145
Farrer's, Kendal 99, **128**
Fayrer Garden House Hotel, Bowness-on-Windermere 14
First Floor Café, Windermere 106, **180**
Flock-In, Rosthwaite **184**
FondEwe Fine Cheeses, Keswick 93, **131**
Food & Company 120, **152**
food festivals 29
Foxfield Brewery **58**
Francine's Coffee House and Restaurant, Windermere **180**
Friendly Food and Drink **94**
Furness Fish, Poultry and Game Supplies 106, 122, **123**
Fusion Café, Brougham 162
Geltsdale Brewery/beers 56, 68, **101**, 119, 131, 164
George and Dragon, Clifton **52**, 82
Gillam's Tea Room, Ulverston **179**
Gilpin Lodge, Windermere 30
The Gincase, Mawbray Hayrigg 172
Gleaston Watermill, near Ulverston **185**
Golden Rule, Ambleside 72
Good Taste, Keswick **184**
Gossipgate Gallery, Alston **182**
J&J Graham, Penrith 93, 98, **137**
Grain Store Restaurant, Kendal **21**, 183
Grange Bakery 124
Grange-over-Sands 74, 124, 183
Grasmere 20, 31, 38, 39, 74, 126, 183
Grasmere Gingerbread Shop 126
Great Taste Awards 92
Greenhouse Restaurant, Kendal 22
Green's Café and Bistro, Grasmere **183**
Greystone Farm Shop, Stainton 90, 91, **141**
Half Moon Wholefoods, Brampton 88, 97, 99, **115**
Hallsford Farm Produce, Hethersgill **80**, 81
Hat Trick Café, Low Newton **171**
Hawkshead 59, 94, 101, 102, 127, 167
Hawkshead Brewery/beers 21, 44, 50, 52, 54, 62, **65**, 66, 68, 72, 73, 74, **102**, 117, 119, 121, 127, 131, 166
Hawkshead Relish Company **94**, 114, 127, 164
Hawkshead Relish (shop), Hawkshead 127
Hazelmere Café and Bakery, Grange **183**
HDM Spice Shop, Carlisle **147**
Her Citi, Maryport **172**
Herdwick sheep 79
Hesket Newmarket 60, 102
Hesket Newmarket Brewery/beers 56, **60**, 62, 66, 70, 73, 102, 119, 131
The Hideaway at Windermere **41**
Hideaway Coffee House, Lupton 98
Higginsons & Daughter, Grange-over-Sands 49, 81, 84, **124**, 178
High Borrow Bridge Farm, near Kendal **80**
High Head Sculpture Valley, Ivegill **182**
Historic Food (Ivan Day) **153**
Holbeck Ghyll, Windermere **32**
Holker Food Hall, Cark-in-Cartmel 84, 85, 91, 93, 94, 95, 98, 99, **117**, 163
The Honeypot, Hawkshead 85, 90, 93, 95, **127**
Hoopers, The Restaurant, Carlisle **164**
Horse and Farrier, Threlkeld **74**
Hot Mango Café, Ulverston **185**
Howbarrow Organic Farm 82, 83, 106, **121**, 124, 170
Jennings Brewery/beers 44, 46, 52, 56, 68, 69, **109**, 119, 131

Jeremy's Soups **109**, 133
Jerichos at the Waverley, Windermere **34**
The Jumble Room, Grasmere **20**
Jumping Jenny, Coniston **166**
Kendal 21, 22, 29, 39, 62, 65, 74, 128, 129, 140, 147, 168, 169, 183
Kendal College Food Festival **29**
Kennedys Fine Chocolates **135**
Keswick 74, 103, 130, 131, 183
Keswick Brewing Company/beers 70, **103**, 131, 184
Kirkby Lonsdale 74, 75, 132, 184
Kirkby Stephen 40, 51, 64, 151, 152, 170
Kirkstile Inn, Loweswater 63
Kitridding Farm Shop, Old Town 109, **133**, 145
Kitridding Tea Room, Old Town **175**
Laird's Larder, Carlisle 88, 90, 93, 95, 99, **119**, 138
Lakeland Pedlar Wholefood Café, Keswick **184**
Lakeland Willow Water **109**
Lakes Chilli Fest 29
Lakeside Hotel, Newby Bridge **23**
Lakes Speciality Foods 109
Lancrigg Vegetarian Country House Hotel **38**
Lanercost Tearooms, near Brampton **182**
Langdale Bar, Ambleside **44**
Langstrath Country Inn, Stonethwaite 74
Larch Cottage Nurseries, Melkinthorpe **184**
Linthwaite House Hotel, Bowness-on-Windermere **16**
Linton Tweeds, Carlisle **182**
Lizzie's Home Made **99**, 106, 113, 119, 133, 164
Lovelady Shield, near Alston **10**
Love the Lakes, Bowness-on-Windermere 94, **147**
Low Lorton, near Cockermouth 22, 73
Low Sizergh Barn Farm Shop, near Kendal 78, 82, 84, 88, 90, 92, 93, 95, 98, 99, **140**
Low Sizergh Farm Tea Room, near Kendal **177**
Lowther Park Farms/Estate 52, 70, **82**
Low Wood Hotel, Ambleside **44**
LucyCooks **154**
Lucy4 Wine Bar and Bistro, Ambleside **72**
Lucy's on a Plate, Ambleside 11, **160**
Lucy's Specialist Grocers, Ambleside 88, 94, 99, **113**, 146
Manor Arms, Broughton-in-Furness 73, **104**
Mansergh Hall Organic Farm 21, 40, **82**, 83, 86, 133, 135, 177
Mardale Inn, Bampton **75**
Maryport 40, 172
Masons Arms, Cartmel Fell **50**, 102
Matson Ground Farm, Windermere **82**, 83
Mawsons **109**, 114
McMenamins **40**
Melmerby 133, 151, 173
Merienda, Cockermouth **183**
Michael's Nook, near Grasmere 10, 31, 39, 68
Michelin star 18, 26, 31, 32
Millbeck Farm, Great Langdale **84**
Miller Howe Hotel, Windermere 34, **35**, 65, 69, 150
Millstones Bakery/Food Hall, Bootle 93, 97, **114**
Mill Yard Café, Morland **174**
The Moody Baker, Alston **112**, 182
D Moore of Dalston **92**
More? The Artisan Bakery **147**
Mosedale Meeting House, Mosedale **185**
Moss Howe Farm Foods **95**, 117, 127, 133
Mutton Renaissance **86**
Narrowbar Café, Penrith **185**
Newfield Inn, Seathwaite 64, **101**
North Lakes Hotel and Spa, Penrith **24**
Number 15, Penrith **185**
Oak Street Bakery, Windermere **146**

Old Crown, Hesket Newmarket **60**, 102
Old Dungeon Ghyll Hotel, Great Langdale **72**
Old Sawmill Tearoom, Mirehouse **184**
Old School Room Tea Shop, Rydal Hall **176**
The Old Smokehouse 24, 63, **84**, 139, 155
Open All Hours, Keswick **131**
Organico, Ambleside 106, **114**
Organico, Staveley
Orton Grange, near Carlisle 138, **175**
Pennington Hotel, Ravenglass **24**, 38
Penrith 24, 26, 40, 52, 70, 75, 90, 97, 135, 136, 137, 141, 184
Pheasant Inn, Bassenthwaite Lake **46**, 58
Pheasant Inn, Cumwhitton **56**, 101
Pie Mill **92**
The Plough, Wreay, near Carlisle **73**
Plumgarths Farm Shop, near Kendal **147**
Poppi Red, Hawkshead **167**
Potter, Beatrix 32, 59, 79, 80, 86, 113, 166
Miss Potter (film) 32, 37, 86
Prickett, Sue **109**, 133, 175
Prince Charles 60, 64, 86, 102, 138
Prince of Wales, Foxfield **58**
Prior's Kitchen, Carlisle **164**
Pub is the Hub **60**, 64
Pudding Room **185**
Punch Bowl Inn and Restaurant, Crosthwaite 55, 60
Queen Inn, Great Corby, near Carlisle **73**
Queen's Head Hotel, Hawkshead **59**
Queen's Head Hotel, Troutbeck **75**
Queen's Head Inn, Tirril 60, **75**
Quince & Medlar, Cockermouth **18**
Rambla, Windermere **185**
Rampsbeck Country House Hotel, Ullswater **40**
Rattle Gill Café, Ambleside **182**
Ravenglass **24**
Ravenstonedale, near Kirkby Stephen 64, 152
Ray's Shrimps **109**
Relish Deli, Kendal **147**
The Restaurant, Kendal College **39**
Rogan and Company, Cartmel **18**
Rothay Manor Hotel, Ambleside **12**, 27
Rough Fell sheep 80, 85, 139
Royal Oak, Appleby **72**
Royal Yew Inn, Dean 52, **56**
Ruskin, John 75, 166, 183
Rustique, Ulverston **41**
Saltmarsh lamb 69, **84**, 117, 124, 136
Saunders Chocolates, Penrith **138**, 147
Sedbergh 51, 139, 176
Pippa Sedgwick Wines **120**
Sella Park House Hotel, Calder Bridge 24, **38**
Sharrow Bay, Ullswater **26**, 73, 162
Shill's of Station Street, Cockermouth **147**
Sillfield Farm (Peter Gott) 21, 40, 81, **85**, 112, 117, 122, 145
Sillfield Farm shop **123**
Silloth 108, 172
Siskins Café, Whinlatter **184**
Sizergh, near Kendal 65, 140, 177
Skelwith Bridge, near Ambleside **178**
Slack House Farm, Gilsland 83, **88**, 112, 115, 164
Slow Food 22, 86, 96, **106**, 107, 144, 157
Smoky Jo's **155**
South Lakes Organic Milk 83, **109**, 170
Spice Enterprise, Carlisle **37**
Staff of Life Bakery, Kendal 21, 97, 106, **129**, 168
Stagger Inn, Stainton-with-Adgarley **72**
Stainton Wines, Kendal 70, **129**, 141

Staveley, near Kendal 65, 66, 94, 102, 144, 154, 179
Steadmans, Sedbergh **139**
Storrs Hall Hotel, Windermere **36**
Strawberry Bank liqueurs 106, **109**
Strickland Arms, Sizergh 65, 74, 101
Sun Hotel, Coniston 73
Sun Inn, Crook 74, 100
Sun Inn, Kirkby Lonsdale **75**, 102
Tapestry Tearooms, Kendal **169**
Taste of Eden, Winskill, near Penrith **89**
Temple Thai, Ulverston **27**
Thornby Moor Dairy 11, 14, 22, 24, 63, 70, 74, **88**, 93, 112, 115, 119, 127, 131, 164
Tirril Brewery/beers 70, 121, 131
The Toffee Shop, Penrith 117, 126, **138**
Torver, near Coniston 68
Truffles Chocolates **99**
Tweedies Bar, Grasmere **74**
Ullswater 26, 40, 185
Ullswater Steamers **185**
Ulverston 27, 41, 47, 69, 147, 150, 179, 185
The Village Bakery, Melmerby 83, 120, **133**, 136, 137, 151, **173**
Mr Vikki's **109**, 112, 164
Wardhall Dairy 22, **109**
Wasdale Head Inn **75**
Waterhead Hotel, Ambleside **11**, 29
Waterhead Hotel Food Week, Ambleside **29**
The Watermill, Little Salkeld 74, 83, **97**, 112, 113, 114, 115, 133, 135, **157**, 170
Watermill Café, Caldbeck **162**
Watermill Inn and Brewing Co, Ings 62, 100, 102, 131
Waterside Wholefood, Kendal **169**
John Watt & Son, Carlisle **182**
Weavers Café, near Sedbergh **176**
Westmorland Damson Association 29, 98
Westmorland Farm Shops, Tebay 78, 80, 82, 84, 85, 88, 90, 91, 92, 93, 94, 95, 99, **145**
Wheatsheaf, Beetham **72**
Wheatsheaf, Brigsteer 74, 101
Wheatsheaf Inn, Low Lorton **73**
White Hart Inn, Bouth **47**
Whitehaven **28**
Whitehaven Brewing Company/beers 56, **104**
White Moss House, near Grasmere **38**
Wigton 93, 95, 104,
Wild and Fruitful **95**, 106, 112, 119, 124, 164
Wilf's Café, Staveley 65, **179**
Winder Hall Country House, Low Lorton **22**
Windermere (the lake) 30, 32, 35, 36, 44, 65, 66, 161
Windermere (the town) 34, 41, 54, 62, 146, 180, 185
Winster, near Bowness-on-Windermere 73, 147
Witherslack, near Grange-over-Sands 74, 95
Richard Woodall, Waberthwaite 14, 21, 40, 44, 54, 59, 74, 81, **85**, 106, 119, 127, 137, 145, **146**, 168
Woodend Cookery **157**
Wooden Spoon Fudge Company **99**, 162
Wordsworth Hotel, Grasmere 31, **39**
Wordsworth, William 18, 38, 39, 59, 64, 101, 126, 127, 176, 184
World Marmalade Festival, Dalemain 29, 122
World Peace Café, Ulverston **185**
Yanwath Gate Inn, Yanwath 70, 101, 102, 103
Yates Brewery/beers 56, 63, 66, 68, 73, **104**, 131
Yew Tree Farm, near Coniston **166**
Yew Tree Farm Heritage Meats, near Coniston 79, **86**
Zeffirellis, Ambleside 13, **44**, 160
Zest Harbourside/Restaurant Whitehaven **28**

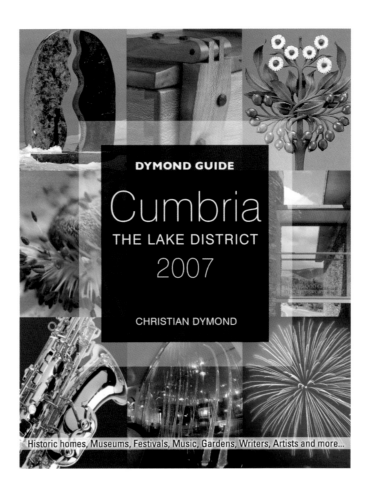

DYMOND GUIDE

Cumbria
THE LAKE DISTRICT
2007

CHRISTIAN DYMOND

Historic homes, Museums, Festivals, Music, Gardens, Writers, Artists and more...

Look out for a new edition of this guidebook. Meanwhile here's what people said about the 2007 Dymond Guide to Cumbria, the Lake District.

'It looks wonderful! The illustrations and presentation are superb. The book will feature very proudly on my bookshelf for all to see.'
Jim Eldridge, author and TV and radio scriptwriter

'It is superb, quite the best thing I've seen on Cumbria.'
Jonathan Denby, chairman, Lakes Hospitality Association.

'You have produced a book of real quality, relevant and interesting content, excellent design and production and simply beautiful to use.'
Euan Cartwright, Cumbrian photographer.

'Congratulations on the Dymond Guide. It looks stylish, informative, well laid out and detailed. I'm sure the guide will be very popular.'
Barney Cunliffe, managing director of Gilpin Lodge Country House Hotel, Windermere.

'I have read numerous guides to Cumbria and the Lake District. I find the Dymond Guide easily the best, being totally comprehensive and eminently readable.'
Dr Alec Brade, Lancashire.

'It is well written, the quality of the photographs is uniformly high and it all looks good to me. I like the design, the paper, typeface and the shape. It feels good in the hand and every home and car owner should have at least one.'
Michael Moon of Michael Moon's Bookshop, Whitehaven, Cumbria.

I've been extremely fortunate in that a great many people have helped me with this guide, so to all of them I say a very big thank you. Heaps of recommendations came my way from within and without Cumbria, which made drawing up a master list of places to visit considerably easier. I'm also immensely grateful to all those listed in the book who contributed to the production costs of the project.

Editor Chris Bagshaw has guided me throughout with skill and knowledge, his encouragement invaluable during 18 months of work. Designer Gary Burge at Walker Ellis Associates (see below) was a joy to work with. His creativity, enthusiasm and meticulous attention to detail were ever present during the period of design. Richard Cook at The Amadeus Press was, as usual, unfailing in his enthusiasm, a Yorkshireman who loves Cumbria and its produce.

I'm also immensely grateful to the main photographer Helen Whitaker (*www.helenwhitaker.com*) whose talent and work rate combined to produce delightful and inviting images of so many places that are mentioned in the book. A few are singled out. Val Corbett (photographer of *Gardens of the Lake District*, the Lakeland Book of the Year in 2008) provided me with almost all of the glorious landscape photographs you see. Martin Campbell of Artisan Food also took photographs, and images were taken or supplied by numerous others listed below. Robert Henry assiduously checked through all the pages before they were sent through to the editor and then did the proof reading.

Friends and family have been tremendously supportive, in particular Charlotte, my wife, who has heard me talk about Cumbrian food and drink for more than two years and still maintained a healthy appetite for this project. I cannot thank her enough for her encouragement.

I also say many thanks to the following: Sue Allan, Linda and Tim Aspinall, John Bailey, Carolyne Baines, Janice Benson, Mike Booth, Chris and Jaqui Carter, Jim Chapple, Dave Cope, Felicity Crowley, Brian Dawes, Ivan Day, Birthe Dymond, Jim Eldridge, Sam Evans, Victoria Farley, Joyce Fisher, Richard Foster, Annette Gibbons, Sue and Dave Goold, Helen Graham, Carole and Martin Greenland, Sue and Phil Harrison, Rebecca Heaton-Cooper, Helen Hinvest, Jon Holdsworth, Howard Hull, Ian Kirton, Sandy Kitching, Jayne Lloyd, John Morrell, Graham and Susie Moss, Gill Nicholson, Penelope Phillips, Sally and Tim Sarginson, Barbara Slack and Jeremy Suter.

Photographs: Ben Barden, Bread Matters, Martin Campbell, Val Corbett, Simon Crouch, Cumbrian Newspapers, Dalemain, Ivan Day, John de Jong, Kevin Gibson, Paul Goodwin, Benjamin Hadwin, Simon Hardy-Graham, Andy Harrison, Christopher Holmes, Bryan Jones, Paul Jones, Lakeland Arts Trust, Made in Cumbria, Tommy Martin, Muncaster Castle, Carajana-ar Ollis, Geoff Pagotto, Jeremy Rata, Madeleine Scott, Kasia Sharp, Ivan Tennant, Simon Tebbey, Andrew Tomkins, Tullie House in Carlisle, James Walker, Helen Whitaker, Jenny Woolgar and Lakes & Cumbria Today.

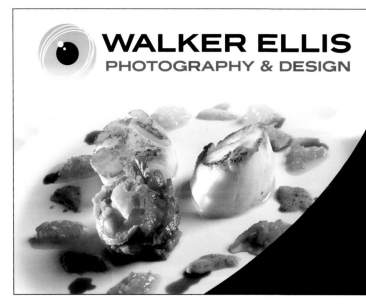

Send us your comments

There are about 300 places listed in this guide but, as I say
in the Preface, there could have been more. So, if you've got
suggestions for other restaurants, pubs and inns, food and
drink producers, food and farm shops, cookery and baking
courses or cafés and tearooms, or even other things you'd
like me to include in the next guide to food and drink in
Cumbria, please let me know.

I'd also like to hear what you think of the places that I have
mentioned – what the food and drink was like, how good the
welcome and service was and so on. The email address is
below. Looking forward to hearing from you.

info@dymondguides.com